PESCAN

# PESCAN

## A FEEL GOOD COOKBOOK

**Abbie Cornish & Jacqueline King Schiller**

ABRAMS, NEW YORK

For Quinn,
You're the best
thing I ever made.
— Jacq

India, Soleil, and in
loving memory of Heath.
♡ Abbie ♥

# ABBIE'S STORY

I grew up on 170 acres of rolling rural land in Lochinvar, New South Wales, Australia, with my mum, dad, and four siblings. We farmed our own cows, pigs, chickens, turkeys, and ducks and raised a myriad of animals, including rabbits, kangaroos, ferrets, birds, cats, and dogs. Ever since I can remember, I've felt a strong connection with animals, the earth, and all living things.

*"I asked Jacqueline, 'Is it really possible to find enlightenment here in the kitchen?' To which she replied with a gentle nod and a knowing smile."*

Anyone who knows me knows I love food. As a child, I ate everything. As a teenager, I became more aware of what was on my plate. I started to make the connection: What am I eating? Where is it from? Do I want to eat it? I read about the meat industry, animal welfare, factory farming, and other inhumane animal practices being conducted on a worldwide scale. After which I decided on a vegetarian diet and lifestyle. In my twenties, I became quite the little foodie. Always on the road, dining in different restaurants and cafés. It was fun, but it wasn't always healthy.

At thirty, I went through a really big shift in my life, mentally, physically, and spiritually. Physically, my body was talking to me, and I needed to listen. I felt like I was running on about 70 percent of my full capacity, and I wasn't sure why. I sought advice and opinions from different doctors and practitioners (mainstream, integrative, and natural) and concluded that it was my diet that needed to change. My nutritionist at the time suggested I reintroduce meat to my diet and cut out processed sugars, dairy, and gluten as much as possible. The change wasn't easy, but as I continued to educate myself and eat with awareness, I became more comfortable. I felt stronger, healthier, and more energetic too. I found myself by forgetting myself, as the Buddhists say, and letting ten thousand things in.

I started shopping locally, organically, and seasonally. I filled my fridge wherever I was in the world, even if that meant clearing out the mini bar in the hotel to make room for the good stuff. I started asking questions in stores, restaurants, and cafés and at markets: What is this? Where is it from? How was it farmed? The next big step for me, and by far the most fun, was learning how to cook.

The turning point was during the summer of 2014 while on vacation with my best friend, Jacqueline. I was standing in the kitchen of a lakeside cottage reading *Bring Me the Rhinoceros,* a collection of Zen koans by John Tarrant,

while Jacq was preparing breakfast. I was at the end of a chapter about a woman who had found enlightenment in the kitchen through cooking and the simplest of domestic activities. It struck a chord with me. I asked Jacqueline, "Is it really possible to find enlightenment here in the kitchen?" To which she replied with a gentle nod and a knowing smile. I knew in that moment that there was something beautiful to learn here, and on that day, Jacqueline became my kitchen guru.

When we returned home to Los Angeles, we started going to the farmers' market on Sundays, then back to Jacqueline's house to cook. This quickly became a weekly ritual. Later, I found myself as a sous chef of sorts to Jacq at parties and on special occasions. Over these years, our friendship grew in the kitchen, and out of this special connection, and the experiences and moments we've shared together, came this book. A cookbook full of Jacq's creations, from her grace, passion, talent, and ingenuity as a chef.

I love this way of eating because it's healthy, conscious, and nutritious (not to mention delicious!), and it makes you feel good. "Do you live to eat or eat to live?" a friend of mine asked me recently. I live to eat. I love to eat! And I appreciate it even more now.

This cookbook is a celebration of food, family, and friendship. A cookbook full of love. I hope it gives you the light it has given me.

# JACQUELINE'S STORY

As a child, I was what you might call pudgy. (I grew up in a Hispanic family, so they went with the only slightly sweeter sounding gordita.) It's not surprising, considering I grew up on a typical American diet of boxed cereal, canned soup, frozen dinners, and fast food. It didn't bother me much as a kid, but by the time I was in high school, my clothes were getting tight and I was wearing the largest "regular" size. I was determined to avoid moving into plus-size clothes, so I began my first diet. I started counting calories with total disregard as to whether what I was eating was actually good for me. Being skinny was the ultimate goal, without a thought about being healthy.

I lost weight, and by the time I was fifteen I was working as a professional model. I happily moved to Europe after high school, and despite being surrounded by a slew of new culinary delights, I focused on how much (or more precisely, how little) I was eating. My idea of healthy food was a chocolate-flavored protein bar, which I would eat up to three times a day. Like many young women, I saw food as the enemy. After a while, I started to notice some unwelcome side effects of my restrictive eating. My skin and hair were dry, my nails were brittle, and the half-moons under my eyes were getting progressively darker. Even worse than the effects on my appearance was how I started to feel. By the time I was in my early twenties I felt tired and moody all the time and began having anxiety attacks. On the outside, I was living what seemed like a glamorous life, traveling all over the world, but I couldn't enjoy it fully because I didn't know how to truly take care of myself.

Things came to a head one humid summer day at a photo shoot for a designer I had been really looking forward to working with. Following a protein bar and diet cola breakfast, I stood up after getting my makeup done and nearly fainted. My heart was pounding. I felt wobbly and needed to sit down. Here I was working my "dream job," but instead of performing at my best, I could barely maintain my composure. I knew something had to change. That night I talked to a friend who seemed to be the most "together" person I knew, and she encouraged me to try yoga. I began a regular practice, which helped me understand that in order to feel good mentally and emotionally, you have to take care of yourself physically. It's simple enough, but at the time, it was a revelation!

*"On the outside, I was living what seemed like a glamorous life, traveling all over the world, but I couldn't enjoy it fully because I didn't know how to truly take care of myself."*

Learning to cook was an extension of learning to take care of myself, to literally find the nourishment I needed. I was living in Milan, and there is no better place to learn about food or cooking than in Italy. The Italians have such a wonderful appreciation for fresh, healthy ingredients and food made from scratch. I couldn't help but change the way I looked at things. Thanks to some great Italian friends I learned to prepare (and enjoy!) fresh, delicious, unprocessed food. We would spend weekend mornings at the markets, cook the afternoon away, and spend evenings at the table eating, talking, and laughing over the meal we created. I discovered a sense of pleasure around food that I never thought possible.

After much experimenting in the kitchen and reading countless books on nutrition and wellness, I found that a diet filled with vegetables, fruits, whole grains, nuts, and legumes, and supplemented with eggs and seafood, made me feel much more energized and healthier than I ever had before. Eating this way means I never have to worry about my weight, count calories, or feel deprived. It's amazing how eating well, exercising regularly, and having tools for relaxation can improve day-to-day life so much. The bottom line is nothing feels or looks better than being healthy.

Finding a sense of joy and freedom around food, rather than anxiety, made me want to share what I had learned with the world. I started a blog called *The Feel Good Kitchen* and went to culinary school with the intention of teaching others, so of course, I was thrilled when my best friend Abbie asked me to teach her how to cook.

It was back to the farmers' markets, the Sunday cooking lessons, the wonderful dinners. I shared my favorite recipes from Italy and all of the techniques I learned in school. Abbie and I grew together cooking for brunches, parties, and holiday meals. Within a matter of months, I saw her bloom in the kitchen. She moved from helping me chop things here and there to making beautiful full-blown meals of her own creation. This book is an expression of the cooking we've explored together. Food that is comforting and indulgent, but also incredibly health-supportive and energizing.

In working on this book, I have come to appreciate how enriched our lives have been by the time we've spent in the kitchen. I've realized that the food we prepare can be an expression of love. There is no greater sign of affection than putting together ingredients from nature that not only give us pleasure on the palate but also contribute to our overall well-being. When we make foods that nourish us, that make us feel good, that help us be our best versions of ourselves, that is nothing short of an act of self-love. When we serve those foods to our family and friends, we are sharing that love. It is in this spirit that we offer these recipes and lessons to you.

# WHAT LED US HERE

When we started cooking together and sharing our food with friends and family, we found that they were impressed and curious about even the simplest dishes. People who initially didn't think they would like our "rabbit food" ended up gobbling up piles of veggies because they tasted amazing. The comment we kept hearing was some variation of "this food tastes delicious, and it makes me feel so good!" We heard it time and time again, and it left us wondering, why don't we all know how to do this?

The answer, of course, is that we never learned. We grew up in a time when processed foods ruled the day. We regularly ate foods in colors and shapes not found in nature without thinking twice about it. Dairy and meat consumption was steadily increasing along with obesity rates. At the same time, there was a boom in low-nutrient, processed foods marketed to us as health foods under the labels "low-calorie," "low-fat," and "all natural." Advertisers promoted the idea that cooking is a tedious chore to be avoided whenever possible. In turn, we have the highest rates in history of chronic diseases that are preventable through a healthy diet and lifestyle.

Thankfully, times are changing! In the last few years there's been a move back into our home kitchens, as we're figuring out that there is a better way. Social media, the Internet, and good old-fashioned books have given us more access to recipes and information about nutrition and wellness than ever before. We're rediscovering the simple joy of preparing and eating flavorful home-cooked meals made with fresh, wholesome ingredients.

We are thrilled to share the recipes and lessons in this book because we believe that they have benefited more than our waistlines and our heart health. In this process of learning to cook and enjoy real whole foods, rather than choosing foods based on convenience, or restricting food in the hopes of getting closer to some false idea of perfection, we gained a connection to some of the most pleasurable experiences in life. We've learned something that was once common knowledge— how to bring the bounty from the earth into our homes and turn it into beautiful food that nourishes our body and feeds our soul. Now, as we cook for ourselves and our friends and family, every meal has the potential to be an experience that can connect us to the earth, connect us to the moment, to each other, and dare we say, to the divine.

These experiences don't have to be complicated. You don't have to be a Michelin-starred chef. Heck, we've had them in sweatpants. Think of the last time you ate a piece of grilled sweet corn on a summer day. Or a peach at the peak of ripeness, its juice flowing down your chin. You taste the soil in those bites, you taste the sunshine. It's transcendent. When you eat food that grows out of the ground, the way nature intended, without transforming it too much, without stripping it of its goodness, using your creativity to enhance it ever so slightly, that's when you can really start to experience food as the gift that it is.

For many of us, the only thing keeping us from feeling really comfortable in the kitchen is a little know-how. With this in mind, we have chosen recipes that not only highlight certain flavors or ingredients but also the techniques that we think have made our lives better. (Sounds bold, but it's true!) Once you make our PB&J overnight oats, you can make overnight oats fifty different ways. The same can be said about risotto or frittatas or broiled fish. We hope these recipes are gratifying on their own and also a launching pad to inspire your own creations. We've made sure to include recipes for everyday use, as well as dishes you'll feel good serving to the people you love on your most special occasions. Now let's get cooking!

*"Good food is the foundation of genuine happiness."*
—AUGUSTE ESCOFFIER

# A GUIDE TO FEELING GOOD IN THE KITCHEN

**1 //  Do not buy into the idea that kitchen work is drudgery.**

We like getting our hands dirty in the kitchen! Cooking, for us, can be a meditation. Sometimes cooking is playtime; sometimes it's making art. We cook to say sorry and we cook to seduce. We cook to see the smiles on the faces of our family and friends. Sometimes we cook together, drink too much wine, laugh a little too loudly, and come out better friends in the end.

**2 //  Make the kitchen your happy place.**

Get organized. When you know where things are, you are the master of your domain. Keep flowers in a vase, listen to music, use the pretty dish towel. Display your fruit in a big bowl. Keep yummy drinks around. Invite friends and/or family over to cook with you. Do whatever makes you feel good in that space.

**3 //  Love, appreciate, and celebrate food.**

For millennia, people celebrated the harvest, said a prayer of thanks at every meal, and revered certain foods for their medicinal qualities. In the last century, most of us have lost any connection to the spirit of these traditions. And yet it's so simple to take a moment to be grateful for the food on our plates. To feast with our eyes, take in the aroma, and savor each bite. We make food with love to celebrate milestones and holidays, to bring people around the table to share a common, delicious experience face to face. We appreciate food as medicine for the body and soul, and take any opportunity to connect with and thank the hardworking farmers and fishermen who bring the food to our plates.

**4 //  Prioritize foods that help us be the people we want to be: strong, healthy, sexy, energetic, powerful, all-around kick-ass people!**

For decades now, marketers have pushed food that makes us overweight while also promoting the idea that women have to be one size (extra small) to be considered beautiful. You can probably picture an ad with a bikini-clad model eating a huge burger with sauce dripping down her face as an example. When we see those ads, we don't buy what they're selling. Instead, we choose food that makes us feel good when we eat it. We choose food that gives us the energy to be the bosses we need to be to live our best lives. We focus

on feeling strong and healthy because when we do, we feel confident. Everyone knows confidence is sexy no matter your size. We also know that being healthy means finding balance. If we eat something gluttonous, you'd better believe we enjoy it. As with anything in life, it's not about being perfect. It's about being happy.

**5 //  Listen to your body.**

When you regularly eat real whole foods, you aren't seduced by labels like "fat-free" or "zero calorie." You don't have to count calories. When you get hungry, instead of grabbing the quickest thing to put in your mouth, you turn your attention inward and ask, "What does my body need right now?" Working out a bunch? "Hmm, I need protein." A little hungover or under the weather? "Give me a green juice, ASAP!" You tune in to subtle cravings and also hear when your body is telling you it's had enough.

**6 //  Eat pescan.**

This is not a traditional diet book. We're not here to tell you exactly what the "perfect diet" is for your body and conscience. That's up to you to decide. What we do want to tell you is what works for us and why. We call it the pescan lifestyle, and we love eating this way because it lands in the sweet spot where good nutrition, conscious living, and culinary pleasures converge.

# THE PESCAN LIFESTYLE

## pes·can
## /peskən/

**1.** not containing red meat, poultry, or dairy; consisting wholly of vegetables, fruits, fungi, grains, legumes, nuts, and sometimes eggs or seafood.

**2.** a person who follows a pescan lifestyle.

## PESCAN BASICS

### Eat fruits and/or vegetables at every meal (aka #eattherainbow).

These days there are about a million different theories on the best way to eat, but the one thing everyone agrees on is that we should be eating more plants. Having a plant-focused diet means you're absorbing a ton of vitamins, minerals, fiber, and healthy fats without even trying. Making vegetables the center of our diet has had the biggest effect on how we feel. It makes your whole body run more efficiently. Good digestion, improved mood, and higher energy levels are all perks. Plus, your immune system will get a huge boost.

As if those health benefits weren't enough, scientists have proven a little secret that we've known for a while—eating lots of fruits and veggies actually makes you look better. They help you maintain a healthy weight thanks to all of the fiber they contain, which gives you that full, satisfied feeling. You'll also notice that a lot of cravings will disappear once your body is getting all of the nutrients it needs. Studies have even shown that what people perceive as a "healthy glow" comes from eating the pigments that give fruits and vegetables their color.

If eating a lot of produce is new to you, don't feel like you have to radically shift your diet immediately to get the benefits. Start by adding veggies to the foods you're already making. Add some onions and spinach to your breakfast scramble, throw some zucchini and carrots into your pasta sauce, add avocado and tomato to your sandwich, and freshen up your granola with sweet berries. You can make vegetables and fruit a bigger part of each meal as you get used to cooking and eating more of them.

### Eat food that is as close to its natural state as possible.

Stick to organic produce, grains, legumes, nuts, sustainable seafood, and free-range eggs whenever possible. This will guarantee that everything you are eating is nutrient-dense and nourishing. It will also help you avoid toxic pesticides and genetically modified foods. Remember whole foods—the way nature intended—are always best, so leave the peel on fruits and veggies, eat whole grains, and keep the yolks in your eggs.

Avoid processed foods with added chemicals, refined sweeteners, or added flavors. Even those "natural flavors" in the ingredients list can include artificial ingredients such as synthetic solvents or preservatives. It's best to stay away from foods with labels like "low-calorie", "low-fat", or "gluten-free" unless those foods are *naturally* that way. Ditch the refined sugars like white or brown sugar and switch to whole-food sweeteners such as honey, maple syrup, and dates.

### Eat fish two to three times per week.

The American Heart Association recommends eating fish at least two times a week and so do we. Fish provides vitamin $B_{12}$ and DHA and EPA omega-3 fatty acids. These nutrients are are impossible to get enough of on a completely plant-based diet without eating fortified foods or taking supplements. This is one of the reasons we prefer the pescan diet rather than a strictly vegan diet. These omega-3 fatty acids are essential for proper brain function and heart health, and vitamin $B_{12}$ helps with a wide array of our body's functions, like keeping our hormones in balance and maintaining healthy nervous and cardiovascular systems.

Aside from being full of nutrients that so beautifully complement a plant-based diet, seafood is quite simply delicious. It makes a wonderful centerpiece for a special-occasion meal, is quick enough to prepare on any weeknight, and can be an easy, nutritious option when eating out. At many restaurants, the only dairy-free vegetarian options might be steamed vegetables and a baked potato. Add some grilled fish, and you have a balanced and satisfying meal.

### Eat seasonally.

While you may not be familiar with the term *pescan*, it is not really a new way of eating. This is the staple diet of many native coastal communities that have some of the highest longevity rates. Its foundation is in macrobiotics and the Mediterranean diet. As with each of those diets, we recommend focusing on local and seasonal ingredients in your cooking. Doing so ensures that you're eating the freshest, most nutritious food possible. It's also generally the most cost-effective and environmentally friendly way to eat. Produce begins to lose nutritional value soon after it has been picked, so the faster it goes from the farm to your table, the better.

### Avoid red meat and dairy.

There are a number of studies linking red meat consumption to increased risk for cancer and heart disease, with processed meats like hot dogs and deli meats being the worst for your body. Exposure to antibiotics and hormones in meat and the negative environmental effects of industrial animal farming are also of concern. As for dairy, giving it up may feel like a bit of a sacrifice initially, but it's so worthwhile! We know that might sound crazy, but if we told you that you could have better skin, less bloating, and never have to count calories again, wouldn't that be worth taking into consideration? Dairy is one of the most common allergens and can make problems like acne, asthma, and irritable bowel syndrome much worse. For a lot of people, it creates inflammatory responses like heartburn, lack of energy, and joint pain. In fact, more than 60 percent of the world's population is believed to have a dairy intolerance.

Cutting out meat and dairy may take some getting used to, but it's really not as hard as you think. Most people who switch to a pescan diet feel and look so much better that the transition is much easier than expected. If you are not ready to give up these animal foods completely, try to incrementally lower your consumption. Buy only pasture-raised or grass-fed meats and dairy, which are more nutritious than factory-farmed products, and think of them as an accent to your meal rather than the star. Switch to veggie burgers and dogs. Try to have at least one completely plant-based meal per day. This isn't about an overnight quick fix; it's about changing your lifestyle for the better in a *sustainable* way that works for you.

### Eggs and gluten are optional, so figure out if they work for you.

We put these foods in the optional category because a big chunk of the population has intolerances or allergies to them. They may be particularly problematic for those with autoimmune or thyroid issues. Others are fine with them and think scrambled eggs on wheat toast is the most fabulous breakfast ever. For that reason, you have to figure out what works for you. If you think you may be intolerant, the best way to find out is either to get tested for food allergies and sensitivities or go the less expensive route and do an elimination diet. This is especially important if you have digestive issues, skin problems, or lack of energy even after getting enough sleep. To try an elimination diet, cut out the food in question for three to four weeks and see if your symptoms improve, then reintroduce it into your diet. Really check in with your body to see if there are any negative reactions like fatigue, joint pain, headaches, indigestion, nausea, rashes, or bloating. If you feel OK, then feel free to eat it in moderation. If you feel better abstaining, then do your best to avoid them altogether. For severe symptoms, consult a medical professional.

We love a slice of fresh-baked whole-grain or sourdough bread on occasion but avoid gluten most of the time, so we have made sure to include gluten-free options for each of the recipes. We also enjoy organic, pasture-raised eggs occasionally. They are a good source of protein, vitamin D, $B_{12}$, and other important nutrients, so we included a chapter with egg recipes (see page 85). We left them out of our other recipes, however, including baked goods and veggie burgers. So, if you're avoiding them, don't worry. Most of the recipes will still work for you.

### Remember, the pescan diet is not a diet!

It's one of the great limitations of the English language that there is only one word to describe both a temporary weight-loss plan and the kinds of food that a person regularly eats. Pescan is the latter, which is why we prefer to call it a lifestyle. This is not a temporary fix or about dropping a few pounds to fit into a dress. It's the process of regularly choosing foods that make you feel amazing until it becomes a habit and a way of life. You may lose weight initially, but once you get to a healthy weight, you'll stay there. You can literally throw away your scale. We did, and it felt great.

# STOCKING YOUR KITCHEN

Empty cupboards are less than inspiring. When you have ingredients on hand and ready to go, it's much easier to get creative in the kitchen and prepare a healthy meal at any given moment. Below are some of the items that we think are must-haves. All are available from natural-food stores such as Whole Foods Market, or online.

### Fresh Fruits and Vegetables
These are really the stars in our kitchen; the other ingredients are there to help them shine. Local produce is usually fresher and therefore more nutritious and tastier. Choose organic whenever possible to avoid consuming carcinogenic pesticides. Buy produce at least once a week. This should include vegetables that can be used raw in salads and wraps, such as lettuce, tomatoes, carrots, baby dark leafy greens, radishes, cucumbers, and celery. Also buy seasonal vegetables for roasting, sautéing, or steaming as well as fresh fruit for breakfast, dessert, and healthy snacking. We recommend keeping a couple of large sweet potatoes and russet potatoes ready to bake for an easy meal. Onions, shallots, fresh ginger, and garlic are fundamental flavor builders. The juice from fresh lemons and limes can be used to brighten many dishes; plus, they make water taste more exciting. Avocado adds richness to sandwiches and wraps and makes a luscious topping for soups, salads, and, yes, toast.

### Frozen Fruit and Peas
Frozen fruit is often less expensive than fresh and makes a great base ingredient for smoothies. Try it in our Go-To Smoothie Bowl (page 71). You can also freeze your own! Simply wash and cut your fruit prior to freezing in zip-top plastic bags. Be sure to peel bananas, hull berries, and discard pits and cores before freezing. Very ripe spotty bananas make the best frozen bananas for smoothies. Frozen peas taste like springtime and are an easy way to add protein and color to rice dishes and pasta dishes. They're also the base for our English Pea Soup with Mint (page 104).

## Grains, Legumes, Nuts, and Seeds

These items are the dry good foundation of your pescan kitchen. If you're starting from scratch, we recommend stocking up on the following basics:

**GRAINS //** quinoa, brown rice, buckwheat or kasha, wild rice, and oats

**LEGUMES //** black beans, garbanzo beans, pinto beans, lentils, and great Northern or cannellini beans

**NUTS/SEEDS //** almonds, cashews, pecans, walnuts, and pistachios, and chia, hemp, pumpkin, sunflower, and sesame seeds

Store these foods in an airtight container to help prevent spoilage and to keep bugs out. Whole grains and dried legumes can be kept for a few years in a cool pantry (below 75°F/24°C). Nuts and seeds have a shorter shelf life, and will generally keep 3 to 6 months in the pantry, or up to one year in the fridge. Discard any items that are discolored or smell musty or rancid. Nuts that taste unusually bitter are spoiled and should not be eaten.

## Eggs

Organic pasture-raised eggs are best from a taste, nutritional, and animal-welfare standpoint. They have higher amounts of vitamin E and beneficial omega-3s compared to conventional eggs. If you have a backyard, chickens are surprisingly easy to keep, just be sure to check your local ordinances to see if they're allowed. Jacq keeps a small four-chicken flock in her backyard in Los Angeles with no trouble at all. If you're interested in keeping chickens, it's best to buy them from a local farm rather than a large hatchery.

## Seafood

The fish counter is a good place to get expert advice. Find a trusted fishmonger and ask questions. They're usually happy to help and can even give you cooking tips. If you live near a body of water, local wild-caught fish is usually freshest, but farmed and frozen fish can be good alternatives.

Fish should smell like the ocean, not "fishy." They should have clear, not cloudy, eyes. The gills should be bright pink or red, not dark or brownish. If you are buying fillets, make certain that there is no brown or yellow discoloration around the edges. When buying frozen fish, choose fish that has been flash frozen at sea and shows no signs of frost or ice particles inside the package.

Look for seafood from the United States, the UK, Europe, or Canada, which have stricter standards for farmed fish and better managed fisheries than many other countries. Aquaculture regulation is still somewhat lax, however, so your best bet is to download the Monterey Bay Aquarium's Seafood Watch app (seafoodwatch.org) and choose fish ranked as "Best Choice" to ensure that you are buying sustainable products. The Environmental Working Group website (ewg.org) provides an online shopping tool that helps people find sustainable seafood that is low in mercury and high in omega-3 fatty acids. You can also look for fresh or frozen farmed products with the blue "Aquaculture Stewardship Council" (ASC) label, or if you are buying wild fish, look for the "Marine Stewardship Council" (MSC) logo.

There are also a growing number of sustainable fish markets in many cities which make buying better seafood easy. The top-ranked supermarket for sustainable seafood is Whole Foods Market—it has higher than government standards for farmed fish and prohibits the use of antibiotics, added growth hormones, pesticides, genetically engineered fish, and poultry by-products in feed. Thrive Market (thrivemarket.com) sells only sustainable wild-caught fish or responsibly farmed fish online and delivers it in eco-friendly packaging.

ACCORDING TO SEAFOOD WATCH'S "SUPER GREEN LIST," THE BEST SEAFOOD CHOICES BASED ON LOW MERCURY LEVELS, BENEFICIAL NUTRIENTS, AND SUSTAINABILITY CURRENTLY ARE:

US-farmed clams, mussels, oysters // Wild Atlantic mackerel from Canada and the United States // Farmed freshwater coho salmon from the United States // Wild-caught Alaskan salmon // Albacore tuna from the United States or British Columbia (troll- or pole-caught) // Sablefish/black cod from Alaska and the Canadian Pacific

FISH WITH THE HIGHEST MERCURY LEVELS THAT SHOULD BE AVOIDED ARE:

King mackerel // Marlin // Orange roughy // Shark // Swordfish // Tilefish from the Gulf of Mexico // Bigeye and ahi tuna // Bluefish // Grouper

You'll want to keep a few types of packaged fish in your kitchen, such as anchovy fillets for sauces and salad dressings like our Green Goddess Dressing (page 107). Good-quality canned or jarred skipjack or albacore tuna, wild salmon, and mackerel (especially those packed in 100 percent olive oil) are delicious and all you need to turn a salad into a well-rounded meal. We like Wild Planet and Safe Catch brands.

Look at individual recipes to learn more about buying shrimp, lobster, mussels, clams, and specific types of fish.

### Tofu

Tofu is made from coagulated soy milk. It comes in different textures that can be used in a variety of applications. You can use soft silken tofu to add creaminess to desserts and smoothies. It's also one of the main ingredients in our savory Creamy White Sauce (page 152). For most of our recipes, we use extra-firm tofu, which is moist but holds its shape well and is excellent for slicing and cubing, and can be used in a variety of cooking techniques. Try it pan-fried in our Crispy Turmeric Spiced Tofu (page 133) recipe. We also use vacuum-packed super-firm tofu, which has a lower moisture content, for recipes such as our Curried Tofu Scramble (page 72).

There has been some controversy surrounding soy foods and cancer risk because of the presence of isoflavones, which are sometimes called plant estrogen. However, a recent research review by the American Institute for Cancer Research noted that human studies show moderate amounts of soy foods including tofu (one to two servings per day) do not increase cancer risk and in some cases may even lower it. Nevertheless, soy is one of the most common genetically modified crops. For this reason, we prefer to use organic soy products.

### Bread

Whole-grain breads contain protein and fiber and are a much better choice than breads made with white flour, which has been stripped of almost all of its fiber and nutrients. Buy 100 percent whole-grain breads with a short list of ingredients that you recognize. Some people have an easier time digesting sourdough breads because they are a fermented food. If you have celiac disease or are avoiding gluten, look for gluten-free bread made from nutritious ingredients like chickpea, buckwheat, or oat flour.

### Pasta

Look for whole-grain pastas, which come in a variety of shapes. There are also some newer pastas made from chickpeas or black beans that are high in protein and a great alternative to traditional pasta.

### Herbs and Spices

These are the ingredients that can take your dish from fine to fabulous. See our guide to cooking with herbs and spices on page 29. The availability of fresh herbs will vary depending on the season. To keep herbs fresh, trim their stems and place them in a glass of water. If you have room to keep the glass in the fridge, the herbs will keep even longer. Another way to keep your herbs fresh is to wrap them in a slightly damp paper towel and cover with plastic wrap, keeping the top and bottom ends open. Herbs are also incredibly easy and rewarding to grow, even in an apartment. We both keep small herb gardens. Look into container gardening, if you're interested.

You can also find organic spices online if your market has a limited selection or low turnover.

### Vinegars/Mustards

These add a ton of flavor to dishes and dressings while adding very few calories. We always keep whole-grain and Dijon mustard in the fridge. Alkalizing Bragg raw apple cider vinegar is our go-to. Good-quality balsamic vinegar and extra-virgin olive oil are all you need for a simple yet delectable salad dressing.

We also make champagne, red wine, and white wine vinegars. All you have to do is add leftover wine or champagne to a clean jar along with a splash of Bragg raw apple cider vinegar. Put some cheesecloth on top and secure with a ring or rubber band; keep adding to the jar anytime you have leftover wine. Eventually you may see a jelly-like blob in your vinegar. Don't worry—it's normal. That's the mother that has grown. You can strain it out and discard it if it bothers you.

Umeboshi vinegar (aka ume plum vinegar) is made from pickled plums and has a complex, salty taste that is a key component in our Mediterranean Tofu Feta (page 203) and our Kale-Walnut Pesto (page 161).

### Oils

For most of our cooking, we use a pure California olive oil simply labeled "olive oil," which has a higher smoke point than extra-virgin olive oil. We use extra-virgin olive oil for raw applications, such as dressings and drizzling. Coconut oil is wonderful in baking and many cooking applications. Virgin coconut oil has a mildly sweet coconut flavor; refined coconut oil has a more neutral flavor and is better for higher-temperature cooking. Sesame oil and truffle oil can be used as finishing oils and add unmatched flavors.

### Sweeteners

Candy-like Medjool dates are the most nutritious sweetener, and you'll find we use them throughout the book. They also make a wonderful snack, especially when stuffed with nut butter, as in our Hazelnut-Stuffed Medjool Dates (page 206). One hundred percent pure maple syrup and raw honey are natural unprocessed liquid sweeteners that also taste amazing. Coconut sugar is our go-to granulated sugar. It's made from the dried sap of the coconut palm tree and contains more nutrients and is lower on the glycemic index than white sugar.

### Salt

Salt is the single most important ingredient you will use to enhance the flavor of your food, but not all salt is created equally. Regular table salt has all of its nutrients refined out of it and usually includes anti-caking agent additives. It tends to have a flat, one-dimensional flavor. Look for unrefined sea salt or natural Himalayan salt instead. All of our recipes have been tested with kosher salt from the brand Real Salt. It is mined in Utah from an ancient ocean and is America's only pink salt. It contains more than sixty trace minerals and can be found at natural-food markets such as Whole Foods. Our favorite flaky sea salt is from Oregon's Jacobsen Salt Co., available at many gourmet shops, but Maldon salt works well also and is widely available. Hepp's Salt Co. out of Venice, California, has truly unparalleled smoked salts and truffle salts that add an incredible savoriness to a plant-forward kitchen. Their 7-Fire smoked sea salt is the best and available at farmers' markets in Los Angeles or online at heppssalt.com.

### Nut Butters/Tahini

Nut butters are a creamy and delicious treat any time of day. They're a great way to add plant protein, healthy fats, and a nutrient boost to whatever you're eating. Try them spread on toast with a drizzle of honey and some apple slices for breakfast, stuffed into celery or dates as a snack, or in a smoothie to add creaminess. You can add a spoonful to your oats or porridge. Almond butter and peanut butter are classics, but pecan, cashew, hazelnut, and macadamia butters are all amazingly delicious. Tahini is a sesame seed butter and a key ingredient in hummus. You can use it as a drizzle on bowls or mix it with lemon juice and olive oil to make a creamy salad dressing that is especially tasty on kale.

### Tamari and Bragg Liquid Aminos

Tamari is a Japanese fermented soy sauce. It has a darker color and richer flavor than most common soy sauces and is generally made without the addition of wheat and therefore gluten-free. Double-check the label if you are avoiding gluten. As with all soy products, it is best to buy organic to avoid genetically modified ingredients. Bragg Liquid Aminos is another gluten-free sauce derived from soybeans. It is useful when you want to add savoriness to a dish that does not have an Asian flavor profile. Try a spoonful stirred into a pot of your favorite grains.

### Miso Paste

Miso is a paste made from fermented soybeans, chickpeas, or grains. It has a salty, savory, and slightly sweet cheesy flavor. In other words, it's an umami bomb. It enhances and deepens other flavors without dramatically changing them. We use it in a variety of recipes to add a little needed funk. A tiny bit goes a long way, and it keeps for ages in the fridge. Try it in our Kale-Walnut Pesto (page 161) or our Creamy White Wine Risotto with Roasted Mushrooms and Thyme (page 142) to get a good idea of what it can do. There are slight differences in flavor depending on the base ingredient, but it's OK to substitute one for the other in recipes; for example chickpea miso instead of sweet white (soy) miso.

### Sun-Dried Tomatoes and Olives

Whenever a dish is lacking flavor, adding just a few slivers of sun-dried tomatoes and/or olives can really turn things around. They keep well in the refrigerator and can be added to sauces, salads, and wraps.

### Hot Sauce

Hot sauce is great as a condiment, and is also a quick and easy way to add a ton of flavor and complexity to sauces and marinades. Two kinds we always have on hand are OrganicVille Sky Valley sriracha sauce to use in bowls, wraps, and Asian-style dishes, and Organic Harvest Foods jalapeño pepper sauce for a Mexican flavor. These are the sauces we like to use in our Spicy Buffalo Tofu Fingers with Avocado Ranch Dressing (page 196). You'll also want to keep a jar of spicy and aromatic harissa, the Moroccan style chile paste, for recipes like our Honey-Harissa Grilled Shrimp with Roasted Vegetables, Charred Grapefruit, and Wild Rice (page 175).

### Fish Sauce

This pungent, salty sauce made from fermented fish adds an irreplaceable depth of flavor to many sauces. It's quite potent, so use sparingly. Look for sauces without additives. We use Red Boat fish sauce made from wild black anchovies and sea salt.

## Dairy Replacements

Vegan cheese and other dairy replacements understandably got a bad reputation. A lot of the early products were highly processed, unhealthy foods that tasted terrible. In the last few years, a new generation of products has emerged that taste incredible and are made from simple ingredients. More are continuously being added, but here's our current list of favorite brands and flavors.

### CHEESE/BUTTER

*Kite Hill (almond based)* Cream Cheese, Ricotta, Truffle Dill & Chive, Soft Fresh Original

*Miyoko's (cashew based)* Vegan Butter, Mozzarella, Smoked Farmhouse, Black Ash, Double Cream Chive

*Treeline (cashew based)* Classic, Herb-Garlic Flavor, Green Peppercorn

### YOGURT

*Forager Project (cashew based)* Unsweetened Plain, Vanilla Bean

*Coyo (coconut milk based)* Natural, Vanilla Bean

*Anita's (coconut milk based)* Plain, Blueberry Chia, Mango

### MILK

*Elmhurst* Milked Almonds, Milked Cashews, Milked Walnuts, Milked Hazelnuts

*New Barn Almondmilk* Unsweetened, Unsweetened Vanilla

## Canned Beans, Tomatoes, and Artichoke Hearts

You can use canned beans as the base for a quick meal, as a side dish, or as a filling for burritos. Add them to salads and wraps for extra fiber and protein. Check out our Quick and Jazzy Canned Beans recipes (page 127) for more ideas. Canned tomatoes make an easy base for sauces like our Veggie Tempeh Bolognese (page 167). Artichokes are a meaty vegetable and make a tasty addition to salads, wraps, bowls, and pastas.

## Flours and Almond Meal

There is a plethora of nutrient-dense flours and nut meals at the market these days. We recommend keeping whole-wheat or gluten-free flour, as well as buckwheat flour, brown rice flour, chickpea flour, and almond meal, on hand. Store whole-grain flours in an airtight container, 4 to 6 months in the pantry, or up to 1 year in the refrigerator. Nut and seed meals should be stored in the fridge and will keep for up to 6 months.

## Baking Soda/Baking Powder/Arrowroot

Baking soda and baking powder are used to create fluffiness in baked goods and pancakes. Arrowroot is a beneficial root starch that can be used as a thickener in place of cornstarch.

## Raw Cacao Powder, Cocoa Powder, and Cacao Nibs

These ingredients allow you to create naturally delicious chocolatey treats that are filled with nutrients. Cacao is thought to be the highest source of antioxidants and magnesium of all foods.

Cacao powder has the richest, most delicious flavor and is simply ground cacao beans. Cocoa powder also comes from ground cacao beans, but is then heat processed at a high temperature. It is slightly less nutritious than cacao powder, but contains fewer calories, is generally easier to find, and is less expensive. We use natural (non-alkalized) cocoa powder with no added sugars. Cacao nibs are broken-up pieces of cacao beans and add a bitter chocolate crunch to oatmeal, yogurt, and desserts.

## Vanilla Beans and Vanilla Extract

Nothing compares to the heady aroma of real whole vanilla beans. The flavor they impart in drinks and desserts borders on magical. Unfortunately, they are priced as such, so we reserve them for special occasions, like when we make our Spiced Rosé Poached Pears with Vanilla-Pine Nut Cream Cheese (page 229). For day-to-day use, vanilla extract makes a fine substitute.

## Spirulina

Due to its powerful nutritional benefits—it's exceptionally high in protein and antioxidants—many cultures around the world include spirulina as part of their daily diets. It is a blue-green algae that has a strong earthy flavor and can be added to smoothies, overnight oats, and porridge. It is an especially nice addition to chocolate desserts, where it can balance sweetness and add depth of flavor, like in our Chocolate Tahini Tart with Fresh Oranges (page 214). Look for it in the supplement or superfood section at the market and be sure to buy it in powdered form rather than pills.

*"Good food is very often, even most often, simple food."*
—ANTHONY BOURDAIN

# Cooking School

## BASICS AND BATCH COOKING

# GETTING STARTED

Abbie: When I first began to learn how to cook with Jacqueline, kitchen basics were exactly where we started. Not only is this a gentle way to ease into cooking, but these recipes are incredibly useful on a daily basis and will help you gain confidence in the kitchen. There's nothing more intimidating than the idea of launching into a full-blown recipe when you barely know how to handle a knife. My first embarrassing moment in the kitchen was when I had to admit that I didn't know how long to boil an egg. Yep, lesson number one was how to boil an egg.

Jacq taught me how to cook with weekly batch cooking lessons for beans, grains, homemade nut milks, and veggies. She showed me where to shop and what to buy, the essential pantry items and utensils I would need at home, and how to use and take care of them. Sunday became our cooking day. During these cooking lessons, we also came up with a list of basic recipes that we can make in one session that will set us up for healthy eating throughout the week. If you get in the habit of making these few items on a regular basis, it will change the way you eat, feel, and live for the better!

This weekly food preparation is an activity that can be nice to do on your own, even meditative, but we highly recommend wrangling up friends or loved ones to join in on the fun. In a couple of hours, you'll have the foundation for endless combinations of bowls, wraps, salads, veggie patties, and snacks that can be prepared in less time than it takes to check your Instagram or catch up on the news. You can even share a meal together when you're done and enjoy the fruits of your labor. Learning how to cook is a beautiful journey. It's endless; it's an ongoing exploration. Start with these basics and build from there. And most importantly, have fun!

**EVERY WEEK MAKE THESE MUST-HAVES**

1 pot of beans (favorites: black, garbanzo, cannellini, pinto)

1 pot of grains (favorites: brown rice, quinoa, wild rice, amaranth)

1 to 2 baked sweet potatoes per person

Roasted seasonal vegetables

1 to 2 dips or spreads (our favorites are: Artichoke Hummus with Za'atar (page 202), Avocado-Lime Cream (page 179), Creamy Cashew Sour Cream (page 139), and Quick Pico de Gallo (page 200))

Plant milk

**IF YOU HAVE A LITTLE EXTRA TIME OR MORE HANDS ON DECK, TRY MAKING**

Raw veggies prepped for snacking, salads, and/or smoothies

A salad dressing

A cheese replacement (like our Mediterranean Tofu Feta (page 203) or Cashew–Pine Nut Parmesan (page 165))

A few jars of PB&J Overnight Oats (page 64) or Carrot Cake Chia Pudding (page 83)

**Game Plan**

Make these basic recipes in the order below to get the most out of your time in the kitchen. Set timers as you go to keep it easy. If this list feels intimidating, don't worry! We'll give you simple detailed instructions on how to cook and store these foods on the following pages. You will be able to get all of this done in an hour and a half to two hours and will be eating like a master chef in no time.

Preheat the oven to 425°F (220°C).

Start cooking the beans first, as they take the longest to make. See page 35.

Once the beans are simmering, get your grains on the stove. See page 29.

When your oven is hot, prick your sweet potatoes a few times with a fork and place them on a baking sheet in the oven. Bake for 45 minutes to 1 hour, until you can prick them easily with a fork.

Get your seasonal veggies ready for roasting (page 41), then add them to the oven. You may also want to make steamed (page 45) or sautéed veggies (page 49) for variety throughout the week.

Prepare your dips, such as Artichoke Hummus with Za'atar (page 202), Fire-Roasted Baba Ghanoush (page 205), or Avocado-Lime Cream (page 179).

Make the plant milk (page 55). We like to make both a sweetened and unsweetened version for the week.

Finish with anything else your heart desires!

# HOW TO COOK LIKE A PRO

Jacq: I don't know what I was expecting when I started culinary school, but almost all of the lessons start off the same way: You are handed a recipe, you make it to the best of your ability, following the instructions exactly, then the rest of the class samples your dish. At first, I thought it was kind of a waste. After all, as an aspiring chef, shouldn't I be focusing on making up dishes and using my creativity? But as I went along, I realized there is no magic trick to becoming a good cook. You learn by doing. Working with trusted recipes is the best way to learn technique and gain an understanding of flavor. At school, they emphasized a few points to keep in mind when cooking from a recipe, so I wanted to share them here with you.

**READ THE ENTIRE RECIPE FIRST SO THERE ARE NO SURPRISES //** This will help you manage your time and avoid any mistakes while you're cooking.

**PREPARE YOUR MISE EN PLACE //** This is the fancy French way of saying get yourself organized. Go down the ingredient list and get all of the items you need in front of you. You don't want to be running back and forth to the pantry as you cook or frantically searching

for curry powder as your pot's about to boil over. Measure your ingredients ahead of time, when possible, and organize them so you can follow each step of the recipe without hesitation. When you get in the habit of doing this, cooking becomes much more relaxing.

**GET YOUR PREP WORK DONE BEFORE YOU START COOKING //** Wash any vegetables that need washing. Chop the vegetables that need chopping. When a recipe calls for "one onion," you can prep by peeling the onion. When it calls for "one onion, thinly sliced," you want to have the onion peeled and thinly sliced before you start. Many recipes move quickly once you get going. If you don't have your ingredients prepared ahead of time, you're much more likely to have something burn.

**USE LEVEL MEASURES UNLESS OTHERWISE STATED //** At school, they made us run the back of a knife over our measuring spoons and cups as we measured spices and flours. The ingredients you are measuring should be precise and in line with the top of the spoon or the cup. The exceptions are when it says "heaping" or "scant." Heaping means you want to use a little extra of the ingredient. For example, a "heaping teaspoon" is a teaspoon plus a little mound over the rim of the spoon. Scant is when it falls just below the rim of the spoon or measuring cup.

**IF THE SIZE OF PRODUCE IS NOT SPECIFIED, IT MEANS MEDIUM //** If a recipe calls for "1 carrot," it is implied that it is not one tiny, adorable baby carrot, or one of those giant state-fair-winning carrots. It's just, you know, an average carrot that you would find at a supermarket. Don't get too caught up in wondering if your carrot is the perfect size. Recipes without precise weights or measurements are generally flexible enough so that a little more or less of one ingredient won't change the outcome.

**DON'T BE AFRAID TO TASTE THINGS AS YOU GO AND TO MAKE ADJUSTMENTS //** In your house, you're the head chef! If you love garlic, throw in an extra clove. If you love spicy food, add a little extra cayenne. And, of course, you can always dial up or down the salt and pepper. For best results, use Real Salt kosher sea salt in our recipes. If unavailable, use any sea salt or kosher salt without additives. If using a fine grain salt, use scant measurements since kosher salt is less dense.

# GRAINS

You've probably heard that eating whole grains can help you lower your cholesterol and cut your risk of heart disease. As with beans and veggies, the high fiber content in grains also helps you maintain a healthy weight. When paired with beans, they make a complete protein and are a nourishing foundation for a limitless number of meals. Serve whole grains alongside sauteed veggies, stir-fries, or curries. Or use them in salads, wraps, and bowls.

**So how should you cook them?**
You can cook grains either by boiling or steaming, or turn them into a risotto or pilaf. The easiest method is to cook them as you would pasta—at a low boil in a lot of salted water until tender, then drain. This technique is great because no measuring is needed and it keeps the grains separate. The only downside to boiling—and it's kind of a biggie—is that many of the nutrients in the grains are lost in the cooking water. For this reason, steaming is the preferred method.

**Steaming and Soaking**
When steaming whole grains, we recommend referring to the package instructions to determine the specific amount of liquid and grains needed for cooking. The package will also indicate whether your grains need to be soaked or rinsed and how long to cook. If you buy your grains from a bulk bin, you can give them a rinse and check the chart on page 30 for cooking times.

Soaking grains overnight can improve digestibility and shorten cooking times. The traditional way to soak grains is to cover them with a two-to-one ratio of warm water to grains, plus 1 tablespoon of apple cider vinegar per cup of water, and allow to soak overnight. This gives the grains a bit of a tangy flavor so we usually skip this step, but health gurus and people who have trouble digesting unsoaked grains swear by this technique. When you're ready to cook the grains, drain, rinse, and be sure to drain well again before cooking.

You can keep your grains simple, or add a little salt or other seasonings. Our favorite way to make flavorful steamed grains is to use a vegetable broth as our cooking liquid and to finish with finely chopped fresh parsley, green onions, or chives. These herbs not only add a boost of vitamins and flavor, but they also pair well with many other dishes.

## COOKING WITH HERBS AND SPICES

*Nothing adds more character and excitement to basic recipes than herbs and spices.*

One of the most common mistakes home cooks make is to not use enough of these ingredients. Not only do they make food come alive, but they also have medicinal qualities. It's a win-win.

It's usually best to add hearty fresh herbs, dried herbs, and spices *before* cooking so that they have time to infuse the other ingredients with flavor. Delicate fresh herbs are best added *after* cooking for a tremendous burst of flavor, nutrients, and color. Finish any dish with a sprinkle of chopped delicate herbs or fold them into grains, beans, scrambles, soups, curries, and pastas. Be sure to add finishing herbs just before serving so they do not have time to wilt or discolor. Some examples of what to use as you play in the kitchen are:

**HEARTY OR DRIED HERBS //** fresh rosemary, oregano, bay leaves, sage or thyme; any dried herbs or herb blends, such as herbes de Provence or Italian seasoning

**SPICES AND SPICE BLENDS //** turmeric, chili powder, ground ginger, cinnamon, cardamom, paprika, cumin, red pepper flakes, curry powder, berbere spice, black pepper

**DELICATE HERBS //** basil, cilantro, dill, chives, parsley, tarragon, and mint

For information on buying and storing herbs and spices, see Stocking Your Kitchen on page 20.

# Perfect Everyday Grains

*Check the package for directions to soak or rinse your grains and follow as instructed. Even if grains do not require soaking, you can still choose to soak them overnight as described on page 29. Just be sure to rinse and drain well afterward. If you are using grains from a bulk bin, it's best to rinse them well in a fine-mesh strainer until the water runs clear. Check the chart below for approximate cooking times. Soaked grains will cook 25 to 30 percent faster than the times listed.*

PREP // **2 minutes**
COOK // **11 to 75 minutes (see chart opposite)**
MAKES // **about 3½ cups (720 g)**
SERVES // **6**

**1 cup (about 200 g) whole grain**

**Vegetable broth (see chart opposite)**

**¼ cup (13 g) finely chopped fresh flat-leaf parsley leaves, chives, or green onion**

**Kosher sea salt and black pepper (optional)**

In a medium heavy pot, combine the grains along with the appropriate amount of vegetable broth as your liquid. Bring up to a boil over medium-high heat, stirring occasionally. Lower the heat until the liquid is gently simmering and cover with a tight-fitting lid. At this point, set your timer according to the chart and don't give in to the temptation to stir or lift the lid.

After the recommended amount of time, check to see if the grains are done. If they are tender, drain any excess water, replace the lid, and proceed to the next step. If the grains are still crunchy, check to see if any liquid remains at the bottom of the pot. If not, add a splash of water, then replace the lid and continue cooking. Check every 5 to 10 minutes until the grains are done.

Turn off the heat and let rest, covered, for 10 minutes. This helps to redistribute moisture evenly and keeps your grains from getting mushy. Fluff the grains with a fork and fold in the herbs. Season with salt and pepper, if desired.

Serve immediately, or cool completely and refrigerate or freeze promptly. The best way to cool grains quickly is to spread them on a baking sheet and then stick them in the fridge or freezer. Once cool, you can store them in an airtight container in the refrigerator for up to 5 days or freeze for up to 3 months. Do not store them in the pot they were cooked in! It will keep the grains warm for too long, which can lead to bacterial growth.

**CHEF'S NOTE** Some people prefer the flavor of grains that have been toasted before they are steamed. To toast your grains, heat 1 teaspoon oil over medium-high heat in the pot in which you'll be steaming your grains. Add the grains and cook, stirring frequently, until the grains are very dry and begin to smell toasted. Add the appropriate amount of liquid and proceed with recipe as written.

## COOKING CHART

*Below is the ratio of liquid to 1 cup (about 200 g) of grain. Grains that have been pre-soaked will cook 25 to 30 percent faster and require about 15 percent less liquid.*

| Grain | Liquid | Steaming Time |
|---|---|---|
| Amaranth | 2 cups (480 ml) | 25 minutes |
| Barley, hulled* | 3 cups (720 ml) | 75 minutes |
| Barley, pearl* | 3 cups (720 ml) | 45 minutes |
| Brown rice | 2 cups (480 ml) | 45 minutes |
| Brown basmati rice | 2 cups (480 ml) | 40 minutes |
| Buckwheat | 2 cups (480 ml) | 15 minutes |
| Farro* | 3 cups (720 ml) | 30 minutes |
| Kasha | 2 cups (480 ml) | 11 minutes |
| Millet | 2½ cups (600 ml) | 50 minutes |
| Quinoa, red | 1¾ cups (420 ml) | 20 minutes |
| Quinoa, white | 1¾ cups (420 ml) | 15 minutes |
| Wild rice | 2¼ cups (540 ml) | 45 minutes |

*Grains marked with an asterisk are not gluten-free*

# Red Quinoa with Herbes

*This simple yet flavorful quinoa recipe is one of our favorites thanks to its versatility. Serve it as a side dish, or use it as a base for bowls and wraps. You can also toss it in salads like The Happy Hippy Quinoa Salad (page 118) to add more substance and protein.*

PREP // **2 minutes**
COOK // **about 20 minutes**
MAKES // **about 3 cups (550 g)**
SERVES // **6**

**1 cup (170 g) red quinoa**
**1¾ cups (420 ml) vegetable broth**
**¾ teaspoon black pepper**
**½ teaspoon herbes de Provence**
**Handful fresh flat-leaf parsley leaves, finely chopped**
**Kosher sea salt (optional)**

Rinse the quinoa in a fine-mesh strainer until the water runs clear, then drain well.

In a medium heavy pot, combine the quinoa with the broth, pepper, and herbes de Provence. Bring to a boil over medium-high heat and give the quinoa a stir. Lower the heat until the broth is gently simmering and cover with a tight-fitting lid. Set your timer for 20 minutes and don't give in to the temptation to stir or lift the lid.

Cook until the water has been absorbed and the grains are tender and appear to have grown little tails, 20 to 25 minutes.

Turn off the heat and let rest, covered, for 10 minutes. Fluff the quinoa with a fork and fold in the parsley. Season with salt, if desired.

Serve immediately, or cool completely and store for later use in bowls, wraps, soups, or salads. Refrigerate in an airtight container for up to 5 days or freeze for up to 3 months.

**FEEL GOOD INGREDIENT // QUINOA** Quinoa is gluten-free and high in fiber and protein. It also contains all nine essential amino acids. The lysine in quinoa improves tissue growth and repair, the high magnesium content can help regulate blood sugar and energy levels, and the $B_2$ (riboflavin) can even improve your metabolism.

# Kasha with Caramelized Onions and Walnuts

*We love kasha because it gives you all of the satisfaction of a hearty grain in a fraction of the cooking time. In this recipe, caramelized onions deepen kasha's earthy, nutty flavor, and the toasted walnuts add meatiness and crunch. Serve it as a side dish or anywhere you would use rice or quinoa.*

PREP // **5 minutes**
COOK // **17 minutes**
MAKES // **about 3½ cups (510 g)**
SERVES // **6**

**1 tablespoon olive oil**
**1 onion, roughly chopped**
**¼ teaspoon kosher sea salt, or to taste**
**2 teaspoons fresh thyme leaves, or ¼ teaspoon dried thyme**
**2 cups (480 ml) mushroom broth (substitute vegetable broth, if necessary)**
**1 cup (175 g) kasha (also called toasted buckwheat groats; see Notes)**
**½ teaspoon black pepper, or to taste**
**1 tablespoon balsamic vinegar**
**½ cup (50 g) chopped walnuts**
**3 tablespoons finely chopped fresh chives**

In a small skillet, heat the oil and onion over medium-high heat for 1 minute. Add the salt and thyme. Lower the heat to medium-low. Cook, stirring occasionally, until the onion is soft and browned, about 15 minutes.

Meanwhile, in a medium heavy pot with a lid, bring the broth to a boil over high heat. Add the kasha and pepper, give it a stir, then lower the heat. When the liquid is gently simmering, cover the pot with a tight-fitting lid. Cook until the grains are just tender, about 11 minutes. Turn off the heat and let rest, uncovered.

When the onion is browned, sprinkle it with the vinegar and stir. Scrape the onion into the kasha, then wipe out the onion pan with a paper towel. Add the walnuts to the same pan and toast over medium-high heat for about 2 minutes, shaking the pan continuously, until they just begin to brown and smell toasted. Fold them into the kasha along with the onion and chives. Taste and adjust seasoning, if needed.

Serve immediately, or cool completely and store for later use in bowls, wraps, soups, or salads. Refrigerate in an airtight container for up to 5 days or freeze for up to 3 months.

**CHEF'S NOTES**  If you can't find kasha at the store, you can toast raw buckwheat groats in a dry pan over medium heat. Stir the buckwheat groats continuously for 4 to 5 minutes, until lightly browned and fragrant.

Turn this recipe into delicious kasha fritters! Whisk 1¼ cups (150 g) of the cooked kasha with 2 eggs and a pinch of salt and pepper. Heat a nonstick skillet over medium heat and use ¼ cup (30 g) of the mixture for each fritter; cook 2 to 3 minutes per side. Makes 5 fritters.

**FEEL GOOD INGREDIENT // KASHA/BUCKWHEAT**
Like quinoa, buckwheat is a pseudo grain—a seed used as a grain. It also is considered a complete protein, containing all nine essential amino acids, and is naturally gluten-free. It's high in fiber and very rich in minerals including manganese, copper, magnesium, iron, and phosphorous. The antioxidants in buckwheat protect against free-radical damage, support cellular function, prevent inflammation, and support brain, liver, digestive, and cardiovascular health.

# Citrus-Herb Wild Rice

*This is what we think of as a great supporting dish. It's not the star, but it plays its role perfectly and helps the rest of the meal shine. It adds color, flavor, freshness, and drama. Try it with our Tilapia al Mojo de Ajo (page 188) or in our Honey-Harissa Grilled Shrimp with Roasted Vegetables, Charred Grapefruit, and Wild Rice (page 175) to see what we mean.*

PREP // **2 minutes**
COOK // **1 hour**
MAKES // **about 3 cups (490 g)**
SERVES // **6**

**1 cup (160 g) wild rice**

**2¼ cups (540 ml) vegetable broth**

**1 scant teaspoon black pepper**

**¼ cup (10 g) finely chopped fresh herbs (see Notes)**

**1 tablespoon fresh lemon, orange, or grapefruit juice**

**1 tablespoon olive oil**

**1 teaspoon lemon, orange, or grapefruit zest**

**Kosher sea salt (optional)**

Rinse the rice in a fine-mesh strainer until the water runs clear, then drain well.

In a medium heavy pot, combine the rice, broth, and pepper and bring to a boil over high heat. Lower the heat to a gentle simmer and cover the pot with a tight-fitting lid. Set your timer for 45 minutes and don't give in to the temptation to stir or lift the lid.

Cook until the grains are tender and the water is absorbed, 45 to 55 minutes. If there is excess water at 45 minutes, leave the lid off for the remaining cooking time.

Turn off the heat and let rest, covered, for 10 minutes. Fluff the wild rice with a fork and fold in the fresh herbs, lemon juice, oil, and lemon zest. Season with salt, if desired.

Serve immediately, or cool completely and store for later use in bowls, wraps, soups, or salads. Refrigerate in an airtight container for up to 5 days or freeze for up to 3 months.

**CHEF'S NOTES**  Any delicate fresh seasonal herb will work here. Basil, tarragon, and mint are great summer herbs. Chives, parsley, and cilantro tend to complement heartier cold-weather dishes as well as spicier foods. Dill is especially lovely with seafood dishes.

You can change the flavor of this dish depending on the type of citrus you use. Lemon is the most versatile, but orange and grapefruit are fantastic as well.

**FEEL GOOD INGREDIENT // WILD RICE**  Wild rice is actually a grass grown in shallow water between two and four feet deep. It is low in fat and high in fiber. It contains about as much protein per serving as quinoa and also includes manganese, phosphorus, magnesium, and zinc. The B vitamins in wild rice enhance the health of your skin, hair, eyes, and liver.

# BEANS

Nothing beats the flavor of a fresh pot of beans simmered on the stovetop. You'll find homemade beans to be deeply rich, creamy, and satisfying. Beans are an excellent source of protein (good for your muscles), soluble and insoluble fiber (good for a healthy gut biome and digestion), and complex carbohydrates (good for your mood and energy levels). They are also extremely satiating, even more filling than animal protein.

Use them in burritos, bowls, or wraps, toss them in salads, add bulk to soups, or puree them for a delicious spread or dip. Or just keep it simple and serve yourself a big dishful. We love them with a drizzle of olive oil and a handful of sprouts as a post-workout snack.

## Sorting and Picking

The older the bean, the longer it takes to cook, so buy your dried beans at a store with high turnover. Before using beans and legumes, spread them out on a baking sheet and sort through them for any little stones or other debris. Also, be sure to remove any shriveled or discolored beans.

## To Soak or Not to Soak: That Is the Question

There is some debate as to whether soaking beans overnight before you cook them is a good idea, and, to be honest, there's not a clear answer to this simple question.

**PROS //** If you soak them, your beans will cook about 25 to 30 percent faster, and also more evenly. Plus, some phytic acid and lectins, which are considered antinutrients, and enzyme inhibitors present in the skins of the bean will be neutralized, making them easier to digest. Overnight soaking reduces the phytic acid by about 50 percent.

**CONS //** Some mineral nutrients and flavor will leach into the soaking water. Darker beans will also lose some color during soaking.

**VERDICT //** Soaking can be really beneficial for large beans and chickpeas, which take longer to cook and soften. For all other beans, we've found that either way works fine. However, if you tend to have trouble digesting beans, we recommend soaking them beforehand.

**TO SOAK BEANS IN THE TRADITIONAL WAY //** Place the beans in a large bowl and cover them with water by 3 inches (7.5 cm). Add 1 tablespoon of salt per pound of beans and let them soak overnight. Drain and rinse before using.

**QUICK-SOAK METHOD //** Place the beans in a pot and cover with water by 2 inches (5 cm). Bring to a boil over high heat and boil the beans for 2 minutes. Turn off the heat and allow the beans to sit in the water for 1 hour. Drain and rinse before using.

**NO SOAK //** If you forget or decide not to soak your beans ahead of time, just sort and give them a really good rinse before cooking. Know that they'll take a little longer on the stovetop, but it will be worth the wait. Lentils and split peas generally do not need soaking.

## Other Tricks for Making Beans Easier to Digest

We like to add a little piece of dried seaweed called kombu to our beans; it not only adds depth of flavor but also helps to soften them and make them more digestible. Kombu contains enzymes that help break down the particular sugars in beans that are the gas-producing culprits. You can find it at any health-food store or Asian market. Also, be sure to skim any foam that rises to the top after you bring your beans to a boil to help increase digestibility.

## BEAN COOKING TIMES

*These are approximate cooking times for unsoaked beans. Older or drier beans may take longer. Beans that have been soaked will cook 25 to 30 percent faster. Beans are done when tender through to the center.*

| | |
|---|---|
| Adzuki | 1 hour |
| Black | 1 to 1½ hours |
| Black-eyed peas | 1 hour |
| Cannellini | 1 hour |
| Chickpeas | 2 to 3 hours |
| Fava | 40 minutes to 1 hour |
| Great Northern | 1 to 2 hours |
| Kidney | 1 hour |
| Lentils, brown | 45 minutes to 1 hour |
| Lentils, green | 30 to 45 minutes |
| Lentils, red | 15 to 25 minutes |
| Mung | 1 hour |
| Pinto | 1 to 2 hours |
| Soy | 3 to 4 hours |
| Split peas, green | 45 minutes |

# Everyday Magic Beans

PREP  //  **2 minutes**

COOK  //  **15 minutes to 4 hours (see chart on page 36)**

MAKES  //  **about 5 cups (925 g), or the equivalent of 3 (15-ounce/425-g) cans of beans**

SERVES  //  **6**

**1 pound (455 g) dried beans (optionally soaked), rinsed and drained**

**1 to 3 teaspoons kosher sea salt**

**1 (3 by 1-inch/7.5 by 2.5-cm) strip kombu**

**½ onion, peeled and root end trimmed**

**2 to 6 garlic cloves, smashed and peeled (depending on your love of garlic; we use 4)**

**1 to 2 bay leaves**

**Herbs or spices (optional; see Cooking with Herbs and Spices on page 29)**

Place the beans in a large heavy pot with a lid. Fill the pot with enough water to cover the beans by 2 inches (5 cm) and bring to a boil over medium-high heat. Skim off any foam that comes up to the surface.

Lower the heat to keep the beans at a gentle simmer. Add 1 teaspoon salt if the beans have been soaked in salted water. If not, add 2 to 3 teaspoons depending on your love of salt. Add the kombu, onion, garlic, bay leaf, and any other seasonings you might enjoy. Be aware that adding any acid, such as vinegar or tomatoes, will toughen the beans and is not recommended until the end of the cooking process. Leave the lid off for firmer beans to use in salads and pasta dishes. If you want creamier beans for dips, creamy soups, curries, and burritos, cover the pot with the lid slightly ajar.

Check on the beans periodically. Add more water if needed during cooking to make sure the beans stay immersed. Give them a stir every once in a while to help them cook evenly and to make sure they don't stick to the bottom. Continue simmering the beans until they are as tender as you like. Remove the onion half.

Serve immediately, or cool completely and refrigerate or freeze promptly. Store them in an airtight container in the refrigerator for up to 5 days or freeze for up to 6 months.

**HOW TO SMASH GARLIC** *The idea is not to smash it to pieces but to break the clove just a bit so its oils can release. The best tool for smashing garlic is a chef's knife. Set the flat side of the knife on top of an unpeeled clove of garlic with the sharp edge facing away from you. Place the heel of your hand on top of the knife and apply enough pressure so that the clove splinters but does not completely fall apart. The skin should separate easily, and the clove should remain in one flattened piece. The garlic is now ready for cooking. This technique is useful to prep garlic for beans, soups, and sauces. It can also be used to flavor oils when sautéing with much less risk of burning compared with minced garlic.*

# Fiesta Black Beans

*Jacq: In my Mexican American family, a party isn't a party without a big pot of beans waiting to feed a crowd. Over the years, I've added a few Californian touches to enhance my family recipe. The orange adds a brightness to complement the spices and just a little touch of good olive oil helps round out the flavor. Pair this with our Fiesta Veggie Rice (page 146) and Broiled Fish Tacos with Smoky Salsa Verde (page 177) and get your dancing shoes ready!*

PREP // **5 minutes**
COOK // **1 to 1½ hours**
MAKES // **about 5 cups (925 g), or the equivalent of 3 (15-ounce/425-g) cans of beans**
SERVES // **6**

1 pound (455 g) dried black beans, unsoaked

½ sweet orange, such as Cara Cara or Valencia

½ yellow onion, peeled and root end trimmed

4 large garlic cloves, smashed and peeled (see page 36)

1 (3 by 1-inch/7.5 by 2.5-cm) strip kombu (optional)

1 tablespoon kosher sea salt

2 teaspoons black pepper

2 teaspoons ground cumin

2 dried bay leaves

Pinch red pepper flakes

1 tablespoon extra-virgin olive oil

Fresh cilantro for garnish (optional)

Spread the beans on a baking sheet and pick out any little stones or shriveled or discolored beans. Rinse the beans well in a colander, then place them in a heavy pot with a lid. Fill the pot with enough water to cover the beans by 2 inches (5 cm). Bring to a boil over medium-high heat and skim off any foam that has risen to the surface.

Lower the heat to keep the beans at a gentle simmer. Add the orange, skin side down, to the pot. Add the onion half, garlic, kombu (if using), salt, pepper, cumin, bay leaves, and red pepper flakes. Do not skim once you have added the spices, as they may rise to the surface.

Cover the pot, leaving the lid slightly ajar. Give the beans a stir every once in a while to help them cook evenly and to make sure they don't stick to the bottom. Add more water if needed during cooking to make sure the beans stay immersed. Continue simmering until they are tender. This should take 1 to 1½ hours.

Remove the orange from the pot and set aside. Discard the onion half, garlic cloves, and bay leaves. When the orange is cool enough to handle, squeeze its juice into the pot. Drizzle with the oil and give it a final stir. Garnish with the cilantro, if desired. Cool and refrigerate in an airtight container for up to 5 days or freeze for up to 6 months.

**FEEL GOOD INGREDIENT** // **BLACK BEANS** High in vitamins A and B$_9$, iron, phosphorus, calcium, magnesium, manganese, copper, and zinc, these beans provide a slow-burn energy release. They support colon health, nervous system care, and aid in lowering blood cholesterol levels.

# Rosemary Great Northern Beans

*Jacq: This recipe is inspired by the delicately fragrant beans I ate when traveling through Tuscany. Not only are they great as a side dish, but they make a wonderful base for soups (just add veggies and broth) and salads like our White Bean and Celery Salad with Pesto Grilled Shrimp (page 122).*

PREP // **6 to 12 hours soaking time**
COOK // **1 to 1½ hours**
MAKES // **about 5 cups (885 g), or the equivalent of 3 (15-ounce/425-g) cans of beans**
SERVES // **6**

1 pound (455 g) dried great Northern beans, soaked (see page 35)

4 cups (960 ml) vegetable broth

½ yellow onion, peeled and root end trimmed

4 large garlic cloves, smashed and peeled (see page 36)

1 (3 by 1-inch/7.5 by 2.5-cm) strip kombu (optional)

2 (3-inch/7.5-cm) sprigs fresh rosemary

2 bay leaves

1 teaspoon kosher sea salt

1 teaspoon white pepper

Pinch ground nutmeg

Pinch red pepper flakes

2 tablespoons dry white wine

Extra-virgin olive oil

Finely chopped fresh flat-leaf parsley leaves

Drain and rinse the beans in a colander. Transfer the beans to a heavy pot with a lid. Pour in the vegetable broth, then add enough water so the beans are covered by 2 to 3 inches (5 to 7.5 cm). Bring to a boil over medium-high heat and skim off any foam that has risen to the surface.

Lower the heat to keep the beans at a gentle simmer. Add the onion half, garlic, kombu (if using), rosemary, bay leaves, salt, white pepper, nutmeg, and red pepper flakes. Do not skim once you have added the spices, as they may rise to the surface.

Cover the pot, leaving the lid slightly ajar. Give the beans a stir every once in a while to help them cook evenly and to make sure they don't stick to the bottom. Add more water if needed during cooking to make sure the beans stay immersed. Continue simmering until they are tender. This should take 1 to 1½ hours. Add the white wine and simmer for a minute more.

Remove the onion half, rosemary, and bay leaves. Serve the beans with a bit of their cooking liquid, a drizzle of olive oil, and a sprinkle of parsley. Cool and refrigerate in an airtight container for up to 5 days or freeze for up to 6 months.

**FEEL GOOD INGREDIENT // ROSEMARY** A good source of iron, calcium, and vitamin B$_6$, rosemary also contains antibacterial and antioxidant acids, along with several essential oils that have anti-inflammatory, anti-fungal, and antiseptic properties. It boosts immunity and helps brain function, and its aroma can lift your mood.

## Old West Pintos

*This is our most quintessentially American bean recipe. A little sweet, spicy, smoky, and salty all at once. Perfect for barbecues and potlucks, they're also our favorite beans to make during our weekly food prep. Pair them with our Whole Roasted Maple Ginger Carrots (page 42), Greens Agrodolce with Almonds and Crispy Shallots (page 50), and a simple grain for the ideal Buddha bowl.*

PREP // **6 to 12 hours soaking time**
COOK // **1 to 2 hours**
MAKES // **about 5 cups (855 g), or the equivalent of 3 (15-ounce/425-g) cans of beans**
SERVES // **6**

**1 pound (455 g) dried pinto beans**

**1 yellow onion, peeled, halved, and root end trimmed, divided**

**4 large garlic cloves, smashed and peeled (see page 36)**

**1 (3 by 1-inch/7.5 by 2.5-cm) strip kombu (optional)**

**1 bay leaf**

**1 teaspoon kosher sea salt plus more to taste**

**1 teaspoon smoked paprika**

**¼ teaspoon cayenne pepper**

**1 tablespoon olive oil**

**2 teaspoons maple syrup**

**Fresh flat-leaf parsley for garnish (optional)**

Drain and rinse the beans in a colander. Transfer them to a heavy pot with a lid and fill the pot with enough water to cover the beans by 2 to 3 inches (5 to 7.5 cm). Bring to a boil over medium-high heat and skim off any foam that has risen to the surface.

Lower the heat to keep the beans at a gentle simmer. Add 1 onion half, the garlic, kombu (if using), bay leaf, salt, paprika, and cayenne. Do not skim once you have added the spices, as they may rise to the surface.

Cover the pot, leaving the lid slightly ajar. Give the beans a stir every once in a while to help them cook evenly and to make sure they don't stick to the bottom. Add more water if needed during cooking to make sure the beans stay immersed. Continue simmering until they are tender. This should take 1½ to 2 hours.

Meanwhile, cut the remaining onion half into ¼-inch- (6-mm-) thick slices. In a small skillet, heat the oil, sliced onion, and a pinch of salt over medium heat for 1 minute, then lower the heat to medium-low and cook, stirring occasionally, until the onion is caramelized, about 20 minutes.

When the beans are tender, remove the onion half, garlic cloves, and bay leaf. Stir in the maple syrup and caramelized onion. Garnish with the parsley, if desired. Serve immediately, or cool and refrigerate in an airtight container for up to 5 days or freeze for up to 6 months.

**FEEL GOOD INGREDIENT // PINTOS** Like most beans, pintos are high in protein and fiber. They are a great source of vitamins B$_1$ and B$_6$, and the minerals copper, phosphorus, iron, magnesium, manganese, and potassium. These nutrients can help detoxify the body, improve heart and brain function, and assist in maintaining normal blood pressure.

# VEGETABLES

# ROASTED VEGETABLES

Roasting is hands down the easiest way to make the most out of almost any vegetable. It brings out the natural sweetness in veggies, giving them a caramelized exterior while keeping the inside moist and tender. Roasting is also perfect for batch cooking or feeding a crowd. You can make several servings at once, or roast a few types of veggies on the same baking sheet to prep for the week ahead.

One of the great advantages of roasting is that you don't need a recipe. Every vegetable will be enhanced by the simple addition of olive oil, salt, pepper, and a little time in a very hot oven. That being said, roasting is also a great opportunity to get creative with your favorite hearty herbs and spices. Once you are comfortable with the basic technique, you can have fun experimenting with different flavor combinations.

## ROASTED VEGETABLES CHEAT SHEET

*These are the vegetables that we love to roast. Smaller or thinner pieces will cook on the lower end of the range while larger pieces take longer. Cooking times also vary depending on your oven and whether you like your veggies to be tender-crisp or charred.*

| Vegetable | Roasting Time |
| --- | --- |
| Asparagus | 10 to 15 minutes |
| Beets, wedges | 35 to 45 minutes |
| Broccoli/Cauliflower, florets | 20 to 30 minutes |
| Brussels Sprouts, halved | 15 to 25 minutes |
| Cabbage, large wedges | 35 to 45 minutes |
| Carrots/Parsnips | 30 to 45 minutes |
| Eggplant, cubes | 25 to 35 minutes |
| Fennel, wedges | 35 to 45 minutes |
| Mushrooms, bite-size | 15 to 25 minutes |
| Potatoes, wedges | 30 to 40 minutes |
| Radishes, halved or whole | 15 to 25 minutes |
| Sweet potato, wedges | 30 to 40 minutes |
| Tomatoes, plum, halved | 35 to 45 minutes |
| Winter Squash, cubed | 30 to 40 minutes |
| Zucchini, rounds | 15 to 25 minutes |

## Easy Everyday Roasted Veggies

Preheat the oven to 425°F (220°C) and line a baking sheet with parchment paper.

Cut veggies into even-size pieces. In general, for larger vegetables like root vegetables or squash, you'll want to cut them into large bite-size pieces (1- to 1½-inch/2.5- to 4-cm chunks). For smaller items, like new potatoes, cherry tomatoes, radishes, or Brussels sprouts, you can cut them in half or quarter them, depending on their size. Again, think bite-size. Really tiny veggies or thinner ones like asparagus can be left whole.

Place the veggies in a large bowl and drizzle with olive oil or melted coconut oil. Toss to coat evenly so the vegetables have a nice sheen. Sprinkle with sea salt and pepper and toss again. At this stage, you could also add a splash of balsamic vinegar, other spices, hearty fresh herbs such as thyme, oregano, rosemary, and sage, or dried herbs such as herbes de Provence.

Place the vegetables on the parchment-lined baking sheet, leaving any extra oil behind in the bowl so the veggies don't get soggy. Using parchment ensures that they won't stick to the pan and makes for easy cleanup. If you want extra browning, like with Brussels sprouts, you may want to skip the parchment. Direct contact with the pan creates more browning.

Spread the veggies in a single layer, creating a little space between each piece so dry air can circulate around it. This will create nice caramelization. If the pieces are crowded and on top of each other, they will start to steam as they cook, which can lead to a mushy, unappealing texture instead of the tender-crisp look you're going for.

Flip or toss vegetables when they're about halfway done cooking so that both sides are browned. The exception to this is cut tomatoes, which you'll want to cook skin side down only, and Brussels sprouts and asparagus, which will likely be cooked through by the time the first side browns.

Once vegetables are tender and lightly browned, remove from the oven and add any toppings such as fresh herbs, seeds, chopped nuts, and/or a squeeze of lemon if you like.

# Whole Roasted Maple-Ginger Carrots

*These carrots are an irresistible sweet and spicy treat! This recipe has become one of our staple dinner party sides because it pairs well with a variety of dishes and people always gobble it up. Look for smaller carrots that are fairly uniform in size. Rainbow carrots make for an especially pretty presentation if you can find them.*

PREP // **5 minutes**
COOK // **35 minutes**
SERVES // **4 as a side**

**14 to 16 small to medium carrots (2 bunches; see Note)**

**1-inch (2.5-cm) piece ginger, peeled**

**1 tablespoon olive oil**

**1 tablespoon maple syrup**

**1 tablespoon water**

**⅛ teaspoon kosher sea salt**

**⅛ teaspoon black pepper**

**⅛ teaspoon cayenne pepper**

**⅛ teaspoon ground cumin**

**2 tablespoons fresh orange juice (from ½ orange)**

**1 tablespoon chopped fresh cilantro leaves**

Preheat the oven to 425°F (220°C) and line a baking sheet with parchment paper. Trim the carrot tops (if necessary) to ¾ inch (2 cm). Rinse and scrub the carrots well with a paper towel for a rustic look or peel them if you want a very smooth look. Place the carrots on the baking sheet.

In a small bowl, grate the ginger, then add the oil, maple syrup, water, salt, black pepper, cayenne, and cumin. Whisk with a fork. Pour the mixture over the carrots and turn them a couple of times to ensure they are well coated. Arrange the carrots in a single layer and make sure there is a little space between each one to allow air to circulate.

Roast the carrots in the oven for 20 minutes. Remove and carefully turn them using tongs. Pour the orange juice over them and sprinkle with the cilantro leaves. Roast for 10 to 15 minutes more, until they are soft and wrinkly on the outside and tender-crisp in the middle.

**CHEF'S NOTE** If you are using carrots that are on the larger side, you can slice them in half lengthwise to cut down on the cooking time. In this case, use fewer carrots so they fit on the baking sheet in a single layer.

**FEEL GOOD INGREDIENT // CARROTS** The idea that carrots are good for your eyes is more than an old wives' tale. Carrots are packed with beta-carotene, which is converted in our liver into vitamin A, helping to maintain healthy skin, hair, nails, and, yes, vision.

# Roasted Brussels Sprouts, Dried Cherries, and Walnuts

*These sprouts are super easy to prepare and totally addictive! We've balanced their slightly bitter earthiness with sweet-tart dried cherries and crunchy, meaty walnuts. You'll want them again and again.*

PREP // **10 minutes**
COOK // **15 minutes**
SERVES // **4 as a side**

**1 pound (455 g) baby Brussels sprouts**

**3 tablespoons olive oil**

**1 tablespoon balsamic vinegar**

**1 tablespoon honey**

**½ teaspoon kosher sea salt**

**½ teaspoon black pepper**

**3 tablespoons dried cherries (or substitute dried cranberries)**

**3 tablespoons chopped walnuts**

**1 heaping tablespoon roughly chopped fresh cilantro**

**Pinch flaky sea salt (optional)**

Preheat the oven to 425°F (220°C). Trim any rough bottoms from the Brussels sprouts and cut them in half. In a large bowl, toss with the oil, vinegar, honey, salt, and pepper and allow to marinate for 5 to 10 minutes.

Arrange the Brussels sprouts in a single layer on a baking sheet, cut-side down. Roast until nicely browned and tender, 12 to 15 minutes, depending on their size. Toss with the dried cherries, walnuts, and cilantro. Finish with flaky sea salt, if desired.

**FEEL GOOD INGREDIENT // BRUSSELS SPROUTS**
Brussels sprouts fall into the cancer-fighting cruciferous vegetable category, along with their cousins broccoli, cauliflower, and kale. They provide you with a whopping twenty essential vitamins and minerals, including vitamins C, K, A, and $B_6$, folate, and manganese.

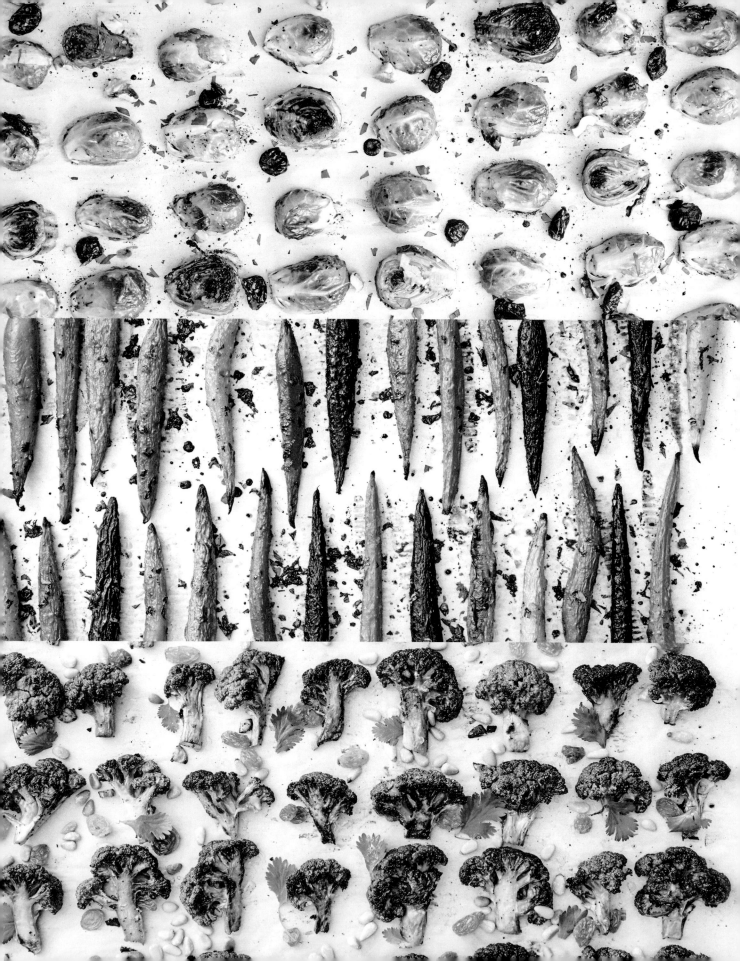

## Roasted Curried Cauliflower with Raisins and Pine Nuts

*There are a lot of ways to enjoy cauliflower, but few as flavorful and easy as this recipe. It's spicy, sweet, and nutty: Try it once, and it's sure to become one of your regulars. Serve it with Red Quinoa with Herbes (page 32) and Quick Curried Garbanzos (page 127) to make hearty bowls or as a side dish for Island-Style Whole-Roasted Fish with Pickled Vegetables (page 184).*

PREP // **5 minutes**
COOK // **30 minutes**
SERVES // **4 to 6 as a side**

3 tablespoons raisins (see Notes)

3 tablespoons olive oil

4 cloves garlic, roughly chopped

½ teaspoon curry powder

¼ teaspoon kosher sea salt, or to taste

⅛ teaspoon black pepper, or to taste

2 tablespoons chopped fresh cilantro, divided

1 large head cauliflower (about 2 pounds/910 g), cut into florets (see Notes)

1 rounded tablespoon pine nuts

Preheat the oven to 425°F (220°C) and line a baking sheet with parchment paper. Set aside.

In a small pot, bring 1 inch (2.5 cm) water to boil, add the raisins, and turn off the heat to allow the raisins to soak and plump up.

Meanwhile, in a large bowl, whisk together the oil, garlic, curry powder, salt, pepper, and 1 tablespoon of the cilantro. Add the cauliflower to the bowl and toss to evenly coat it with the oil. Spread the florets on the baking sheet and roast for 15 minutes, turn once, and return to the oven. Roast until it is tender-crisp and browned, about 10 minutes more, and transfer to a serving bowl.

Place the pine nuts on the hot baking sheet and toast them in the oven for 2 minutes. Be sure to remove them promptly, as they burn easily. Drain the raisins in a strainer and sprinkle over the cauliflower. Fold in the pine nuts and the remaining 1 tablespoon cilantro. Taste and add a little more salt and pepper, if needed.

**CHEF'S NOTES** If you can get your hands on a purple cauliflower, pair it with golden raisins in this recipe for a beautifully colorful dish.

This recipe can be multiplied. Just make sure to keep the florets in a single layer when roasting. Use two baking sheets, if necessary.

**FEEL GOOD INGREDIENT // CAULIFLOWER** Cauliflower is one of the top food sources of vitamin C. You get 77 percent of your daily value in a 1-cup (135-g) serving. It helps to reduce inflammation and boost immunity against common colds and infections, making it a truly feel-good food!

**STEAM TO REHEAT** *Steaming is the best way to reheat foods quickly and keep them moist without ruining the integrity of the flavors. For vegetables, you can add them directly back to the steamer basket. For other items that need to stay contained, such as grains, you can place them in a small oven-safe dish and add them to the steamer basket. For foods that you'd like to keep drier, such as muffins or burritos, wrap them in parchment paper first. You'll be surprised by how quickly the food heats up and how much better the texture remains compared with microwaving.*

# STEAMED VEGETABLES

Steaming can be a great way to highlight the flavors of fresh seasonal ingredients. Steam cooks food at a temperature that is higher than boiling water with no oil needed, making it one of the fastest and cleanest cooking techniques. Another benefit of steaming is that it helps preserve water-soluble vitamins, like B-complex vitamins and vitamin C, both of which are essential to feeling good.

Keep in mind that steaming doesn't add flavor to your food; it only brings out the natural flavor, so it's important to use the best-tasting, freshest ingredients with this method. The only special equipment you'll need is a perforated steamer basket or colander that can fit inside a pot with a tight-fitting lid. The rest is easy.

## Steamed Clean Veggies

Cut the vegetables of your choice into even-size pieces. Delicate greens such as baby bok choy or baby spinach can be left whole. Sturdier greens such as kale or Swiss chard should be torn or cut into pieces to make them easier to eat.

Fill a pot with about 1 inch (2.5 cm) water and place a steamer basket inside. Make sure the water does not touch the bottom of the basket.

Bring the water to a boil, add the vegetables, and cover the pot with a lid. Most bite-size vegetables take between 5 and 7 minutes to cook: Harder vegetables such as carrots, sweet potatoes, and beets will take a few minutes longer. Dark leafy green will take a little less time, about 3 minutes.

Be very careful to open the lid away from you when you check on your veggies to avoid getting burned. The vegetables are done when they are tender but not mushy and still have a vibrant color.

Enjoy your steamed vegetables plain, or finish them in a variety of ways. A squeeze of lemon, a drizzle of good-quality olive oil, and a pinch of flaky sea salt and black pepper is always nice. You can also dress your steamed vegetables in a vinaigrette and sprinkle with fresh herbs for a vibrant flavor, or use a little soy sauce and toasted sesame oil for an Asian-inspired taste.

## Steamed Sesame Spinach Salad

*Abbie: The first time I tried this recipe I ended up eating the whole lot! It's so yummy and rich with goodies. Every bite is a delight for the taste buds and a healthy boost for the mind and body. I love the nod to Japanese cuisine here too, as it is my absolute favorite.*

PREP // **2 minutes**
COOK // **5 minutes**
SERVES // **2 as a side**

**12 ounces baby spinach (about 11 cups/340 g raw)**
**2 tablespoons sesame seeds**
**2 teaspoons coconut sugar**
**2 tablespoons tamari**
**1 teaspoon seasoned rice wine vinegar**
**1 teaspoon water**
**½ teaspoon toasted sesame oil**

Fill a large pot with 1 inch (2.5 cm) water and place a steamer basket inside. Bring the water to a boil over medium heat, then add the baby spinach. Cover with a lid and steam until just wilted and bright green, about 3 minutes. Turn off the heat.

Lay a clean dish towel flat on the counter. Using tongs, spread the spinach on the towel to cool. When the spinach is cool enough to handle, place it in the middle of the towel. Bundle the towel around the spinach and squeeze out all of the excess water. Spread the squeezed spinach on a plate and place in the refrigerator to chill.

Meanwhile, make the dressing: Toast the sesame seeds in a dry skillet over medium heat, shaking the pan constantly. When the seeds begin to brown and pop, immediately remove from the heat and transfer the seeds to a mortar. Add the sugar and grind the sesame seeds and sugar together with a pestle until the seeds are fragrant and just crushed. Add the tamari, vinegar, water, and sesame oil to the sesame seeds and mix with a fork.

In a medium bowl, toss the spinach with the dressing and serve immediately, or keep in the fridge for up to 3 days.

# Garlic-Lemon Steamed Broccoli

*You'll be hard-pressed to find another broccoli recipe that gives you this much flavor in such a short amount of time. Use it as a scrumtious side dish or nutritious addition to salads, wraps, and bowls.*

PREP // **5 minutes**
COOK // **5 minutes**
SERVES // **3 as a side**

**1 head of broccoli (about 1 pound/455 g)**

**2 tablespoons olive oil**

**1 tablespoon fresh lemon juice**

**1 large garlic clove, finely chopped**

**Pinch red pepper flakes**

**4 basil leaves, cut into chiffonade**

**Kosher sea salt and black pepper**

**Cashew–Pine Nut Parmesan (page 167; optional)**

Place a steamer basket in a pot filled with 1 inch (2.5 cm) water. Bring the water to a boil over medium heat.

Cut off the bottom third of the broccoli stem and discard. Cut the crown of the broccoli into 2-inch (5-cm) florets. Peel the remaining stem using a paring knife, then cut the stem into ½-inch- (12-mm-) thick coins.

When the water is boiling, add the broccoli to the steamer basket and cover the pot with a tight-fitting lid. Steam the broccoli until bright green and just tender, 4 to 5 minutes.

Meanwhile, in a small skillet, heat the oil over medium heat, then add the lemon juice, garlic, and red pepper flakes. Cook for about 1 minute, swirling the pan occasionally, until the garlic is just fragrant. Turn off the heat immediately to avoid burning. Throw the basil in the pan and swirl again.

Place the steamed broccoli in a serving bowl and sprinkle with a generous pinch of salt and pepper. Drizzle with the garlic oil and toss to coat. Finish with a sprinkle of the Parmesan, if you like. Refrigerate leftovers for up to 3 days.

**FEEL GOOD INGREDIENT // BROCCOLI** Broccoli is full of beneficial nutrients, such as vitamins C, K, A, B₆, folate, potassium, and manganese, all of which are great for your skin, eyes, digestion, and immune system.

# Steamed Bok Choy with Spicy Lime Dressing

*Abbie: I am always looking for simple ways to prepare greens that lets them shine on their own but with a bit of flavor to enhance their deliciousness. This recipe does just that. The dressing has a springtime lightness to it along with a spicy little kick that really brings the bok choy to life and has you going back for more.*

PREP // **5 minutes**
COOK // **10 minutes**
SERVES // **4 as a side**

**4 baby bok choy (about 1 pound/455 g)**

**2 tablespoons tamari**

**2 tablespoons fresh lime juice (from 1 big lime)**

**½ teaspoon lime zest**

**½ teaspoon sambal oelek (substitute sriracha, if unavailable)**

**¼ teaspoon grated fresh ginger (grated on a Microplane; see Note)**

**1 teaspoon toasted sesame oil**

**1 teaspoon honey**

**1 tablespoon minced fresh chives or cilantro**

Place a steamer basket in a pot filled with 1 inch (2.5 cm) water. Bring the water to a boil over medium heat.

Cut each bok choy in half lengthwise. When the water is boiling, add the bok choy to the steamer basket and cover with a tight-fitting lid. Steam until the base of the bok choy is just tender·when pierced with a knife, about 5 minutes.

Meanwhile, in a small bowl, whisk together the tamari, lime juice, lime zest, sambal oelek, ginger, sesame oil, and honey. Transfer the bok choy to a platter and drizzle with the dressing. Garnish with the minced herbs.

**CHEF'S NOTE** If you do not have a Microplane, you can mince the ginger.

**FEEL GOOD INGREDIENT // BOK CHOY** Bok choy is a quick-cooking, mild-flavored Chinese cabbage ideal for sides, soups, and stir-frys. This nutrient-dense food is full of vitamins C, A, and K and the minerals calcium, magnesium, potassium, manganese, and iron.

# SAUTÉED VEGETABLES

If you're looking to make super-tasty vegetables in a short amount of time, sautéing is the way to go. Cooked at a high temperature with a little fat, it's not only fast but also flavorful. The key is to keep your veggies moving in the pan so they cook evenly and don't burn on the outside before they're cooked through.

## Sautéed Veggie Basics

Cut your vegetables into small, even-size pieces.

Use a pan big enough to spread food in a single layer. This helps to ensure even browning.

Heat the pan over medium-high heat, and when hot, add enough oil to coat the bottom of the pan. Heating the pan first helps to prevent the food from sticking.

Add the vegetables and toss or stir regularly to help them cook evenly. The exception is when you are cooking starchy food such as potatoes or sweet potatoes. In this case, it's best not to toss them until a crispy crust has formed to avoid sticking and seal in their moisture. Once they have a golden crust on one side, toss, then lower the heat to give the food a chance to soften.

Season at the right time. Most sautéed veggies are best seasoned toward the end of cooking to help prevent moisture loss. The exceptions are mushrooms and onions, which benefit from a little bit of salt at the beginning to help draw out their moisture.

Cook until just tender. Timing will vary depending on the vegetable and the size of your cuts. Here are some general guidelines:

Root vegetables such as potatoes, sweet potatoes, beets, carrots, and onions take the longest to cook, upward of 15 minutes. Cutting them in a small dice will help quicken the process, or if you're using a larger cut, you can parboil them first.

Vegetables with medium cooking times include broccoli, cauliflower, bell peppers, thick asparagus, and Brussels sprouts. These can take 5 to 8 minutes.

Vegetables with shorter cooking times include leafy greens, corn, tomatoes, and thin asparagus. These can cook in as little as 2 to 4 minutes.

# Sautéed Garlic-Rosemary Mushrooms

*This simple preparation enhances the savory flavor of mushrooms. Try them on toasted bread for a quick crostini or tossed into pasta for an easy dinner. They're great as a side dish, or paired with Greens Agrodolce with Almonds and Crispy Shallots (page 50) and Rosemary Great Northern Beans (page 38) for a Mediterranean-inspired bowl.*

PREP // **10 minutes**
COOK // **10 minutes**
SERVES // **4 as a side**

**2 tablespoons olive oil or refined coconut oil**

**1 pound (455 g) sliced cremini mushrooms (see Notes)**

**2 teaspoons finely chopped fresh rosemary**

**¼ teaspoon kosher sea salt**

**3 garlic cloves, finely chopped**

**Generous splash dry red wine (about 3 tablespoons; see Notes)**

**Flaky sea salt**

**Freshly ground black pepper**

**1 tablespoon chopped fresh flat-leaf parsley leaves**

Heat a large sauté pan over medium-high heat, then add the oil and swirl to coat the bottom of the pan. Add the mushrooms, rosemary, and salt and cook, stirring or tossing frequently, for 2 minutes. Add the garlic and continue to cook until the mushrooms have released their juices and are tender and browned, about 8 minutes. Pour in the wine and stir until most of the liquid has evaporated. Finish with a generous pinch of flaky sea salt, pepper to taste, and the parsley.

**CHEF'S NOTES** Substitute the mushrooms of your choice. Wild mushrooms are always wonderful, but even plain white button mushrooms are delicious when prepared this way. Slice whole mushrooms into ¼-inch- (6-mm-) thick slices.

If you don't have a wine bottle open, add a tablespoon of balsamic vinegar in its place.

**FEEL GOOD INGREDIENT // GARLIC** The most potent medicinal compound in garlic is called allicin, which can help reduce blood pressure and lower cholesterol.

# Greens Agrodolce with Almonds and Crispy Shallots

*Jacq: After trying the best sautéed greens of my life in Rome, I found out that the simple combo of honey and vinegar creates an amazing flavor. Here we've re-created that Italian-style sweet and sour (known as agrodolce) and added meaty almonds and savory shallots for the perfect balance of flavors and textures.*

PREP // **5 minutes**
COOK // **15 minutes**
SERVES // **4 as a side**

1 pound (455 g) dark leafy greens (mustard greens, kale, Swiss chard, and/or beet greens)

2 tablespoons olive oil, plus more for frying

½ red onion, thinly sliced

Kosher sea salt and freshly ground black pepper

1 tablespoon balsamic vinegar

1 tablespoon honey or maple syrup

Pinch red pepper flakes

1 shallot, thinly sliced crosswise and separated into rings

¼ cup (30 g) Marcona almonds

Trim any woody stems from the bottom of the greens. Tear the center ribs from the leaves and thinly slice the ribs. Heat a large sauté pan over medium-high heat, then add the oil and swirl to coat the pan. Add the sliced ribs, onion, and a pinch of salt; stir. Sauté until the onion is softened and beginning to brown, about 4 minutes.

Roughly chop the remaining greens and add them to the pan. Sprinkle with vinegar, honey, and red pepper flakes and toss to coat. Sauté for about 4 minutes, until the greens are wilted, then turn off the heat. Season with generous pinches of salt and black pepper. Set aside.

Line a plate with paper towels and set it next to the stovetop. In a small skillet, heat ¼ inch (6 mm) oil over medium heat. When the oil is shimmering hot, add the shallot and fry until lightly browned. Remove the rings with tongs as they're done, and transfer to the plate to crisp for 2 minutes. Serve the greens with the almonds and crispy shallots on top.

**FEEL GOOD INGREDIENT // LEAFY GREENS** Dark leafy greens such as kale, spinach, mustard greens, Swiss chard, arugula, and collard greens are full of energizing B vitamins. They have anti-aging properties thanks to their high vitamin K, folate, beta-carotene, and lutein content.

# Calabacitas con Elote

*This is a classic side dish with fresh zucchini and sweet corn. It's particularly delicious in summertime when the ingredients are at their peak. Use this recipe to accompany Tilapia al Mojo de Ajo (page 188), or serve it with Fiesta Black Beans (page 32), Fiesta Veggie Rice (page 146), and Avocado-Lime Cream (page 179) for a Mexican-style bowl with an irresistible combination of flavors.*

PREP // **5 minutes**
COOK // **10 minutes**
SERVES // **4 as a side**

2 tablespoons coconut or olive oil

½ onion, diced

½ red bell pepper, diced

1 poblano or Anaheim chile, seeded and finely chopped

Kernels from 3 ears of corn (see Note)

1 teaspoon dried oregano

2 garlic cloves, thinly sliced

½ (15-ounce/425-g) can diced tomatoes, preferably fire-roasted

2 zucchini, cut into ⅛-inch- (3-mm-) thick slices

Big handful fresh cilantro leaves (¼ cup/10 g)

Kosher sea salt and freshly ground black pepper

Heat a large sauté pan over medium-high heat, then add the oil and swirl to coat the bottom of the pan. Add the onion, bell pepper, chile, corn, and oregano and sauté until the onion is softened and translucent, about 3 minutes. Add the garlic and cook for about 30 seconds more, then add the tomatoes and zucchini.

Stir, then lower the heat to medium-low and partially cover. Cook until the zucchini is tender but not mushy, about 7 minutes. Sprinkle with the cilantro and season with salt and black pepper.

**CHEF'S NOTE** If fresh corn is not available, use 1 (5-ounce/425-g) drained can of corn instead.

**FEEL GOOD INGREDIENT // ZUCCHINI** Zucchini is high in vitamins C, B₆, and K, manganese, riboflavin, potassium, and folate. It contains antioxidants known to improve digestion and heart health, strengthen bones, and support weight loss.

# THE SECRET SAVORY WOW FACTOR

When you think of the basic tastes you probably think of sweet, sour, salty, and bitter, but there is a very important fifth taste: umami. You know that perfect accessory that makes every outfit a little bit better? Umami is like the food version of that. It's not only nice on its own, but it also enhances other flavors. If you think about the taste of a really good mushroom soup or risotto, a rich olive tapenade, or a particularly flavorful stir-fry, you're thinking about umami. It is a taste of savoriness, or fullness of flavor.

Umami is a general term typically used to describe foods containing high levels of the amino acid glutamate. We are programmed to crave umami because it signals to the brain that what we are eating contains life-sustaining protein. While there are plenty of vegetable and seafood sources of umami, in the American diet, the most common sources are meats and aged cheeses. When you cut these out of your savory dishes, it is important to add other umami-rich ingredients to create a deliciously full flavor. Try to include at least one of the ingredients listed opposite in all of your savory dishes.

## Top Pescan Sources of Umami

Soy sauce, tamari, Bragg Liquid Aminos

Miso

Nutritional yeast

Mushrooms, dried or fresh, especially shiitake, maitake, and porcini

Tomatoes, especially roasted or sun-dried

Truffles

Olives

Seaweed

Kimchi and sauerkraut

Roasted or grilled vegetables

Umeboshi plums and ume plum vinegar

Red wine

Aged balsamic vinegar

Roasted garlic

Caramelized onions, leeks, and shallots

Meaty fish, especially anchovies and dried bonito flakes

Shellfish

Fish and oyster sauce

Caviar and bottarga

# HOW TO KEEP YOUR COLORS POPPING

If you've ever had a beautiful purple cauliflower that looked like it had the life drained out of it or made a batch of broccoli that turned a color that can only be described as puke green, you probably thought you had some bad luck or bad produce. In reality, it was neither; it was just plant pigments doing their thing. There are three main categories of pigments that give vegetables their vibrant colors, and they each need to be treated differently to keep your veggies looking their best and brightest.

**GREEN (CHLOROPHYLL) //** Includes asparagus, green beans, broccoli, green bell peppers, and leafy greens.

These pigments are sensitive to overcooking. They initially turn bright green when cooked for a short time but will turn a drab olive color if overcooked. Cooking them with acids such as lemon juice or vinegar will also turn them that unappealing color, so if you use lemon juice or a vinaigrette on your greens to enhance their flavor, do so just before serving.

**PURPLE AND WHITE (FLAVONOIDS) //** Includes purple cabbage, red onion, red radishes, red beets, purple cauliflower, white cauliflower, white asparagus, button mushrooms, and parsnips.

These pigments are water soluble. If you are cooking purple or white vegetables in liquid, the addition of an acid such as lemon juice, vinegar, or wine will help brighten their color. You'll notice this more with purple foods like cabbage, which will turn bright magenta rather than purplish gray, but even white foods like cauliflower will stay a brighter shade of white if you add an acid to the cooking liquid. One to two tablespoons of vinegar, lemon juice or lime juice, or ½ cup (120 ml) white wine added to 1 quart (1 L) water should do the trick.

**ORANGE/YELLOW/RED (CAROTENOIDS) //** Includes squash, carrots, sweet potatoes, tomatoes, and orange, yellow, and red bell peppers.

These colors are stable and not affected much by cooking times or the addition of an acid.

**FOODS THAT BROWN //** Avocados, potatoes, apples, pears, and bananas.

These foods begin to oxidize and discolor soon after they are cut, which is due to a process called enzymatic browning. Good news: It can be slowed by squeezing lemon or lime juice over the food. You can also place the food in acidulated water, which can be made by adding 1½ tablespoons apple cider vinegar or 3 tablespoons lemon juice to 1 quart (1 L) of water. This is especially helpful when you are prepping fruits to use in desserts or fruit salad. Potatoes can simply be placed in plain water to prevent oxygen from hitting their surface.

"A good cook is like a
sorceress who dispenses
happiness"
—ELSA SCHIAPARELLI

# PLANT MILK

It's pretty easy to find nondairy milks at the super-market these days, but those can be made from as little as 2 percent nuts and filled with strange thickeners, emulsifiers, and preservatives. Homemade milks, on the other hand, have a pure flavor and rich, creamy texture and are made with just a few wholesome ingredients.

When making your own, it's best to soak the ingredients ahead of time to soften them, and then to strain the milk after blending to get the smoothest results. We highly recommend investing in a nut milk bag to do this. As with beans and grains, soaking nuts will help remove phytic acid and improve their digestibility. Be sure to use nuts that taste fresh, not bitter or musty. Store them in the fridge or even the freezer until they are ready to use. If you have a nut allergy or are on a budget, oats or sunflower seeds are a great option in place of the nuts. You can use the basic recipe that follows as a substitute for milk or cream in savory recipes, or jazz it up with any number of flavors or sweeteners for a creamy treat.

## SOAKING

*Before making milks, soak the raw ingredients by placing them in a bowl with a two-to-one ratio of filtered water to nuts, seeds, or oats. Cover the bowl with a kitchen towel and soak for the recommended time listed below. Drain, discard the soaking water, and rinse with fresh water. Now you're ready to create some delicious plant milk goodness!*

| | |
|---|---|
| Almonds | 8 to 12 hours |
| Brazil nuts | 2 to 4 hours |
| Cashews | 2 to 4 hours |
| Hazelnuts | 8 to 12 hours |
| Macadamias | 1 to 2 hours |
| Pecans | 4 to 6 hours |
| Pistachios | 4 to 6 hours |
| Rolled Oats | 30 minutes to 8 hours |
| Sunflower seeds | 8 hours |
| Walnuts | 4 to 6 hours |

# Basic Unsweetened Milk Formula

PREP  //  **3 to 5 minutes**
MAKES  //  **1 quart (946 ml)**

**1 cup (about 125 g) soaked raw nuts, seeds, or oats, drained and rinsed**

**3 cups (720 ml) filtered water**

**Tiny pinch kosher sea salt**

Place the nuts, water, and salt in a blender and blend until smooth. This takes about 1 minute in a high-speed blender, up to 3 minutes in a regular blender. Strain through a nut milk bag or cheesecloth. Store your milk in a bottle or jar with a lid in the coldest part of your refrigerator for up 5 days. Shake before using.

**CHEF'S NOTE**  Cashew milk does not require straining.

**PRACTICE RECIPES**

# Creamy Vanilla Cashew Milk

*Abbie: This is one of the first recipes Jacq taught me how to make. This nut milk can be used as a base for smoothies, as a coffee creamer, and also in a variety of breakfast recipes, such as our Millet Porridge with Strawberries, Pine Nuts, and Rosemary Syrup (page 80) and PB&J Overnight Oats (page 64). It's creamy, decadent, and delicious. Not bad for a three-minute recipe.*

PREP  //  **3 minutes**
MAKES  //  **1 quart (960 ml)**

**1 cup (125 g) raw cashews, soaked for 2 to 4 hours, drained, and rinsed**

**3 cups (720 ml) filtered water**

**1 to 2 teaspoons maple syrup (or 1 to 2 dates)**

**Pinch kosher sea salt**

**1 vanilla bean, split down the middle lengthwise, or 1 teaspoon vanilla extract**

CONTINUES

In a blender, combine the soaked cashews, water, maple syrup, and salt. If using a vanilla bean, scrape the black seeds with a butter knife and add them to the blender, or alternatively, use vanilla extract.

Blend, starting on low and bring it up to high speed, for 1 to 3 minutes, until smooth and creamy. Store your milk in a bottle or jar with a lid in the coldest part of your refrigerator for up to 5 days. Shake before using.

**FEEL GOOD INGREDIENT // VANILLA** Coming from the only fruit-bearing orchid that exists in the world, the vanilla bean is great for enhancing our brains and mood. An aphrodisiac that contains magnesium, potassium, calcium, and manganese, this delicious ingredient can be used in its original form, in a powder, or in a liquid extract.

## Strawberry Rose Milk

*Abbie: This is a gorgeous, grown-up version of strawberry milk. Rosewater is a natural mood enhancer, so just a few sips of this pretty pink drink will make you feel soothed and satisfied.*

PREP // **3 minutes**
SERVES // **1**

1 cup (240 ml) unsweetened cashew milk
4 strawberries, hulled
½ teaspoon vanilla extract
1 teaspoon honey, plus more for serving
2 to 3 drops rosewater (see Note)

In a high-speed blender, combine the milk, strawberries, vanilla, honey, and rosewater, and blend, starting on low and bringing it up to high speed, until smooth, about 1 minute. Serve in a glass over ice and drizzle with a bit more honey.

**CHEF'S NOTE** Rosewater is available at many supermarkets, usually in the baking section near the vanilla extract, or in the Middle Eastern food section. It's extremely concentrated, so be careful to add only one drop at a time! Any leftovers can be added to your bathwater for a luxurious soak.

**FEEL GOOD INGREDIENT // ROSEWATER** Rosewater is a natural anti-inflammatory, and it's been proven that the scent can lower levels of the stress hormone cortisol. Cleopatra was apparently so enamored with the fragrance that she dipped her sails in rosewater, leading Shakespeare to write they were "so perfumed that the winds were lovesick with them."

## Mexican Spiced Hot Chocolate

*Jacq: Mexican chocolate was one of my favorite winter drinks growing up. Now when the weather gets chilly I make this healthy sweet and spicy version for a warming treat.*

PREP // **3 minutes**
SERVES // **1**

1 cup (240 ml) walnut or almond milk
1 heaping teaspoon cacao powder
1 teaspoon vanilla extract
1 to 2 teaspoons maple syrup
Pinch ground cardamom
Pinch ground cinnamon
Pinch smoked salt
Tiny pinch cayenne pepper
Freshly grated nutmeg, for serving

In a blender, combine the milk, cacao powder, vanilla, maple syrup, cardamom, cinnamon, salt, and cayenne and blend for a few seconds until smooth. Pour the milk into a small pot and heat over medium-low heat until warm. Serve with a small sprinkle of nutmeg on top.

**FEEL GOOD INGREDIENT // WALNUTS** Walnuts are amazing brain food thanks to their neuroprotective compounds, including vitamin E, folate, melatonin, and omega-3 fatty acids.

# Salted Caramel Pecan Milk

*Jacq: Pecan pairs perfectly with dates and sea salt to create a smooth caramel treat that makes a great afternoon pick-me-up or post-workout beverage. Kids also love the sweet taste of this milk, making it a perfect alternative to drinks made with refined sugar and artificial flavors.*

PREP // **3 minutes**
SERVES // **1**

**2 Medjool dates, pitted**
**1 cup (240 ml) pecan milk (see Note)**
**Pinch kosher sea salt**

If you are not using a high-speed blender, chop the dates first. In a blender, blend the dates with the pecan milk and salt, starting on low and bringing it up to high speed, until smooth, 1 to 3 minutes. Enjoy over ice.

**CHEF'S NOTE** While pecan milk is our favorite for this recipe, feel free to substitute any nondairy milk you prefer. We've tried it with cashew, almond, hazelnut, and macadamia milks. You really can't go wrong with any of them.

**FEEL GOOD INGREDIENT // MEDJOOL DATES** Dates contain a particularly beneficial type of soluble fiber known as beta-D-glucan, and have more potassium per serving than a banana. They're also a source of copper, manganese, magnesium, vitamin B₆, and iron.

*"First we eat, then we do everything else."*
—M.F.K. FISHER

# Breakfast

PREP  //  **5 minutes**

MAKES  //  **about 2½ cups (600 ml)**

SERVES  //  **2 to 3**

# GOOD MORNING GREEN JUICE

1 large (about 11 ounces/310 g) hothouse English cucumber

2 celery ribs

1 navel orange, peeled and segmented (see Note)

¼ cup (60 ml) fresh lemon juice (from 1 to 2 lemons)

1 cup (20 g) lightly packed spinach leaves

¼ cup (13 g) lightly packed fresh mint leaves

1-inch (2.5-cm) piece ginger, peeled (minced if not using a high-speed blender)

Pinch ground turmeric

*Jacq: There's absolutely nothing that makes your body feel better than starting your day off with a fresh green juice! As a chef, I also believe it's important to start your day with something that tastes amazing. Here you get hydrating and nourishing ingredients along with a combination of refreshing flavors that taste as good as they are good for you.*

Juice the cucumber, celery, and orange in a juicer. Pour the juice into a blender and add the lemon juice, spinach, mint, ginger, and turmeric. Blend on high speed until smooth. Enjoy straight or over ice. Refrigerate leftovers for up to 3 days.

**CHEF'S NOTE**  Add an extra orange to the recipe if you prefer your juice on the sweeter side. If you like a "greener" taste (or your liver needs a little extra help in the morning), add a handful of fresh parsley to the blender. And, of course, nothing is stopping you from doing both.

**FEEL GOOD INGREDIENT  //  CELERY** Celery is an excellent source of antioxidants and beneficial enzymes, along with vitamins K, C, and B₆, potassium, and folate. Celery is mainly water and fiber, which makes it very low-calorie. It's a natural diuretic, can help reduce bloating, and may help lower bad cholesterol and blood pressure.

# PEAR-GINGER-CITRUS SMOOTHIE

1 small avocado (or ½ large avocado)

2 oranges, peeled and segmented, with seeds removed

1 Anjou, Bosc, or Asian pear, cut into wedges, with core and stem removed

2 kale leaves, roughly chopped

2 romaine lettuce leaves, roughly chopped

½ cup (120 ml) Creamy Vanilla Cashew Milk (page 55), or any vanilla-flavored nondairy milk

¼ cup (30 g) raw cashews, preferably soaked for 2 to 4 hours, drained, and rinsed

1-inch (2.5-cm) piece ginger, peeled (minced if not using a high-speed blender)

1 tablespoon fresh lemon juice

1 teaspoon apple cider vinegar

½ cup (120 ml) filtered water, plus more as needed

1 cup (150 g) ice cubes

*Abbie: With my lifestyle, smoothies make for a quick, easy, and healthy snack or meal substitute on the go. I particularly love this one for breakfast, as it gives a light and zesty boost. It's also great before or after a workout, as it provides you with the kick you need for peak performance and to maintain steady energy levels.*

Scoop the avocado flesh into a blender and add the oranges, pear, kale, lettuce, milk, cashews, ginger, lemon juice, vinegar, and water. Blend until smooth, about 1 minute in a high-speed blender or 2 minutes in a regular blender.

Add the ice cubes to the smoothie and blend briefly again. If the smoothie is too thick, add a bit more water and blend for a few seconds more, until it's your desired consistency. Pour into glasses and serve.

**FEEL GOOD INGREDIENT // GINGER** Ginger can help prevent bloating by aiding in digestion and removing excess gas. It also has anti-inflammatory compounds which can help relieve period pain, nausea from overindulgences in food and booze, and even the symptoms of morning sickness.

# GOLDEN TEA FOR TWO

**1 quart (946 ml) unsweetened almond milk**

**4 organic Earl Grey tea bags (tags and strings removed)**

**2 teaspoons roughly chopped fresh ginger**

**3 tablespoons maple syrup**

**¾ teaspoon ground turmeric**

**2 tablespoons MCT oil or virgin coconut oil**

**2 pinches ground cinnamon**

*Abbie: Two years ago, I moved to the West Hollywood Hills into a sweet little hillside cottage with Jessie, one of my best friends from Australia. Every weekend we enjoy this delightful turmeric tea, an Ayurvedic-inspired concoction that she picked up during her travels to India. This latte is a healthy, healing brunch-time mimosa substitute (before the mimosas, that is!). Looking out over Los Angeles, a long way from home, it's a magical elixir that is key to unwinding and a golden tea time for two.*

In a medium saucepan, combine the milk, tea bags, and ginger and bring to a boil over high heat. Boil for 3 minutes.

Remove the tea bags and add the maple syrup and turmeric, then reduce the heat to medium-low and simmer for another minute.

Remove from the heat and pour into a blender. Add the oil, and while holding a towel on the lid of the blender, blend for 45 to 60 seconds, starting on low and ending on high speed, until creamy and smooth. If the blender cover does not have steam vents, remove the center portion of the cover to allow steam to escape and place a kitchen towel over the opening to avoid splashes while blending.

Pour the milk tea into two mugs. Sprinkle each with a pinch of ground cinnamon.

**CHEF'S NOTE**  This tea can also be refrigerated for up to 3 days and enjoyed as a cold beverage.

**FEEL GOOD INGREDIENT // EARL GREY TEA**  This black tea is flavored with the oil of the bergamot orange, which is grown in southern Italy. Used for centuries to promote good health, it's both energizing and relaxing. Black tea can improve mental focus and help boost your immunity, digestion, and heart health.

# BLENDED VANILLA ICED MOCHA

1 shot espresso or small cup strong coffee

3 Medjool dates, pitted

1 tablespoon raw cacao nibs

2 tablespoons cocoa powder

2 teaspoons vanilla extract

½ avocado

¼ cup (35 g) raw almonds

¼ cup (30 g) raw cashews

½ cup (120 ml) filtered water

Pinch kosher sea salt

Pinch ground cinnamon

Small pinch cayenne pepper (optional)

1½ cups (225 g) ice cubes

*Jacq: I used to be in love with those blended coffeehouse drinks before I started paying attention to what I put in my body. Once I began reading labels, I realized they were a no-go, so I came up with this version that uses only natural, whole-food ingredients. Not only is it rich and delicious, but it's filled with antioxidants, plant protein, and healthy fats, so it gives you energy to burn for hours.*

In a blender, combine the coffee, dates, cacao nibs, cocoa powder, vanilla, avocado, almonds, cashews, water, salt, cinnamon, and cayenne, if desired. Blend, starting on low and bringing it up to high speed, until smooth. Depending on the strength of your blender, you may need to scrape down the sides of the blender or add more water if the blades get stuck.

Add the ice cubes and blend again until smooth and creamy. Pour into glasses and serve.

**FEEL GOOD INGREDIENT** // **CACAO** Cacao is nutritionally dense and has one of the highest antioxidant ratings of any food, even more so than blueberries. It's also one of the best sources of magnesium, one of the most common mineral deficiencies in the American diet. A neurotransmitter called anandamide, produced naturally in the brain, has also been isolated in cacao. It's known as the "bliss chemical" because it is released when we are feeling pleasure.

*"Let's start at the very beginning, a very good place to start."*

—JULIE ANDREWS
*The Sound of Music*

# PB&J OVERNIGHT OATS

⅓ cup (30 g) old-fashioned or gluten-free rolled oats

⅔ cup (165 ml) cashew or almond milk

1 tablespoon chia seeds

1 tablespoon raisins

Pinch ground cinnamon

TOPPINGS

1 heaping teaspoon peanut butter

1 heaping teaspoon Strawberry-Lemon Chia Seed Jam (recipe follows) or jam of your choice

Sliced fresh fruit

*Jacq: There's no reason such a classic flavor pairing should be limited to the confines of a brown paper bag. Here they move into the morning sunshine to dress up a delicious heart-healthy serving of overnight oats. Like many of our breakfast favorites, you can quickly put this together at night and wake up to something delicious in the morning.*

In a half-pint jar or small bowl, combine the oats, milk, chia seeds, raisins, and cinnamon. Mix well with a fork. Cover with a lid or plastic wrap. Place in the refrigerator for a minimum of 4 hours and up to 3 days. Top with the peanut butter, jam, and fresh fruit just before serving.

**CHEF'S NOTE** Depending on the season, you may want to use fig jam with fresh figs, peach preserves with fresh peaches, or even a mix of flavors, such as apricot jam with fresh blackberries.

**FEEL GOOD INGREDIENT // OATS** The humble oat has been a darling of the health-food world since studies showed that regular consumption can help regulate blood sugar and cholesterol levels. Oats are soothing, inside and out. They contain avenanthramides—antioxidants that have anti-inflammatory effects, both when consumed and applied topically.

## STRAWBERRY-LEMON CHIA SEED JAM

*Chia seeds have a great little party trick: When you mix them with water they turn into a gel. Ta-da! This makes them perfect for jam making. Just mix your strawberries (or any other fruits you love) with these tiny seeds, and you'll get a beautiful, fresh-tasting jam that is just the right consistency without using tons of sugar.*

PREP // **5 minutes**
COOK // **7 minutes**
MAKES // **about 1 cup (240 ml)**

3 cups (495 g) sliced strawberries, plus 8 whole strawberries, hulled

2 tablespoons chia seeds

2 tablespoons maple syrup or honey

1 teaspoon vanilla extract

½ teaspoon fresh lemon juice

¼ teaspoon lemon zest

Place the sliced strawberries in a medium skillet and heat over medium heat. Gently stir until the strawberries begin to break down and the liquid evaporates, about 5 minutes.

Transfer the cooked berries to a high-speed blender and add the fresh berries, chia seeds, syrup or honey, vanilla, lemon juice, and lemon zest and briefly blend until it reaches a jam-like consistency.

Allow the jam to cool to room temperature. Serve immediately, or pour it into a jar with a lid, cool, and place it in the fridge. The jam will continue to thicken as it chills. Store in an airtight container in the refrigerator for up to 10 days.

# STRAWBERRY-MINT BREAKFAST PUDDING WITH VANILLA CASHEW CREAM

### PUDDING

**1 large or 2 small avocados (1 cup/155 g mashed)**

**2 cups (330 g) sliced strawberries**

**2 Medjool dates, pitted**

**1 tablespoon chopped fresh ginger**

**½ cup (25 g) lightly packed fresh mint**

**½ cup (120 ml) orange juice**

**½ cup (60 g) raw cashews, preferably soaked for 2 to 4 hours, rinsed, and drained**

**1½ cups (225 g) ice cubes**

### VANILLA CREAM

**1 cup (120 g) raw cashews, preferably soaked for 2 to 4 hours, rinsed, and drained**

**½ vanilla bean, end trimmed (or 1 teaspoon vanilla extract)**

**1 tablespoon maple syrup**

**⅓ cup (75 ml) filtered water**

**Small pinch kosher sea salt**

### TOPPING

**3 teaspoons Strawberry-Lemon Chia Seed Jam (page 64) or jam of your choice**

**¾ cup (125 g) sliced strawberries**

**Fresh mint leaves**

*When strawberries are in season, life is just better! You can make the most of them in this pretty pink breakfast pudding. The sweet berries are blended with invigorating mint and vitamin C–packed orange juice. It's an indulgent-tasting change of pace from your typical smoothie that will leave you feeling refreshed and ready to take on the day.*

**MAKE THE PUDDING** In a high-speed blender, combine the avocado, strawberries, dates, ginger, mint, orange juice, and cashews and blend until smooth, about 1 minute. Add the ice cubes and blend again to incorporate, about 30 seconds.

**MAKE THE VANILLA CREAM** In a high-speed blender, combine the cashews, vanilla, maple syrup, water, and salt and blend, starting on low, then bringing it up to high speed, until smooth, about 1 minute. Scrape down the sides as needed. If the mixture is too thick, add more water, 1 tablespoon at a time, until you achieve the desired consistency.

**TO SERVE** Divide the pudding into three drinking glasses or pint jars. Top each pudding with vanilla cream, one teaspoon strawberry jam, ¼ cup (40 g) strawberries, and a couple of mint leaves. Or, if you'd like, press a few thinly sliced strawberries against the side of the serving glass with your finger or a kebab skewer until they stick—this will happen naturally thanks to the moisture in the berries. Carefully spoon or pour in the pudding to avoid knocking down the sliced berries and serve with the toppings.

**CHEF'S NOTES** If time does not permit soaking the cashews, you may need to add a bit more water to achieve the perfect consistency.

The color of the pudding may vary depending on how ripe and red your berries are.

**FEEL GOOD INGREDIENT // MINT** Mint is full of potent antioxidants and is a natural stimulant, making it an ideal herb to eat in the morning. Even the smell can boost your energy and kick your brain into a higher gear. It's great for digestion and is high in vitamin A, which promotes healthy skin and supports your immune system.

PREP // **3 minutes**
COOK // **5 minutes**
SERVES // **12**

# LIFE-CHANGING INSTANT SUPERFOOD PORRIDGE

**1 cup (175 g) buckwheat groats**

**2 cups (180 g) old-fashioned, gluten-free, or extra-thick rolled oats**

**1 cup (165 g) chia seeds**

**1 cup (165 g) hemp seeds**

**1 cup (85 g) dried coconut flakes**

**Nondairy milk or yogurt**

*Jacq: I came up with this recipe when my baby was a newborn and mornings were a little hectic. I needed to come up with a breakfast that was nutrient-dense, energizing, and easy to throw together. This recipe was the answer. Thanks to the chia seeds in it, all you have to do to turn it into a thick, delicious porridge is pour it in a bowl and mix it with milk or yogurt. Add your favorite toppings and you're off to a good start in an instant.*

Toast the buckwheat in a dry skillet over medium heat for 1 minute. Add the oats and stir frequently, until lightly toasted, about 3 minutes more. Add the chia and hemp seeds and toast for another minute. Turn off the heat, toss in the coconut, and stir. Let cool and store in an airtight container in a cupboard for up to 1 month.

For each serving, pour ½ cup (60 g) porridge into a bowl and cover it with the milk or yogurt of your choice. Let stand for 3 minutes to thicken. You can use warm or cold milk. Add any desired toppings (see Note).

**CHEF'S NOTE** Try this recipe with a variety of toppings. These are some of our favorites:

*Raspberries, pine nuts, and fresh mint with vanilla cashew yogurt*

*Mangoes, cashews, dates, and a pinch turmeric with coconut milk*

*Sweet potatoes, raisins, cinnamon, walnuts, and maple syrup with almond milk*

*Peanut butter, banana, and cacao nibs with chocolate cashew milk*

**FEEL GOOD INGREDIENT // HEMP SEEDS** Hemp seeds (also known as hemp hearts) won't get you high, but they are a high-quality plant food worth adding to your diet. Each tablespoon gives you more than 5 grams of protein. They are considered a perfect protein because they contain all twenty amino acids, including the nine essential amino acids that our bodies can't produce.

# THE GO-TO SMOOTHIE BOWL

¾ cup (180 ml) Good Morning Green Juice (page 60) or store-bought green juice (see Notes)

1 cup (150 g) frozen mixed berries

⅓ cup (40 g) raw nuts, preferably soaked, drained, and rinsed, or ½ avocado

½ banana or 1 Medjool date, pitted

1 portion plant protein or superfood powder (optional; see Notes)

**OPTIONAL TOPPINGS**

Fresh and/or dried fruit

Granola

Hemp, chia, or sunflower seeds

Cacao nibs

Small edible flowers, such as borage or pansies

*Turn your morning smoothie into a beautiful sit-down experience. The green juice and berries make a nutritious base, then add nuts or avocado for creaminess and banana or a date for sweetness. Once blended, you can add a limitless variety of toppings so each bowl can be filled with exactly what you're craving. It's why we call it the go-to. It never gets old.*

In a high-speed blender, combine the green juice, berries, nuts or avocado, banana or date, and protein powder, if using, and blend until smooth. You may need to scrape down the sides and add a splash of juice or water to get the blades to turn. The consistency should be a little thicker than a traditional smoothie. Pour into a bowl and arrange the toppings nicely.

**CHEF'S NOTES** Look for organic cold-pressed green juice at the supermarket or make your own. Beware of juices that are green in color but are made mostly of high-sugar fruits. Juices that have 5 grams or less sugar per serving are ideal.

If you need an extra nutrient boost, add your favorite superfood or plant protein powder to your smoothie bowl. Our favorite protein powders are Garden of Life organic plant protein and PlantFusion complete plant protein.

**FEEL GOOD INGREDIENT // FROZEN BERRIES** When it comes to food, we usually think fresh is best, but in reality, sometimes frozen is, brace yourself, *better*. As soon as a fruit or veggie is picked, its nutrients begin to degrade. Frozen berries are picked at their peak and frozen shortly after harvest so they retain more nutrients than berries that were picked early and transported long distances. Berries have a great antioxidant capacity, are high in fiber, and are some of the lowest-calorie fruits.

# CURRIED TOFU SCRAMBLE

2 tablespoons olive or coconut oil

1 onion, diced

½ cup (30 g) sliced cremini mushrooms

Pinch kosher sea salt

1 (16-ounce/455-g) package super-firm tofu, crumbled (see Notes)

2 teaspoons nutritional yeast

½ teaspoon black salt (optional; see Notes)

½ teaspoon black pepper

½ teaspoon ground turmeric

½ teaspoon curry powder

Pinch red pepper flakes

½ cup (120 ml) vegetable broth

1 tablespoon tamari

½ cup (70 g) grape or cherry tomatoes, halved

1 cup (20 g) lightly packed baby spinach

Handful (about ¼ cup/13 g) fresh cilantro or flat-leaf parsley leaves, plus additional for garnish

1 avocado, thinly sliced

*People who say they don't like tofu probably haven't had it prepared the right way. If you'd only eaten plain boiled (or worse, uncooked!) pasta, you would think it was pretty boring too. Well, like pasta, tofu needs to be dressed up. This scramble is sure to convert any skeptic. It's bursting with umami-rich ingredients and fragrant spices that transform the tofu into a gorgeously piquant dish.*

Heat a large sauté pan over medium heat. Add the oil and swirl to coat the bottom of the pan. Add the onion and cook, stirring frequently, until it begins to soften, about 3 minutes, then add the mushrooms and salt and sauté until the onion begins to brown, about 2 minutes more.

Add the tofu to the pan and stir to coat it in the oil. Sprinkle the tofu with the nutritional yeast, black salt, if using, the black pepper, turmeric, curry powder, and red pepper flakes. Pour in the vegetable broth and tamari and stir to distribute the spices evenly. Bring to a simmer and cook for about 3 minutes, until most of the moisture has been absorbed, then fold in the tomatoes, spinach, and cilantro. Cook until the spinach is just wilted and the tomatoes are warmed through, about 1 minute more.

Serve the scramble with the avocado slices and a sprinkle of the fresh herb of your choice.

**CHEF'S NOTES** Look for vacuum-packed super-firm tofu, which is sometimes called high-protein tofu. If this is not available, you can substitute water-packed extra-firm tofu. Just be sure to drain the tofu well, wrap it in a dish towel, and gently squeeze to remove excess moisture before crumbling it. Tempeh also works nicely here.

Black salt, or *kala namak*, is an Indian volcanic rock salt with a distinctive sulfur smell. It can add a desirable eggy note to egg-free dishes such as this one. Find it at any Indian or Pakistani spice market or order it online.

You can turn this scramble into awesome breakfast tacos. Simply divide the filling among 8 warm corn tortillas, top with the avocado and fresh herbs, and serve with hot sauce and lime wedges.

**FEEL GOOD INGREDIENT // SPINACH** Full of fiber, vitamins, and minerals (in particular vitamins A, K, B₁, and folate), this low-calorie immune-boosting veggie is great for your hair, teeth, and nails, maintaining healthy blood pressure, repairing muscles, and strengthening bones.

PREP // **5 minutes**

SERVES // **1**

# CHOCOLATE-PECAN-COCONUT OVERNIGHT KASHA

¼ cup (40 g) kasha (also called toasted buckwheat groats; see Note)

½ cup (120 ml) Creamy Vanilla Cashew Milk (page 55) or nondairy milk of your choice, plus more for serving

1 tablespoon chia seeds

1 heaping tablespoon pecan pieces, plus more for garnish

1 tablespoon coconut flakes, plus more for garnish

1 teaspoon cacao powder

1 teaspoon cacao nibs, plus more for garnish

1 Medjool date, pitted and chopped

Pinch kosher sea salt

Maple syrup for serving (optional)

*The flavors in this recipe are inspired by a candy bar, but it's made with simple, healthy ingredients that make it a feel-good way to start the day. Mild, earthy kasha takes a sweeter turn as the groats soften overnight and absorb the chocolatey goodness of the cacao. This recipe also has a great balance of whole-grain carbohydrates, plant proteins, and healthy fats to keep you energized for hours! It takes only a couple of minutes to throw together at night, and in the morning you have a heavenly breakfast to enjoy at home or on the run.*

In a jar or small bowl, combine the kasha, milk, chia seeds, pecans, coconut, cacao powder, cacao nibs, date, and salt. Mix well with a fork. Cover with a lid or plastic wrap.

Place in the refrigerator for a minimum of 4 hours and up to 3 days. Add a splash of milk and sprinkle with additional pecans, coconut, and cacao nibs just before serving. Drizzle with maple syrup for added sweetness, if you like.

**CHEF'S NOTE** If you can't find kasha at the store, you can toast raw buckwheat groats in a dry pan over medium heat, stirring continuously for 4 to 5 minutes, until lightly browned and fragrant.

**FEEL GOOD INGREDIENT // COCONUT FLAKES** The phosphorous and iron in the coconut flakes aid the body's blood cell, teeth, and bone formation. They also contain zinc, which supports a healthy immune system and can help wounds heal faster.

# BANANA PANCAKES WITH CARDAMOM SPICED BERRIES

### SPICED BERRIES

**1 cup (140 g) blackberries**

**1 cup (125 g) raspberries**

**1 tablespoon filtered water**

**2 tablespoons maple syrup**

**¼ teaspoon ground cardamom**

### PANCAKES

**2 ripe bananas**

**½ cup (120 ml) almond milk**

**½ cup (120 ml) filtered water**

**1 cup (90 g) old-fashioned or gluten-free rolled oats**

**½ cup (45 g) almond meal**

**2 teaspoons baking powder**

**½ teaspoon vanilla extract**

**½ teaspoon ground cinnamon**

**¼ teaspoon kosher sea salt**

**2 tablespoons chia seeds or 1 large egg**

**2 teaspoons coconut oil or nondairy butter (preferably Miyoko's Vegan Butter)**

**2 tablespoons coconut butter**

*Abbie: Who doesn't love pancakes? I'm pretty sure not loving pancakes falls into the same percentage of people who don't love chocolate or dogs. Not many! These pancakes are healthy and filling and put a smile on your face. The flavor of banana and berries together is just perfect, and with coconut butter on top . . . yes, please! I'm always excited when vegan food tastes this good. Just try them. I'm sure you'll agree.*

**MAKE THE SPICED BERRIES** Place the blackberries, raspberries, and water in an 8-inch (20-cm) pan. Cook the berries over medium heat, stirring occasionally, until the raspberries begin to break down, about 3 minutes. Stir in the maple syrup and cardamom, lower the heat to medium-low, and cook for about 3 minutes more, until the raspberries have broken down into a sauce. The blackberries may stay intact depending on how firm they are. The sauce will continue to thicken as it sits.

**MAKE THE PANCAKES** In a blender, combine the bananas, milk, water, oats, almond meal, baking powder, vanilla, cinnamon, salt, and chia seeds or egg. Blend, starting on low, then bringing it up to medium-high speed, until smooth, 30 seconds to 1 minute.

Heat a large nonstick skillet or griddle over medium heat, add 1 teaspoon of the coconut oil, and swirl to coat the bottom of the pan. When the pan is hot, after about 1 minute, make 2 pancakes using half of the batter (about ½ cup (60 ml) each), spreading the batter out with the back of a tablespoon. Cook until set on the bottom and a few bubbles appear on the surface, about 2 minutes, then flip and cook on the second side until lightly browned on the bottom, about another 2 minutes. Transfer the pancakes to a plate. Swirl the remaining teaspoon oil into the pan and repeat with the remaining batter.

Meanwhile, reheat the berry sauce over medium-low heat. Transfer the pancakes from the pan onto individual serving plates and top each with one quarter of the berry sauce. Reheat the first two pancakes in the pan over medium heat for 30 seconds per side, then transfer to serving plates and top with the rest of the berry sauce. Finish with a bit of softened coconut butter on top.

**FEEL GOOD INGREDIENT // BANANA** The original scientific name of the banana was *Musa sapientum*, which means "fruit of the wise man." Bananas are low in fat and sodium and provide a variety of vitamins and minerals, especially potassium, fiber, and vitamins C and B$_6$. These all contribute to good blood pressure, heart health, strong bones, a sharper mind, and good digestion.

PREP // **5 minutes**
COOK // **15 minutes**
MAKES // **12 cookies**

# QUINN'S BREAKFAST COOKIES

1 cup (90 g) old-fashioned or gluten-free rolled oats

1 cup (240 ml) creamy almond butter (see Note)

1 medium banana, mashed well with a fork

⅓ cup (65 g) coconut sugar

¼ teaspoon ground cinnamon

Pinch kosher sea salt

⅓ cup (60 g) dairy-free chocolate chips or raisins

*Jacq: My little man loves a good cookie, so I came up with this quick recipe that tastes like a treat, but is nutritious enough to eat at breakfast. I like to whip up a batch before bedtime, when I know I'm going to have a busy morning the next day. They keep well for several days and are filled with ingredients that give you a boost of energy. Plus, there is no denying that eating cookies for breakfast is just plain fun!*

Preheat the oven to 350°F (175°C) and line a baking sheet with parchment paper. Set aside.

In a medium bowl, use a fork to mix the oats, almond butter, banana, coconut sugar, cinnamon, and salt. If the mixture is too dry to stick together, add 1 tablespoon water and mix again. Fold in the chocolate chips or raisins.

Spoon 1 heaping tablespoon of the mixture onto the baking sheet to make each cookie. Spread the mixture evenly with the back of the spoon to create a ¼- to ½-inch- (6- to 12-mm-) thick round cookie.

Bake for about 15 minutes, until the tops of the cookies are lightly golden and the bottoms begin to brown. Use a spatula to transfer the cookies to a plate or cooling rack and cool completely before serving. Store in an airtight container for up to 5 days.

**CHEF'S NOTE** If almond butter is unavailable, you can substitute any nut butter of your choice.

**FEEL GOOD INGREDIENT // ALMOND BUTTER** Eating almonds can help you both inside and out. They contain monounsaturated fatty acids that help support heart health and riboflavin and L-carnitine, which are key in healthy brain function. Almond butter is also a rich source of vitamin E and biotin, which are beneficial for your hair, skin, and nails.

PREP // **5 minutes, plus Creamy Vanilla Cashew Milk (page 55)**

COOK // **35 minutes**

SERVES // **4 as a main dish**

# MILLET PORRIDGE WITH STRAWBERRIES, PINE NUTS, AND ROSEMARY SYRUP

### PORRIDGE

**1 cup (240 ml) Creamy Vanilla Cashew Milk (page 55) or nondairy milk of your choice, plus more for serving**

**2½ cups (600 ml) filtered water, plus more as needed**

**1 cup (200 g) millet**

**1 cup (240 ml) canned coconut milk**

**¼ teaspoon kosher sea salt**

### SYRUP

**¼ cup (60 ml) maple syrup**

**¼ cup (60 ml) filtered water**

**3-inch (7.5-cm) sprig rosemary**

**2 teaspoons fresh lemon juice**

### TOPPINGS

**1⅓ cups (220 g) strawberries, hulled and sliced**

**¼ cup (35 g) pine nuts**

**¼ cup (20 g) toasted coconut flakes**

*Abbie: This is lazy Sunday comfort food at its finest. We love to make this porridge for brunch between reading the paper and catching up over coffee. Yes, it takes a while to cook, but that will just make you appreciate the delicious balance of sweet, nutty, and herbal flavors even more when it's ready. Even baby Quinn is a fan.*

**MAKE THE PORRIDGE** In a medium pot, bring the cashew milk and 1½ cups (360 ml) of the water to a boil. Stir in the millet, reduce the heat to medium-low, and simmer for about 15 minutes, stirring occasionally and making sure to scrape the sides and bottom of the pan to avoid scorching until the millet has absorbed most of the liquid.

Add the coconut milk and the remaining 1 cup (240 ml) water and stir gently. Cover and cook, stirring occasionally, for 15 to 20 minutes more, until the millet is creamy, tender, and slightly chewy. If the millet starts looking dry, add additional water as needed.

**MEANWHILE, MAKE THE SYRUP** Pour the maple syrup and water into a small pan and stir using the rosemary sprig, then add the sprig to the pan. Bring to a simmer over medium heat and simmer until it's reduced to about ¼ cup (60 ml), about 5 minutes. Add the lemon juice and discard the rosemary.

When the millet is ready, add a splash of cashew milk and remove the pot from the heat. Stir in the salt and half of the syrup.

**TO SERVE** Top with the strawberries, pine nuts, and toasted coconut flakes. Finish with a drizzle of the remaining rosemary syrup.

Millet does not keep very well, so immediately refrigerate any leftovers in an airtight container and enjoy within a day or two.

**CHEF'S NOTE** Serve this in individual bowls as a main dish or as part of a brunch spread in one large bowl so your guests can help themselves to a few scoops.

**FEEL GOOD INGREDIENT // MILLET** Millet is one of the least allergenic and most easily digestible grains. Its high protein content and gluten-free status make it a good choice for grown-ups and babies alike. It's also a good source of magnesium, copper, and manganese, all essential for a healthy metabolism.

# CARROT CAKE CHIA PUDDING

2 cups (480 ml) unsweetened cashew or almond milk

2-inch (5-cm) chunk of carrot, plus 2 tablespoons packed grated carrot

1 teaspoon vanilla extract

¼ teaspoon ground cinnamon

⅛ teaspoon ground ginger

Pinch ground nutmeg

Tiny pinch ground cloves

4 Medjool dates, pitted

⅓ cup (55 g) white chia seeds (see Notes)

3 tablespoons golden raisins

3 tablespoons walnut pieces

TOPPINGS

2 tablespoons golden raisins

2 tablespoons walnuts

1 tablespoon carrot ribbons

1 (5.3 ounce/150-g) container plain or vanilla nondairy yogurt (optional)

*Our favorite superfood seed is at it again. This chia pudding has all of the sweet and spicy flavor of carrot cake, but is made with ingredients that give you a nourishing start to your morning. It's the perfect thing to throw together before bed. When you wake up, you can just add your toppings and go. We use a vegetable peeler to make the carrot ribbons, which makes it easy and pretty, just how we like it.*

Combine the milk, carrot chunk, vanilla, cinnamon, ginger, nutmeg, cloves, and dates in a high-speed blender and blend for about 1 minute (or about 2 minutes in a regular blender) until smooth.

Pour the mixture into two mason jars and add half of the chia seeds, grated carrot, raisins, and walnuts to each. Place lids on the jars and shake to combine. Refrigerate for a minimum of 2 hours or up to 3 days to allow the pudding to thicken and the chia seeds to soften. To serve, top with the raisins, walnuts, carrot ribbons, and yogurt, if using.

**CHEF'S NOTES** White chia seeds look nicer in this pudding, but black ones work too.

Turn this into an easy dessert by adding candied walnuts on top. Another nice touch is to top it off with a dollop of Creamy Cashew Sour Cream (page 138) mixed with 2 tablespoons maple syrup, to give it that cream cheese frosting flavor.

**FEEL GOOD INGREDIENT // CHIA SEEDS** Though it seems chia seeds only burst on the scene a few years ago, the Aztecs and Mayans recognized their superfood powers and used them as sustenance during battle and long-running expeditions. It makes sense since they're packed with antioxidants, proteins, omega-3 fatty acids, vitamins, and minerals, and according to a new study, provide a performance boost on the same level as sugary sports drinks. The Aztecs so revered the chia that they were often used as legal tender, giving new meaning to term "seed money."

*"If anyone does not have three minutes in his life to make an omelette, then life is not worth living."*
—RAYMOND BLANC

# Eggs

PREP // **under 5 minutes**
COOK // **2½ hours**
SERVES // **4**

# SOFT SCRAMBLED EGGS WITH OVEN-ROASTED TOMATOES AND CARAMELIZED ONIONS

6 Roma tomatoes, halved

2 tablespoons olive oil, divided

1 tablespoon balsamic vinegar

1½ teaspoons coconut sugar

Kosher sea salt and black pepper

½ small onion

12 large eggs

¼ cup (60 ml) unsweetened cashew or almond milk

Pinch paprika

1 teaspoon finely chopped fresh tarragon, plus whole leaves for garnish

*This dish is inspired by a favorite Ottolenghi couscous recipe. The slow-cooking process coaxes beautifully deep flavors out of the tomatoes and onions. We usually prep them the night before, then stir them into the creamy soft scrambled eggs in the morning for an elegant, crave-worthy brunch dish.*

Preheat the oven to 300°F (150°C). Place the tomato halves on a parchment-lined baking sheet. Drizzle with 1 tablespoon of the oil and the vinegar and toss to coat. Arrange the tomato halves skin side down and sprinkle with the sugar and a big pinch salt and pepper. Place in the oven and bake for about 2 hours, until the tomatoes have lost most of their moisture.

Meanwhile, cut the onion into ¼-inch- (6-mm-) thick slices. In a skillet, heat the remaining 1 tablespoon oil; add the onion and a pinch of salt. Cook for 1 minute, then lower the heat to medium-low and cook, stirring occasionally, until the onion is golden and caramelized, about 20 minutes. Remove from the heat and set aside.

When the tomatoes and onion are ready, whisk the eggs, milk, paprika, ¾ teaspoon salt, and a big pinch of pepper together in a large bowl.

Pour the eggs into a large sauté pan or skillet and heat over medium heat for 1 minute. Lower the heat to medium-low and continuously stir the eggs with a wooden or silicone spoon while scraping the sides and the bottom of the pan. Small curds will appear first, then the eggs will begin to set. Turn off the heat when the eggs still look very moist but not runny. This will take 6 to 10 minutes.

Gently fold the chopped tarragon into the eggs and top with tomatoes and onion. Garnish with tarragon leaves and serve immediately on warm plates.

**CHEF'S NOTE** If you make the onion and tomatoes ahead of time, you can reheat them on a baking sheet in a 350°F (175°C) oven for about 5 minutes, until warmed through.

**FEEL GOOD INGREDIENT // TARRAGON** Tarragon is a popular herb in French cooking with a robust anise-like flavor. It has one of the highest antioxidant values among the common herbs. Though eaten in small amounts, tarragon will still give you a dose of iron, calcium, and vitamins A and C.

# SPINACH, MUSHROOM, AND EGG BREAKFAST BURRITO WITH AVOCADO

### BEANS

**1½ cups (277 g) cooked black beans, or 1 (15-ounce/425-g) can, drained**

**Pinch kosher sea salt**

**Pinch black pepper**

**Pinch ground cumin**

### EGGS

**3 large eggs**

**Pinch kosher sea salt**

**Pinch black pepper**

**Pinch paprika**

**1½ tablespoons coconut oil**

**¼ small onion, diced**

**1 cup (70 g) sliced mushrooms**

**2 cups (40 g) baby spinach**

### BURRITO

**2 (8-inch/20-cm) whole-grain or gluten-free tortillas of your choice**

**¾ cup (180 ml) Quick Pico de Gallo (page 200) or store-bought salsa**

**½ avocado, sliced**

**2 tablespoons Creamy Cashew Sour Cream (page 138) or unsweetened coconut milk yogurt (optional)**

**1 tablespoon packed fresh cilantro leaves**

*Food trucks were a common sight on the streets of L.A. long before the craze started nationwide. One of the most popular items on the menu has always been—and will always be—the breakfast burrito. Even in the land of smoothies, sometimes you need a warm, spicy start to your morning. We created this recipe so that you can enjoy a street-food favorite at home, but with an extra dose of veggies, in just fifteen minutes. It's filling, nutritious, and super flavorful.*

**MAKE THE BEANS** In a small pot, combine the beans, salt, pepper, and cumin, and cook over low heat, stirring occasionally, until heated through, about 4 minutes.

**MEANWHILE, MAKE THE EGGS** In a small bowl, beat the eggs with the salt, pepper, and paprika.

Heat a medium skillet over medium heat. Add the oil, onion, and mushrooms, and sauté until the onion starts to brown, about 3 minutes, then add the spinach. When it starts to wilt, pour in the eggs and allow to set for about 1 minute, then scramble gently for about another minute, until cooked through but still moist.

**MAKE THE BURRITOS** Heat a tortilla directly on the burner over a medium flame, or in a dry skillet over high heat if using an electric range, for about 30 seconds per side. Repeat with the second tortilla. Divide the eggs, beans, salsa, avocado, sour cream, and cilantro between the tortillas. Leave room to fold the bottom third of the tortilla up, then fold the sides over to make a burrito.

**CHEF'S NOTE** You can substitute heartier greens like kale or Swiss chard for the spinach. They'll just take an extra couple of minutes to cook down.

**FEEL GOOD INGREDIENT // PAPRIKA** Paprika gets its beautiful red color from carotenoids, the type of plant pigments that can help the body fight inflammation and disease. Paprika has a mild heat, so it's a great way to add flavor to foods without adding extra calories. The capsaicin in paprika can even help stimulate your metabolism.

PREP // **under 5 minutes**
COOK // **10 minutes**
MAKES // **1 omelette**

# SMOKED SALMON AND CREAM CHEESE OMELETTE

### FILLING

**2 teaspoons olive oil**

**2 tablespoons diced red onion**

**⅓ cup (45 g) diced tomato or halved cherry tomatoes**

**Kosher sea salt and black pepper**

**2 ounces (55 g) smoked salmon**

**½ teaspoon capers (optional)**

**1 tablespoon nondairy cream cheese (preferably Kite Hill)**

**1 tablespoon lightly packed fresh dill fronds, plus 1 frond for garnish**

### EGGS

**2 extra-large eggs (see Note)**

**1 tablespoon water**

**Pinch smoked paprika**

**Kosher sea salt and black pepper**

**1 teaspoon olive oil**

*Jacq: A plain French-style omelette is a beautiful thing, but stuff it with some smoked salmon and cream cheese and you've got yourself something really special. It's the kind of breakfast I feed my husband when I want to make him fall in love with me all over again. It's quite rich, so serve it with a simple salad dressed in a little lemon juice and olive oil.*

**MAKE THE FILLING** Heat the oil in a small skillet over medium-high heat. Add the onion, tomato, and a pinch of salt and pepper. Sauté until the onion begins to soften and brown, 2 to 3 minutes. Add the salmon and capers, if using, and stir, then turn off the heat.

**MAKE THE EGGS** Crack the eggs into a small bowl. Add the water and a pinch of paprika, salt, and pepper. Whisk with a fork until well blended.

Heat the oil in an 8-inch (20-mm) nonstick skillet over medium heat. Pour in the eggs and cook undisturbed until the edges set, about 1 minute. Cut the set egg into quarters with the tip of a rubber spatula (liquid egg will fill up the cut), then use the spatula to pull the outside edge away from the side of the pan. Run the spatula around the perimeter of the pan, allowing most of the liquid eggs to flow underneath as you go, tilting the pan as necessary. Cover and cook for 30 seconds to 1 minute more, until the bottom is set and the top is just slightly runny. Uncover and turn off the heat.

Dot half the eggs with the cream cheese, then top with the salmon filling and dill fronds. Slip the spatula under the unfilled side and fold over the filled half. To serve, slide the omelette onto a plate and garnish with the additional dill frond.

**CHEF'S NOTE** Two extra-large eggs make a perfect omelette for one. If you are using smaller eggs or feeling extra hungry, you may want to use three eggs.

**FEEL GOOD INGREDIENT // DILL** Dill has been used in both culinary and medicinal applications dating back to ancient Egypt. The essential oils in dill contain flavonoids, known for their antioxidant, anti-inflammatory, and antiviral properties. It also gives you vitamins A and C, manganese, folate, and iron.

PREP // **5 minutes**

COOK // **25 minutes**

SERVES // **4**

# ZUCCHINI CURRY TORTILLA WITH ARUGULA SALAD

### TORTILLA

6 large eggs

¼ cup (60 ml) unsweetened cashew or almond milk

¾ teaspoon curry powder

Pinch paprika

Kosher sea salt and freshly ground black pepper

2 tablespoons olive oil

1 onion, diced (about 2 cups/250 g)

1 green zucchini

1 golden zucchini or summer squash

1 tablespoon roughly chopped fresh cilantro leaves

2 ounces (55 g) Gooey Cashew Mozzarella (page 164) or Miyoko's Vegan Mozzarella, sliced (see Note)

### SALAD

2 tablespoons extra virgin olive oil

2 teaspoons balsamic vinegar

1 teaspoon coarse-ground mustard

4 cups (3 ounces/85 g) lightly packed baby arugula

½ cup (50 g) halved cherry or grape tomatoes

Kosher salt and freshly ground black pepper

*Abbie: This is one of the first recipes Jacqueline taught me how to cook. I still remember it by heart. I love the depth of flavor that the curry adds to the tortilla, and it also pairs perfectly with the zucchini. This recipe can be enjoyed for breakfast, lunch, or dinner. I've made this for my family and friends many times, as my fridge is usually stocked with all of the ingredients.*

**MAKE THE TORTILLA**  Preheat the broiler.

In a medium bowl, beat the eggs with the milk, curry powder, paprika, ½ teaspoon salt, and ¼ teaspoon pepper.

In a 12-inch (30.5-cm) broiler-safe skillet, heat the oil over medium-high heat. Add the onion and a pinch salt and sauté for about 3 minutes, until the onion starts to soften and become translucent, then lower the heat to medium-low and stir occasionally.

While the onion is cooking, thinly slice the zucchini and squash. When the onion just begins to brown, after about 3 minutes more, add the zucchini and squash, stir, and raise the heat to medium. Cook, stirring occasionally, until the zucchini softens and begins to brown, about 8 minutes. Season the vegetables with a pinch of salt and pepper, then lower the heat to medium-low.

Pour in the eggs and cover the pan. Cook for 5 minutes, remove the lid, and sprinkle with the cilantro leaves. Dot with the mozzarella and broil for 1 to 3 minutes, until lightly browned and fluffy; keep a close eye so it doesn't burn. Remove from the broiler and let stand.

**MAKE THE SALAD**  In a large bowl, whisk the oil, vinegar, and mustard. Add the arugula and tomatoes, sprinkle with a pinch of salt and pepper, and toss to coat.

**TO SERVE**  Transfer the tortilla to a serving platter and mound the salad on top nicely.

**CHEF'S NOTE**  Feel free to use any nondairy cheese of your choice, but always look for cheeses that have ingredients you can pronounce!

**FEEL GOOD INGREDIENT // CURRY POWDER**  Curry powder is a generic term for a spice blend commonly associated with East Indian cooking. Each blend is different, but it's almost guaranteed to have turmeric, which is a powerful anti-inflammatory, as well as lots of spices that aid in digestion such as black pepper, ginger, cinnamon, and cumin.

PREP // **5 minutes**

COOK // **30 to 45 minutes**

SERVES // **6 to 8**

# LOBSTER, CORN, AND CARAMELIZED LEEK FRITTATA

**1 cup (6½ ounces/145 g) cooked lobster meat or 1 (2-pound/910-g) live lobster (see Notes)**

**12 large eggs**

**⅓ cup (75 ml) unsweetened cashew or almond milk**

**1¼ teaspoons kosher sea salt, plus more to taste**

**½ teaspoon black pepper, plus more to taste**

**2 tablespoons finely chopped fresh chives**

**¼ cup (13 g) chopped fresh dill fronds, divided**

**¼ cup (60 ml) olive oil**

**2 leeks, white and light green parts only, halved lengthwise, thinly sliced, and rinsed well**

**1 shallot, thinly sliced**

**Kernels from 2 ears corn, or 1 (11-ounce/310-g) can of corn**

**1 teaspoon fresh thyme leaves, or ¼ teaspoon dried thyme**

**1 cup (145 g) cherry tomatoes, halved**

**8 ounces (225 g) broccolini, ends trimmed, cut into 2-inch (5-cm) pieces**

**4 ounces (115 g) nondairy ricotta or cream cheese (preferably Kite Hill)**

**CHEF'S NOTES** You can also use 2 frozen (4-ounce/115-g) lobster tails. Allow them to thaw completely, then steam them for 3 minutes following the instructions for cooking a fresh lobster.

Live American lobsters from Maine and California Spiny lobsters are the most sustainable and delicious choice. Avoid limp lobsters. A healthy one will move energetically when lifted from the tank.

*Nothing makes eating eggs feel more like a special occasion than adding a little lobster. This frittata is particularly spectacular in summertime when the corn is sweet and the tomatoes are ripe. It's perfect for those long, lazy holiday weekends when friends and family gather to enjoy great food and fun times. We like to serve it with roasted potatoes and a simple salad for breakfast, lunch, or dinner.*

Preheat the oven to 350°F (175°C).

**PREPARE THE LOBSTER** If you need to cook your lobster, fill a large stockpot with 1½ inches (4 cm) water. Place a steamer basket or colander inside and bring the water to a rolling boil. Place the lobster in the pot and cover. Lower the heat to maintain a simmer and steam for 12 minutes, then remove the lobster from the pot using tongs. It should be slightly undercooked.

Once the lobster is cool enough to handle, cut the feathery tail fins off the bottom of the tail, then use kitchen shears to cut the shell on the underside of the lobster. Remove the tail meat and cut it into bite-size pieces. Twist off the claws, then use a nut cracker, kitchen shears, or the back of a heavy knife to crack the claws. Remove the meat from the claws and knuckles. Set the lobster meat aside.

**MAKE THE FRITTATA** In a large bowl, whisk together the eggs, milk, salt, pepper, chives, and half of the dill. Set aside.

Heat a 12-inch (30.5-cm) oven-safe skillet over medium-high heat, then add the oil. When hot and shimmering, add the leeks, shallot, and a pinch of salt. Sauté for 3 minutes, then add the corn and thyme and cook for 3 minutes more, stirring occasionally. Add the tomatoes and broccolini and continue cooking until the broccolini turns bright green, about 3 minutes more. Season the veggies with salt and pepper.

Toss the lobster meat in the pan and spread it around evenly. Dot the pan with spoonfuls of the cheese, then pour in the eggs. Cook until the edges begin to set, 2 to 4 minutes, then use a spatula to pull the edges away from the sides of the pan. Run the spatula around the entire pan, allowing the liquid eggs to flow underneath as you go, tilting the pan as necessary. Shake the pan to smooth out the top, then transfer the pan to the oven.

Bake for 8 to 12 minutes, until the eggs are just set and the frittata begins to puff up. Do not overcook. It's OK if the very center is a little runny. Remove from the oven and let rest 5 minutes, then sprinkle with the remaining dill, cut into wedges, and serve.

**FEEL GOOD INGREDIENT // LOBSTER**
Though it tastes rich and buttery, lobster is actually very low in fat and calories while high in protein. It's a good source of zinc, copper, selenium, vitamin $B_{12}$, and heart-healthy EPA and DHA omega-3 fatty acids.

# AUSSIE-STYLE FRENCH TOAST

DRESSING

2 teaspoons balsamic vinegar

2 teaspoons olive oil

2 teaspoons diced red onion

FRENCH TOAST

2 eggs

Generous pinch paprika

Tiny pinch ground nutmeg

Kosher sea salt and black pepper

2 slices whole-grain or gluten-free bread

1 tablespoon nondairy butter

1 tablespoon olive oil

½ cup (55 g) sliced red onion

1 large garlic clove, minced

1½ cups (220 g) whole grape or cherry tomatoes

2 cups (40 g) medium packed baby spinach

1 avocado, thinly sliced

¼ cup (10 g) loosely packed fresh basil leaves

*Abbie: I love French toast (who doesn't?), so I came up with a savory spin on this much-loved classic. I've topped the toast with cherry tomatoes, baby spinach, avocado, and basil leaves cooked with onion, garlic, and a hint of spice. The balsamic vinegar dressing tops the toast off nicely, adding a high note to this earthy meal. A fast, easy, and satisfying start to the day.*

**MAKE THE DRESSING** In a small bowl, whisk the oil and vinegar together and stir in the onion. Set aside.

**MAKE THE FRENCH TOAST** In a medium bowl, whisk the eggs with a fork. Add the paprika, nutmeg, and a pinch of salt and pepper and whisk again. Dip the bread into the egg mixture and let soak for 30 seconds to 1 minute, flipping the bread while soaking and making sure to coat both sides.

Heat a large skillet over medium heat. Add the butter and swirl to coat the bottom of the pan. Place the bread in the pan and cook until golden brown, about 2 minutes per side. Sprinkle with a small pinch of salt and pepper. Remove the bread from the pan and set aside onto a plate.

In the same pan, reduce the heat to medium-low, pour in the oil, and swirl to coat the bottom of the pan. Add the onion, garlic, and a pinch of salt and pepper and cook, stirring frequently, until the onion softens, about 2 minutes. Add the tomatoes and cook until they soften and the onion begins to lightly brown, about 3 minutes more. Add the spinach and a pinch of salt and pepper and stir until very lightly wilted, about 30 seconds.

Move the onion, tomatoes, and spinach to one side of the pan. Place the bread back in the pan and heat for 45 seconds. Turn over the bread and place the onion, tomatoes, and spinach on top of the bread. Cook for about 2 minutes more, until heated through.

**TO SERVE** Using a spatula, transfer the bread to two serving plates, keeping the onion, tomatoes, and spinach on top. Layer the sliced avocado on top of the tomatoes and season with salt and pepper. Drizzle with the dressing and garnish with the basil. Finish with salt and pepper to taste.

**FEEL GOOD INGREDIENT // WHOLE GRAINS** Whole grains contain three parts. The bran is the outer shell, which has fiber, minerals, and antioxidants. The endosperm, the middle layer, is mostly made up of carbs, and the germ, the inner layer, houses vitamins, minerals, and protein. Refined grains are mainly composed of the endosperm, and therefore much less nutritious than whole grains.

# SALAD LYONNAISE TARTINE WITH POACHED EGG

1 tablespoon plus 1 teaspoon olive oil

1 tablespoon chopped shallot

2 pieces tempeh bacon

1 tablespoon plus 1 teaspoon red wine vinegar

1 teaspoon whole-grain mustard

Kosher sea salt

2 large eggs

2 pieces whole-grain or gluten-free bread

3 ounces (85 g) frisée, torn into pieces (about 3 cups/85 g lightly packed)

Flaky sea salt and freshly cracked black pepper

Truffle salt

4 French breakfast radishes

*This was one of our go-to recipes when we were busy writing this book. It's simple to make but has a flavor that is somehow greater than the sum of its parts. The richness of the egg yolk is balanced with the bright acidity of the dressing, and the tempeh bacon adds a kiss of smokiness. Don't forget the little sprinkle of truffle salt at the end for a sublime finishing touch.*

Heat the oil in a skillet over medium heat. Add the shallot and bacon and sauté until the shallot has softened and is just beginning to brown, 1 to 2 minutes. Add the vinegar and mustard, stir, then turn off the heat.

To poach the eggs, in a medium sauté pan or pot, heat 2 inches (5 cm) salted water over medium heat until tiny bubbles cover the bottom and sides of the pan. Crack the eggs one at a time into a teacup, and when a few bubbles have broken the surface of the water, gently slide each egg into the pan, leaving room between them. Adjust the heat so the water is barely simmering.

Cook the eggs, undisturbed, until the whites are set and the yolks have filmed over but are still soft to the touch and runny in the middle, 2 to 3 minutes. Use a fish spatula to gently release the eggs from the bottom of the pan, then transfer the eggs to a clean folded kitchen towel to drain.

Meanwhile, toast the bread in a toaster.

Add the frisée to the pan with the dressing, season with flaky sea salt and pepper, and toss to coat.

Place one piece of toast on each serving plate. Top each with half of the salad and a poached egg. Sprinkle each egg with a pinch of truffle salt and a little pepper. Serve each tartine with 2 radishes.

**FEEL GOOD INGREDIENT // EGGS** One large egg has just 72 calories and 6.5 grams of protein, along with vitamins and minerals such as vitamins A, D, E, B5, B12, and B2, selenium, phosphorous, and folate. Eggs are also a powerhouse of disease-fighting carotenoids lutein and zeaxanthin, which help protect your eyes and skin.

# KASHA AND KALE BOWL WITH BERBERE SPICE FRIED EGG

**Kasha with Caramelized Onions and Walnuts (page 32)**

PICKLED RADISH

**¼ cup (60 ml) red wine vinegar**

**¼ cup (60 ml) filtered water**

**¾ teaspoon kosher sea salt**

**2 teaspoons coconut sugar**

**4 watermelon, red, or Easter egg radishes, thinly sliced**

**1 bay leaf**

**4 peppercorns**

KALE

**1 bunch kale (about 10 ounces/280 g)**

**1 tablespoon olive oil**

**3 garlic cloves, thinly sliced**

**Pinch red pepper flakes**

**½ cup (120 ml) water, divided**

**Kosher sea salt and black pepper**

EGGS

**3 tablespoons olive oil**

**½ teaspoon berbere spice (substitute with turmeric, if unavailable)**

**4 large eggs**

**Flaky sea salt and freshly cracked black pepper**

TOPPING

**¼ teaspoon kosher sea salt**

**1 (5.3-ounce/150-g) container unsweetened coconut milk yogurt (see Note)**

**1 heaping tablespoon snipped fresh chives**

*Jacq: A recipe from my favorite magazine, Bon Appétit, inspired this bowl. It has become a go-to because it doesn't require hours at the stove. It's creamy, spicy, tangy, and earthy, and has a beautiful, lacy olive oil–fried egg on top. As good as it tastes, the best thing about it is the way that it makes you feel—nourished and fortified!*

Prepare the kasha according to the recipe.

**MEANWHILE, MAKE THE PICKLED RADISH** In a small bowl, whisk together the vinegar, water, salt, and sugar. Add the radishes, bay leaf, and peppercorns and place in the refrigerator while you prepare the remaining ingredients.

**MAKE THE KALE** Trim the bottom of the kale stems and discard. Remove the leaves from the center ribs and tear them into fairly large pieces. Thinly slice the stems and ribs.

In a large skillet, combine the oil, garlic, red pepper flakes, and kale stems and heat over medium-high heat. Sauté for about 2 minutes, until the garlic is fragrant, then add ¼ cup (60 ml) of the water. Continue to cook, stirring, until the water evaporates, about 3 minutes. Add the kale leaves and the remaining ¼ cup (60 ml) water and cook, stirring frequently, until they soften but still have some shape to them, about 4 minutes more. Season with a big pinch of salt and pepper. Turn off the heat and transfer to a bowl.

**MAKE THE EGGS** Wipe out the skillet with a paper towel. Add the oil and berbere spice to the pan and swirl to distribute the spice. Heat the oil over medium heat and when hot, add the eggs. Wait a few seconds after adding each egg to allow the edges to set so they don't stick together. (Work in batches, if necessary.) Tilt the pan and use a tablespoon to scoop up the hot oil and spoon it over the whites until they are opaque with lacy edges, about 2 minutes. Lightly season with flaky sea salt and pepper.

**TO SERVE** Fill four serving bowls with ¾ cup (125 g) each of the kasha. Top each with kale, a fried egg, and pickled radish. Whisk the salt into the yogurt with a fork, then add a dollop to each bowl. Garnish with the fresh chives.

**CHEF'S NOTE** Look for thick yogurt such as Coyo or Anita's brands.

**FEEL GOOD INGREDIENT // KALE** Kale is one of the most nutrient-filled foods! Eating it regularly may lower your risk for heart disease. An added bonus, it can help with shiny locks and good complexion thanks to its high beta-carotene content.

*"If you really want to make a friend, go to someone's house and eat with him. . . . The people who give you their food give you their heart."*

—CESAR CHAVEZ

# Soups and Salads

# ENGLISH PEA SOUP WITH MINT

### SOUP

3 tablespoons olive oil

½ white onion, diced (about 1 cup/125 g)

1 shallot, roughly chopped (about ¼ cup/30 g)

2 garlic cloves, thinly sliced

4 cups (960 ml) vegetable broth

½ teaspoon black pepper

1 (10-ounce/280-g) package frozen green peas

¼ cup (13 g) lightly packed fresh mint leaves

2 tablespoons fresh flat-leaf parsley leaves

1 tablespoon fresh lemon juice

¼ cup (40 g) mashed avocado (½ small avocado)

2 teaspoons nutritional yeast

### TOPPING

1 (5.3-ounce/150-g) container unsweetened coconut milk yogurt (see Notes)

2 teaspoons fresh lemon juice

¼ teaspoon kosher sea salt

1 tablespoon finely chopped fresh chives

1 tablespoon finely chopped fresh mint

*Jacq: Peas and fresh mint are a match made in heaven! I first had the combination at a wedding in the English countryside. When I started experimenting with the recipe at home, I knew I had to give it a Californian touch with a little creamy avocado thrown in. The coconut milk yogurt and fresh herb topping make it extra luscious. Serve it with our Spring Salad with Green Goddess Dressing (page 107) for a light and refreshing meal.*

**MAKE THE SOUP**  In a large heavy pot, heat the oil over medium heat. Add the onion and shallot and cook, stirring often, until softened but not browned, about 4 minutes. Add the garlic and cook until the garlic is fragrant, about 1 minute more.

Add the broth and pepper and bring to a boil. Add the peas and cook, stirring occasionally, until just tender and bright green, 2 to 4 minutes. Do not overcook the peas; as soon as they are heated through, they are done.

Remove the pot from the heat and add the mint, parsley, lemon juice, avocado, and nutritional yeast. Puree the soup in a blender, starting on low and bringing it up to high speed, until smooth. If the blender cover does not have steam vents, remove the center portion of the cover to allow steam to escape and place a kitchen towel over the opening to avoid splashes while blending.

**MAKE THE TOPPING**  In a small serving bowl, whisk the coconut yogurt with the lemon juice and salt. Fold in the herbs and serve alongside the soup as a topping. Refrigerate any leftovers for up to 3 days.

**CHEF'S NOTES**  Look for thick yogurt such as Coyo or Anita's brands.

This soup is also lovely served chilled on hot days.

**FEEL GOOD INGREDIENT // GREEN PEAS**  High in fiber and rich in protein and flavor, green peas are very filling despite being low in calories. Eating foods with these qualities regularly can be helpful in weight management, supporting blood sugar levels, and promoting healthy digestion.

PREP // **15 minutes**

SERVES // **6 as an appetizer or side**
(see Notes)

# SPRING SALAD WITH GREEN GODDESS DRESSING

### DRESSING

**⅓ cup (75 ml) cool filtered water**

**2 tablespoons extra-virgin olive oil**

**3 tablespoons fresh lemon juice (from 1 lemon)**

**1 tablespoon champagne vinegar (substitute red wine vinegar, if unavailable)**

**¼ cup (13 g) lightly packed fresh flat-leaf parsley leaves and tender stems**

**¼ cup (11 g) lightly packed fresh chives**

**3 tablespoons lightly packed fresh tarragon leaves**

**1 large garlic clove, peeled**

**1 shallot, chopped (about 3 tablespoons)**

**3 oil-packed anchovy fillets, drained**

**1 teaspoon Dijon mustard**

**1 cup (155 g) mashed avocado (about 2 avocados)**

**½ teaspoon kosher sea salt**

**½ teaspoon honey**

### SALAD

**1 head romaine or butter lettuce, torn into pieces**

**1 cup (60 g) sugar snap peas**

**2 Persian cucumbers, thinly sliced**

**2 celery ribs, thinly sliced**

**2 carrots, cut into ribbons with a vegetable peeler**

**1 bunch French breakfast radishes, tops removed, halved**

**¾ cup (110 g) halved cherry tomatoes**

**¼ cup (13 g) loosely packed fresh flat-leaf parsley leaves**

**½ lemon**

**2 teaspoons extra-virgin olive oil**

**Flaky sea salt and freshly cracked black pepper**

*The original green goddess dressing recipe uses sour cream and mayo as a base. Here we've substituted our favorite creamy superfood: the avocado. This highly flavored, herbaceous dressing can turn a basic garden salad into a showstopper. It may seem a little strange to put anchovies into a salad dressing, but think of Caesar dressing. Instead of tasting fishy, the anchovy simply adds an undertone of savoriness.*

**MAKE THE DRESSING** In a blender, combine the water, oil, lemon juice, vinegar, parsley, chives, tarragon, garlic, shallot, anchovies, mustard, avocado, salt, and honey. Blend, starting on low and bringing it up to high speed, until smooth and creamy.

**MAKE THE SALAD** In a large bowl, gently toss the lettuce with half of the dressing until well coated. (Use more or less dressing to taste.) Spread the lettuce on a platter and top with the snap peas, cucumbers, celery, carrots, radishes, tomatoes, and parsley leaves. Squeeze the juice from the lemon over the veggies and drizzle with the oil. Finish with a big pinch of flaky sea salt and pepper to taste. Serve with the remaining dressing on the side.

**CHEF'S NOTES** Make this a main dish for four by adding two 6- to 7-ounce (170- to 200-g) jars or cans of solid packed tuna, mackerel, or salmon fillets in olive oil. Look for the blue MSC label, which indicates it is a certified sustainable seafood product.

We've suggested vegetables to include in the salad, but feel free to include the fresh veggies of your choosing.

**FEEL GOOD INGREDIENT // ANCHOVIES** Preserved anchovies are packed with glutamates and one of the easiest ways to add umami to a dressing or sauce. They are also high in protein and healthy omega-3 fatty acids, low in mercury, and full of an assortment of important vitamins and minerals, including potassium, iron, niacin, and B$_{12}$.

# CREAMY TRUFFLE MUSHROOM SOUP

¼ cup (15 g) dried porcini mushrooms

¼ cup (30 g) raw unsalted cashews

¼ cup (60 ml) olive oil

1 onion, thinly sliced

Smoked salt

8 ounces (225 g) cremini mushrooms, roughly chopped

14 ounces (400 g) mixed wild mushrooms (such as shiitake, oyster, chanterelle, and maitake), roughly chopped

3 garlic cloves, thinly sliced

2 teaspoons fresh thyme leaves

Generous splash red wine (about ¼ cup/60 ml)

4 cups (960 ml) vegetable broth

Kosher sea salt and freshly ground black pepper

¾ cup (180 ml) hot water

½ teaspoon red wine vinegar

1 to 2 tablespoons truffle oil

1 tablespoon finely chopped flat-leaf parsley leaves

1 recipe Shiitake Mushroom Bacon (page 153; optional)

**FEEL GOOD INGREDIENT // PORCINI MUSHROOMS**

One of the most prized mushrooms due to their unique savory, earthy flavor, porcini mushrooms are a wonderful way to amplify flavor in dishes while giving a boost of iron, fiber, protein, and antioxidants.

*We've spent the holidays together for years now, and this elegant soup has become the traditional start to our Christmas meal. It has a rich, earthy flavor that makes even those who swear they don't like mushrooms ask for seconds. We feel good serving it to family and friends, knowing mushrooms help strengthen the immune system and bolster energy reserves for the busy season.*

In a small pot, bring 2 cups (480 ml) water to a boil. Place the porcini and cashews into two separate small bowls, pour half of the boiling water over each, and leave to soak.

Meanwhile, heat the olive oil in a large pot or Dutch oven over medium heat. Add the onion and a pinch of smoked salt and sauté until the onion begins to soften and become translucent, about 3 minutes. Lower the heat to medium-low and cook, stirring occasionally, until the onion is softened and golden, about 15 minutes.

Add the cremini and mixed mushrooms, the garlic, thyme, and a pinch of smoked salt to the pot and raise the heat to medium. Cook, stirring, for about 3 minutes, until the moisture begins to release from the mushrooms.

Remove the porcini from the bowl using a fork and add them to the other mushrooms. Strain the soaking liquid through a coffee filter or fine-mesh sieve to remove any grit and add the liquid to the pot. Lower the heat to maintain a simmer and cook uncovered for about 20 minutes, stirring occasionally, until most of the moisture is evaporated.

Add the wine and stir, scraping any browned bits loose from the bottom of the pan. Cook until the wine is almost evaporated. Add the broth, bring to a boil, then lower the heat and simmer for 20 minutes more. Season with ½ teaspoon sea salt, ¼ teaspoon smoked salt, and ¼ teaspoon pepper.

Drain and rinse the cashews. In a blender, blend the cashews with the hot water on high until smooth, 1 to 2 minutes, then pour the cashew cream into the pot and stir. Add the vinegar.

In two batches, pour the soup into the blender and blend until smooth. If the blender cover does not have steam vents, remove the center portion of the cover to allow steam to escape and place a kitchen towel over the opening to avoid splashes while blending.

Pour the soup into bowls and drizzle with the truffle oil. Garnish with the parsley and a couple of slices of shiitake bacon, if desired. Refrigerate any leftovers for up 3 days.

PREP // **10 minutes**

COOK // **1 hour 15 minutes**

SERVES // **4 to 6**

# ROASTED ACORN SQUASH SOUP WITH ROSEMARY-SPICE CANDIED PECANS

### SOUP

**2 large acorn squash (about 1½ pounds/ 680 g each)**

**1 tablespoon olive oil**

**1 shallot, roughly chopped**

**1½ teaspoons plus a pinch of kosher sea salt**

**⅛ teaspoon plus a pinch of black pepper**

**2 garlic cloves, roughly chopped**

**2½ cups (600 ml) vegetable broth, divided, plus more as needed**

**½ cup (120 ml) unsweetened cashew or almond milk**

**1 tablespoon maple syrup**

**¼ teaspoon cayenne pepper**

**2 tablespoons finely chopped chives for garnish**

### CANDIED PECANS

**2 tablespoons plus 2 teaspoons maple sugar**

**½ teaspoon kosher sea salt**

**¼ teaspoon cayenne pepper**

**½ teaspoon cocoa powder**

**⅛ teaspoon ground nutmeg**

**⅛ teaspoon ground cinnamon**

**2 teaspoons filtered water**

**1 cup (120 g) pecan halves**

**¼ teaspoon minced fresh rosemary**

*Nothing will brighten a chilly day like this sunny golden soup! Roasting the squash brings out a rich natural sweetness that is perfectly complemented by the spicy sweet pecans. A touch of rosemary adds an alluring herbal note. It's one of those soups that will tempt you to lick the bowl at the end. Go ahead—we won't tell!*

**MAKE THE SOUP** Preheat the oven to 400°F (205°C). Cut the squash in half lengthwise, avoiding the stem. Scrape out the seeds and strings using a spoon. You can discard them or save the seeds for roasting (see Notes). Pierce the flesh of the squash several times with a fork.

Fill a rimmed baking sheet with ¼ inch (6 mm) water. Arrange the squash on the sheet cut-side down. Bake in the oven until tender and easily pierced with a fork, about 45 minutes.

Meanwhile, in a small skillet, heat the oil over medium heat. Add the shallot and a pinch of salt and pepper and sauté until the shallot begins to brown, about 2 minutes, then add the garlic and cook for 1 minute more, stirring frequently. Add ½ cup (120 ml) of the vegetable broth and scrape up any browned bits on the bottom of the pan. Lower the heat to medium-low and cook until most of the liquid has evaporated and the shallot has softened, about 5 minutes. Transfer the garlic and shallots to a blender.

When the squash is done, remove it from the oven and allow to cool slightly. When cool enough to handle, scoop the flesh into a large blender (see Notes). Add the remaining 2 cups (480 ml) broth, the milk, maple syrup, the remaining 1½ teaspoons salt, the cayenne, and the remaining ⅛ teaspoon black pepper. Puree the soup, starting on low and bringing it up to high speed, until smooth. If the blender cover does not have steam vents, remove the center portion of the cover to allow steam to escape and place a kitchen towel over the opening to avoid splashes while blending. If the soup is too thick, add a bit more vegetable broth until it reaches your preferred consistency.

**MAKE THE CANDIED PECANS** Lower the oven temperature to 350°F (175°C). Line a baking sheet with parchment paper.

In a medium bowl, whisk together the maple sugar, salt, cayenne, cocoa powder, nutmeg, and cinnamon. Add the water and whisk again to form a paste, then toss the pecans in the mixture to coat well. Sprinkle with the rosemary and toss again.

CONTINUES

Arrange the nuts in a single layer on the baking sheet with a little space between each one and roast for 5 to 8 minutes, until lightly browned and fragrant. Remove the pan from the oven and carefully lift the parchment (with the nuts) off of the hot pan and set on a cooling rack or counter. Allow the nuts to cool slightly, then roughly chop half of them. The remaining nuts are for snacking. You're welcome.

**TO SERVE** Pour the soup into bowls and sprinkle generously with the chopped candied nuts. Garnish with the chives.

**CHEF'S NOTES** If you are using a blender that is smaller than 64 ounces (2 L), blend in batches.

To roast squash seeds, rinse them in a colander and remove the pulp with your fingers. Spread the seeds in an even layer on a baking sheet and drizzle with olive oil. Toss to coat and then sprinkle generously with seasoned salt and black pepper. Bake in the oven at 300°F (150°C) for about 20 minutes, stirring halfway, until lightly browned.

**FEEL GOOD INGREDIENT // CAYENNE PEPPER** Cayenne pepper doesn't just turn up the heat in your foods, it can also slightly raise your body temperature, which revs up your immune system, making it a great addition to your fall and winter dishes. The beta-carotene and vitamin C in cayenne also support your immune system, helping you fight off colds and flu.

# POACHED SALMON WITH FRENCH GREEN BEANS AND STRAWBERRY SALAD

### SALMON

1 cup (240 ml) dry white wine

3 cups (720 ml) warm filtered water

2 lemons, one juiced and one thinly sliced

4 sprigs fresh dill, plus 1 tablespoon chopped dill for garnish

1 bay leaf

2 teaspoons black peppercorns

1 teaspoon kosher sea salt

4 skinless salmon fillets (6-ounce/170-g each)

### GREEN BEAN SALAD

Kosher sea salt

¼ cup (60 ml) olive oil

1 medium shallot, thinly sliced

1 pound thin French green beans (haricots verts)

2 small garlic cloves, thinly sliced

2 tablespoons lemon juice

½ teaspoon lemon zest

1 teaspoon Dijon mustard

2 small heads endive, core removed, cut into 1-inch- (2.5-cm-) thick slices (about 3 cups/165 g)

4 strawberries, thinly sliced

2 tablespoons pine nuts

1 tablespoon mint, chiffonade

⅛ teaspoon black pepper

¼ teaspoon flaky sea salt

1 lemon, cut into 4 wedges

*Abbie: This is one of my favorite salads. It's crisp, colorful, summery, and it leaves you feeling as good as it looks. The luscious green beans, fresh-cut strawberries, and tender salmon really brighten up the table.*

**MAKE THE SALMON** Pour the wine and water into a medium sauté pan with a lid. Add the lemon juice and slices, the dill sprigs, bay leaf, peppercorns, and salt and bring to a boil over medium-high heat. Reduce the heat until the liquid is just simmering, add the salmon, and cover. Gently simmer for 4 minutes, or until the fish is mostly opaque on the outside but still pink in the middle. Turn off the heat and leave uncovered. The fish will continue to cook as it sits in the hot liquid while you prepare the green beans.

**MAKE THE SALAD** Fill a large pot three-quarters of the way full with water. Salt the water as if you were making pasta; it should be salty like the ocean. Bring the water to a boil over medium-high heat.

Meanwhile, in a small skillet, heat the oil and shallot over medium heat until the shallot just starts to become translucent, about 2 minutes. Lower the heat to medium-low and continue cooking until softened and golden, stirring occasionally, while you cook the green beans.

Once the water is boiling, add the green beans. Add the garlic to the pan with the shallot. If the garlic begins to brown, lower the heat.

Fill a large bowl with ice water and set aside. Cook the green beans until they turn bright green and are slightly tender but still crisp. This will take 90 seconds to 3 minutes, depending on their thickness. Drain the beans in a colander then place in the ice water to cool. Drain again and pat dry.

When the shallot is golden, turn off the heat. Add the lemon juice, lemon zest, and mustard to the shallot and whisk with a fork.

**TO SERVE** Spread the green beans on a serving platter. Drizzle with the shallot dressing, and toss to coat. Scatter the endive, strawberries, pine nuts, and mint on top. Use a slotted spatula to lift the fish out of the poaching liquid, allowing excess liquid to drip away. Lay the fillets on top of the salad and sprinkle with the chopped dill. Finish with the pepper and flaky sea salt. Serve with the lemon wedges.

CONTINUES

**FEEL GOOD INGREDIENT // GREEN BEANS**
Known as nature's multivitamin, green beans
are technically a fruit, provide the benefits
of legumes (like being rich in fiber, protein,
and iron), are low-calorie, and are high in
antioxidants like a green vegetable. They also
contain significant levels of folate and iron, both
important for fertility and fetal development.

PREP // **5 minutes**

COOK // **15 minutes, plus Cashew-Pine Nut Parmesan (page 167)**

SERVES // **2**

# GREEN SOUP

**10 cups (900 g) broccoli florets**

**⅓ cup (75 g) nondairy butter (preferably Miyoko's Vegan Butter)**

**½ teaspoon kosher sea salt, plus more for finishing**

**¼ teaspoon black pepper, plus more for finishing**

**3 tablespoons olive oil, divided**

**7 cups (140 g) lightly packed baby spinach**

**1 tablespoon Cashew–Pine Nut Parmesan (page 167) or other nondairy Parmesan**

**1 tablespoon fresh flat-leaf parsley leaves**

**1 tablespoon fresh cilantro leaves**

**¼ teaspoon red pepper flakes**

**1 lemon wedge**

*Abbie: My friend Jessie woke up one day to a kitchen stocked with only water, broccoli, butter, baby spinach, olive oil, salt, and pepper. This green soup is one of those magical spontaneous recipes that come from having a few random ingredients, a hungry belly, and a good imagination. It's energizing, alkalizing, and easy to digest, and gives you that healthy clear glow that only a powerful punch of green veggies can.*

In a large saucepan, bring 3 quarts (2.8 L) water to a boil over high heat.

Add the broccoli and cook with the lid off until the broccoli is tender and bright green, about 8 minutes.

Set a colander over a large bowl and strain the broccoli, reserving the broccoli broth.

In a blender, combine the broccoli, 2 cups (480 ml) of the broccoli broth, the butter, salt, and pepper and blend, starting on low and bringing it up to high speed, until smooth, about 30 seconds. If the blender cover does not have steam vents, remove the center portion of the cover to allow steam to escape and place a kitchen towel over the opening to avoid splashes while blending. Leave the blender container on the base while you make the spinach.

In a medium skillet, heat 1 tablespoon of the olive oil over medium heat. Add the spinach and stir with a wooden spoon until the spinach is wilted, 1 to 2 minutes.

Add the spinach to the blender and blend again, starting on low and bringing it up to high speed, until smooth.

To serve, pour the soup into two bowls and drizzle 1 tablespoon of the remaining olive oil over each bowl. Garnish with the Parmesan, parsley, cilantro, red pepper flakes, and a squeeze of lemon. Finish with salt and pepper to taste.

**FEEL GOOD INGREDIENT // PARSLEY** Ancient Greeks deemed parsley as sacred and used it to decorate the victors of athletic contests. Perhaps they knew that parsley is fantastically good for you. It contains high levels of vitamins K, C, and A, and has anti-inflammatory and antioxidant properties that boost liver health and help maintain a good immune system. It's also one of the many herbs considered to be a cancer-fighting food.

PREP // **10 minutes, plus Red Quinoa with Herbes (page 32)**

COOK // **40 minutes**

SERVES // **6 as a main dish**

# THE HAPPY HIPPY QUINOA SALAD

*Often we'll get friends together on the weekends to do a little yoga and have lunch afterward. A few downward dogs and a plate of this salad take you at least halfway to nirvana. Healthy favorites like protein-rich quinoa, super-food golden berries, vitamin-packed orange juice, nutrient-dense avocado, and liver-cleansing radishes come together in a kaleidoscope of colors and flavors that do wonders for your body and your taste buds.*

### PICKLED RED ONIONS

½ cup (45 g) very thinly sliced red onion

2 tablespoons kosher sea salt

2 tablespoons maple syrup

Red wine vinegar

### DRESSING

2 tablespoons finely chopped shallot (1 small shallot)

½ cup (120 ml) freshly squeezed orange juice (from 1 to 2 oranges)

2 tablespoons red wine vinegar

2 teaspoons whole-grain mustard

1 teaspoon maple syrup

½ teaspoon kosher sea salt

⅛ teaspoon black pepper

½ cup (120 ml) extra-virgin olive oil

### SALAD

⅓ cup (40 g) shelled pistachios

8 ounces (225 g) loosely packed baby kale

½ head (185 g) radicchio, leaves separated

1 recipe Red Quinoa with Herbes (page 32)

⅓ cup (45 g) dried golden berries (substitute dried cranberries, if unavailable)

2 small watermelon radishes, thinly sliced

1 avocado, sliced

**MAKE THE PICKLED RED ONIONS** In a small bowl, combine the onion and salt and toss. Add the maple syrup and toss again. Allow to sit to release liquid for at least 30 minutes.

Make the quinoa according to the recipe. When the quinoa is done cooking, drain the red onion and rinse with water in a fine-mesh sieve. Rinse the bowl. Squeeze the onion slices to remove excess water, then return them to the same bowl and add enough vinegar to cover the onion completely. Set aside and let stand for at least 5 minutes. (The quinoa and onions can be made up to 3 days in advance and stored in an airtight container in the refrigerator.)

**MEANWHILE, MAKE THE DRESSING** Blend the shallot, orange juice, vinegar, mustard, maple syrup, salt, and black pepper in a blender on high speed until smooth. Turn down to low speed and slowly add the olive oil through the lid plug opening until thoroughly emulsified.

**MAKE THE SALAD** In a small skillet, toast the pistachios over medium-high heat, until they just begin to brown and smell toasty, about 2 minutes.

In a large bowl, toss the kale and radicchio with ½ cup (120 ml) of the dressing, then spread the kale on a serving platter.

Toss the quinoa with ½ cup (120 ml) of the remaining dressing and add it to the kale.

Sprinkle with the golden berries, pistachios, watermelon radishes, and avocado. Use a fork to lift the pickled onion slices out of their liquid and scatter them on top. Serve with the extra dressing in a small bowl on the side, if desired.

**FEEL GOOD INGREDIENT // GOLDEN BERRIES** Sweet-tart golden berries are more closely related to tomatillos than to other berries. They also contain protein, something rarely found in a berry. They're rich in antioxidant polyphenols and carotenoids, and they help strengthen the immune system, optimize kidney function, and reduce inflammation.

PREP // **See Fiesta Black Beans (page 38)**
COOK // **5 minutes**
SERVES // **4**

# BLACK BEAN SOUP

**3 cups (555 g) drained Fiesta Black Beans (page 38)**

**1 cup (240 ml) of the bean cooking liquid**

**1 cup (240 ml) vegetable broth**

**1 avocado, cubed or sliced**

**¼ cup (60 ml) The Savory Everything Spread (recipe follows)**

**¼ cup (25 g) shredded red cabbage**

**Handful of fresh cilantro leaves**

**2 limes, cut into wedges**

*Abbie: This soup is a pleasant surprise that came out of us using leftovers during our testing days. Jacq put our Fiesta Black Beans (page 38) into the blender and added her magic touch, and what came out became one of my favorite recipes in this book. It's thick, flavorful, filling, and has a delightful little spicy kick to it.*

In a blender, combine the beans, cooking liquid, and broth and blend, starting on low and bringing it up to high speed, until smooth.

Pour into four bowls and top each with the avocado, The Savory Everything Spread, cabbage, and cilantro. Serve with lime wedges. Refrigerate leftovers in an airtight container for up to 5 days.

**FEEL GOOD INGREDIENT // RED CABBAGE** Red cabbage is more nutritious than the green variety. It contains more vitamin C and a high level of powerful antioxidant plant pigments called anthocyanins, which can support your body in fighting against disease.

## THE SAVORY EVERYTHING SPREAD

*This recipe is everything. But no . . . like, really, everything. It's a dip, it's a spread, it's a topping. It can be a replacement for cheese in veggie wraps or a topping on our Top-Secret Veggie Chili (page 137). Spread it on sandwiches, pile it on baked sweet potatoes, or use it to make cheese-less veggie quesadillas. Add it to anything in need of a little burst of flavor and richness.*

PREP // **5 minutes, plus 2 to 4 hours soaking time**
MAKES // **1 cup (240 ml)**

**1 cup (120 g) raw cashews, preferably soaked in warm water for 2 to 4 hours, drained, and rinsed**

**¼ cup (60 ml) cool filtered water**

**¼ cup (45 g) nutritional yeast**

**2 garlic cloves, peeled**

**1 tablespoon plus 1 teaspoon Bragg Liquid Aminos or tamari**

**1 tablespoon fresh lemon juice**

**1 tablespoon raw apple cider vinegar**

**1 tablespoon dry white wine**

**1 heaping teaspoon Dijon mustard**

**Kosher sea salt and black pepper**

In a high-speed blender, combine the cashews, water, nutritional yeast, garlic, liquid aminos, lemon juice, vinegar, wine, mustard, and a pinch of salt and pepper and blend until smooth, 1 to 2 minutes. At this point, it will have more of a thick sauce consistency, but it will firm up to a texture similar to cream cheese once chilled.

Transfer the spread to a jar with a lid and store in the refrigerator for up to 2 weeks.

**FEEL GOOD INGREDIENT // APPLE CIDER VINEGAR** Hippocrates prescribed apple cider vinegar mixed with honey for coughs and colds, and even for treating diabetes in the 4th century BCE. Research has found that the acetic acid in apple cider vinegar may help stabilize blood-sugar levels, suppress appetite, improve metabolism, and reduce fat storage. It also has powerful antibacterial and anti-fungal properties, which can help keep your gut healthy.

PREP // 10 minutes

COOK // 15 minutes, plus Rosemary Great Northern Beans (page 38) and Tastes Like Summer Pesto (page 160)

SERVES // 4

# WHITE BEAN AND CELERY SALAD WITH PESTO GRILLED SHRIMP

### SALAD

3 cups (555 g) Rosemary Great Northern Beans (page 38)

1 cup (145 g) halved cherry tomatoes

3 celery ribs, thinly sliced

5 ounces (140 g) arugula

Small handful torn fresh basil leaves

Small handful torn fresh celery leaves

1 lemon, quartered

### DRESSING

¼ cup (60 ml) extra-virgin olive oil

¼ cup (60 ml) fresh lemon juice (from 2 lemons)

½ teaspoon kosher sea salt

¼ teaspoon freshly ground black pepper

### SHRIMP

1 pound (455 g) large white shrimp, peeled and deveined (see page 176)

Kosher sea salt and black pepper

½ cup Tastes Like Summer Pesto (page 160) or store-bought dairy-free pesto, divided

*Jacq: I was lucky to learn this recipe from my friend's grandma, who grew up in Genoa, Italy. It's light enough to be the perfect summer fare but substantial enough to give you energy all day long. Whether you're hiking through the Italian Riviera or slogging through a long day at the office, it's the kind of salad that tastes incredible and fuels you without weighing you down.*

Make the beans according to the recipe and use a slotted spoon to measure out 3 cups (555 g) drained beans. Spread the beans on a large plate to cool slightly and refrigerate any leftovers.

**MAKE THE DRESSING** In a medium bowl, whisk together the oil, lemon juice, salt, and pepper and set aside.

**MAKE THE SHRIMP** Heat a grill pan over medium-high heat. Meanwhile, place the shrimp in a bowl and sprinkle with a pinch of salt and pepper. Add 3 tablespoons of the pesto and toss to coat. When the grill pan is hot, grill the shrimp until they turn pink and opaque, about 2 minutes per side.

**MAKE THE SALAD** In a large serving bowl, combine the beans, tomatoes, and celery. Pour half of the dressing over the beans and toss. Add the arugula to the bowl containing the remaining dressing and toss to coat. Transfer the arugula to the serving bowl and gently fold it into the beans.

Top the salad with the grilled shrimp and the basil and celery leaves. Serve with lemon wedges and the remaining pesto on the side. Refrigerate leftovers in an airtight container for up to 2 days.

**CHEF'S NOTE** Source wild-caught shrimp from sustainable US fisheries or farmed shrimp from recirculating aquaculture farms in the United States and Canada. Imported shrimp, both wild and farmed, should be avoided due to concerns about sustainability, contamination, and unethical labor practices.

**FEEL GOOD INGREDIENT // CELERY LEAVES** Often discarded, celery leaves make a lovely addition to salads with a flavor that sits somewhere between a leafy green and a fresh herb. They also offer nutrients that can boost your health. In fact, celery leaves are more nutritious than the stalks! They're low in calories and provide vitamin E, calcium, and fiber.

*"One of the very best things about life is the way we must regularly stop whatever it is we are doing and devote our attention to eating."*

—LUCIANO PAVAROTTI

# Beans and Grains

# QUICK AND JAZZY CANNED BEANS

We've waxed poetic about home-cooked beans in Cooking School (page 34), but we live in the real world and know that time doesn't always allow for beans from scratch. Good news: It doesn't take much to transform plain canned beans into something truly appetizing and nutritious. The next four recipes give you a quick spin on some international classics.

## Quick Curried Garbanzos

*Jacq: The first time I tried a dish flavored with curry powder, I was eighteen years old in London. There was an immediate realization that there was a world of flavors that I had yet to explore. This recipe is an easy way to evoke that feeling. Serve it with Roasted Curried Cauliflower with Raisins and Pine Nuts (page 44), simple sautéed spinach, and steamed brown rice.*

PREP // **5 minutes**
COOK // **7 minutes**
SERVES // **4 as a side**

1 tablespoon virgin coconut oil

½ onion, finely diced (about 1 cup/125 g)

Kosher sea salt and freshly ground black pepper

3 garlic cloves, smashed and peeled (see page 36)

2 (15-ounce/425-g) cans garbanzo beans, drained and rinsed

½ cup (120 ml) light coconut milk

1 teaspoon curry powder

Small handful (2 to 3 tablespoons) fresh cilantro leaves

In a large sauté pan or skillet, heat the oil over medium-high heat until melted and shimmering, then add the onion and a generous pinch of salt. Sauté for 3 minutes, then add the garlic and continue cooking until the onion begins to brown, about 1 minute more.

Add the beans, gently stir to coat them in the oil, then add the coconut milk and curry powder. Season with salt and pepper. Simmer for a couple of minutes to allow the flavors to meld, then fold in the cilantro. Allow any leftovers to cool, then store in an airtight container in the refrigerator for up to 3 days.

**FEEL GOOD INGREDIENT // COCONUT MILK** Coconut milk contains lauric acid, which can have antiviral, antifungal, and antibacterial effects on the body.

# White Beans Provençal

*These make an ideal base for a Mediterranean-style meal or an effortless side for your favorite grilled fish, such as our Italian-Style Grilled Halibut (page 191).*

PREP // **3 minutes**
COOK // **7 minutes**
SERVES // **4 as a side**

1 tablespoon olive oil

1 shallot, finely chopped

¼ teaspoon herbes de Provence

1 large garlic clove, minced

2 (15-ounce/425-g) cans cannellini beans, drained and rinsed

2 tablespoons dry white wine or vegetable broth

Flaky sea salt and freshly ground black pepper

Small handful (2 to 3 tablespoons) fresh flat-leaf parsley leaves, chopped

In a large sauté pan or skillet, heat the oil over medium heat until hot and shimmering, then add the shallot. Sauté until it is just beginning to brown, about 3 minutes. Add the herbes de Provence and garlic and continue sautéing until the garlic is fragrant, 30 seconds to 1 minute more.

Add the beans and wine and gently stir. Season with salt and pepper to taste and gently stir again. After a couple of minutes, when the beans have warmed through, fold in the parsley. Allow any leftovers to cool, then store in an airtight container in the refrigerator for up to 3 days.

**CHEF'S NOTE** Turn this recipe into a delicious dip! Simply put it into a food processor or blender along with 1 garlic clove and 3 tablespoons olive oil and process into a chunky puree. If it's too thick, add a splash of veggie broth. Serve with crudités or pita chips.

**FEEL GOOD INGREDIENT // CANNELLINI BEANS**
Cannellini beans, also known as white kidney beans, are popular in Italian and French cooking. They are versatile, have a mild flavor, and are typically inexpensive, making them a good choice for a variety of dishes including soups, sides, and salads. Cannellini beans can also be helpful if you're looking to lose weight because they are rich in fiber, protein, and other beneficial nutrients that are super satisfying.

# Spicy Black Beans

*Abbie: As simple as it is, this is one of the recipes that I use the most often. Spicy black beans make a welcome addition to almost any meal and even make a yummy post-workout snack, especially with a little Quick Pico de Gallo (page 200) and Avocado-Lime Cream (page 179) on top.*

PREP // **2 minutes**
COOK // **4 minutes**
SERVES // **4 as a side**

**2 garlic cloves, minced**

**½ teaspoon ground cumin**

**1 tablespoon coconut or olive oil**

**2 (15-ounce/425-g) cans black beans, drained and rinsed**

**Kosher sea salt and black pepper**

**Pinch cayenne pepper**

**Small handful (2 to 3 tablespoons) fresh cilantro leaves, chopped**

In a large sauté pan or skillet, sauté the garlic and cumin in the oil over medium heat until fragrant, about 1 minute. Add the beans and season with salt, black pepper, and the cayenne. Lower the heat to medium-low and continue cooking for a few minutes until the beans are warmed through.

Garnish with the cilantro. Store any leftovers in an airtight container in the refrigerator for up to 3 days.

**FEEL GOOD INGREDIENT // CUMIN** Cumin is the second most popular spice after black pepper. It is widely used in Latin American, North African, Middle Eastern, Asian, and Indian cuisines and has long been used as a digestive aid. Cooking regularly with ground cumin can help prevent iron deficiency; each teaspoon provides 4 milligrams of iron (or 22 percent of the daily value).

# World's Best Refried Beans

*Jacq: Surprisingly, one of the best things I ever ate in Mexico was beans on toast. The chef who made them was kind enough to let me in on a couple of secret ingredients—cocoa butter and beer! The cocoa butter lends a wonderful complexity while beer adds a subtle earthy flavor and a touch of acidity. I've thrown in tempeh bacon for a meaty smokiness.*

PREP // **5 minutes**
COOK // **10 minutes**
SERVES // **4 as a side**

**2 tablespoons food-grade cocoa butter**

**½ onion, finely chopped (about 1 cup/125 g)**

**½ jalapeño, stemmed and seeded, finely chopped**

**2 slices tempeh or seitan bacon, chopped (see Note)**

**Kosher sea salt**

**2 garlic cloves, minced**

**2 (15-ounce/425-g) cans pinto beans including their liquid**

**¼ teaspoon dried oregano, preferably Mexican**

**¼ teaspoon smoked paprika**

**¼ cup (60 ml) beer (see Note)**

**Freshly ground black pepper**

**Small handful (2 to 3 tablespoons) fresh cilantro leaves, chopped (optional)**

In a large sauté pan or skillet, heat the cocoa butter over medium heat until melted and shimmering, then add the onion, jalapeño, bacon, and a generous pinch of salt. Sauté for 3 minutes, add the garlic, and continue cooking until the onion begins to brown, about 1 minute more.

Add the beans, including the liquid from the cans. Sprinkle in the oregano and paprika and pour in the beer. Lower the heat if needed to keep the beans at a simmer and cook, stirring occasionally, for 5 minutes. Using a potato masher or large fork, mash the beans well until nearly smooth. Season with salt and pepper. Garnish with the cilantro, if desired. Store any leftovers in an airtight container in the refrigerator for up to 3 days.

**CHEF'S NOTE** If you are avoiding gluten, choose tempeh and be sure to use a gluten-free beer.

**FEEL GOOD INGREDIENT // COCOA BUTTER** Cocoa butter is probably best known as a fantastic moisturizer. However, the same antioxidant plant polyphenols that help fight signs of aging and soothe sensitive skin can also fight inflammation internally and contribute to brain health and balanced hormones.

# TACO MEAT COLLARD GREEN WRAPS WITH COCONUT SOUR CREAM

### FILLING

1 tablespoon virgin olive oil or coconut oil

½ cup (55 g) chopped onion

6 ounces (170 g) sliced cremini mushrooms

1 garlic clove, finely chopped

½ teaspoon smoked salt

½ teaspoon ground cumin

¼ teaspoon chili powder

¼ teaspoon black pepper

Pinch cayenne pepper (optional)

2 tablespoons dry red wine (substitute vegetable broth or water, if necessary)

½ cup (60 g) raw walnuts

¼ cup (30 g) raw pecans

½ cup (90 g) cooked or canned black beans, drained (rinse if using canned)

½ cup (55 g) oil-packed sun-dried tomatoes, drained

2 teaspoons oil from the sun-dried tomatoes

¼ cup (10 g) fresh cilantro leaves and tender stems

### SOUR CREAM

1 (13.5-ounce/398-ml) can coconut milk, refrigerated overnight (see Notes)

2 tablespoons unsweetened cashew or almond milk

¾ teaspoon apple cider vinegar

Pinch kosher sea salt

*The filling in these wraps is made with protein-rich beans, meaty mushrooms, and nutritious nuts. You get all of the taco flavor you crave in a light and nutrient-dense package. You can almost feel your cells absorbing their goodness. They're especially great at lunchtime; instead of putting you in a post-lunch slump, they give you a boost of energy that makes you ready to take on the world.*

**MAKE THE FILLING** Heat the oil and onion in a sauté pan over medium-low heat. When the onion softens and becomes translucent, after about 8 minutes, raise the heat to medium and add the mushrooms, garlic, smoked salt, cumin, chili powder, black pepper, cayenne (if using), and wine and sauté, stirring frequently. Once the mushrooms are cooked down, after about 6 minutes, add the walnuts and pecans and cook for 2 minutes more.

Transfer the mixture to a food processor along with the beans, sun-dried tomatoes, oil from the tomatoes, and cilantro. Process until the mixture is approximately the texture of ground meat, or alternatively, finely chop the mixture with a chef's knife. Set aside.

**MAKE THE SOUR CREAM** Remove the coconut milk from the refrigerator. Without shaking or tipping, remove the lid and scoop out ¼ cup (60 ml) of the solid cream from the top into a chilled mixing bowl. Refrigerate the remaining liquid in a small container with a lid to use later in smoothies. This will keep for up to 5 days.

Add the nut milk, vinegar, and salt to the bowl and mix with a fork until smooth. Refrigerate until ready to use.

CONTINUES

**WRAPS**

4 large collard greens leaves

1 avocado, sliced

1 cup (135 g) grape tomatoes, halved

⅛ onion, thinly sliced

3 carrots, julienned

4 radishes, thinly sliced

1 cup (70 g) shredded red cabbage

Sriracha

4 sprigs fresh cilantro

1 lime, quartered

Kosher sea salt

**MAKE THE WRAPS** Trim the stems off of the collard greens below the leaf. Place a leaf rough-side up on a cutting board with the bottom (stem side) facing away from you. Using a paring knife, shave down the center rib so that it is about the same thickness as the rest of the leaf, cutting away from your body. This will keep the leaf from breaking when you roll it. Repeat with the other leaves.

Lay the trimmed leaves next to each other with the stem side facing you. Arrange the avocado slices horizontally on the bottom third of each leaf, leaving 1 inch (2.5 cm) of leaf on either side. Next, divide the filling evenly among the leaves, piling it on top of the avocado slices. Stack the veggies in layers on top of the filling and top with a few dollops of sour cream, a few drops of sriracha, and a sprig of cilantro. Squeeze the juice from the lime wedges over the top and sprinkle the veggies with a pinch of salt.

Fold the bottom of the collard green leaves up over the filling, then fold in the sides. Fold over from the bottom one more time while keeping the sides tucked in to form a burrito. Make 4 burritos and cut them in half to serve. Refrigerate any leftovers (see Notes).

**CHEF'S NOTES** Use only full-fat coconut milk. If your can is not refrigerated, you can place it upright in the freezer for 1 hour.

These wraps keep well for a day. If you are not going to serve them right away, give the avocados an extra little squeeze of lime juice to help prevent browning.

**FEEL GOOD INGREDIENT // COLLARD GREENS** Collard greens are extremely low in calories. They have a similar, impressively high, vitamin content to other leafy greens. Collard greens have even more protein, fiber, and calcium than both kale and Swiss chard.

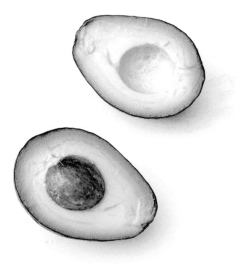

**FEEL GOOD INGREDIENT // TURMERIC**
This powerful spice can help prevent disease and elevate mood as it soothes and repairs the neurological system. It blocks free radicals from interfering with the body's cells, and works as a positive stimulant, actively repairing the body's molecular structure and encouraging new and healthy cellular growth.

# CRISPY TURMERIC SPICED TOFU WITH CILANTRO-MINT COCONUT CREAM

### TOFU

1 (16-ounce/455-g) package extra-firm tofu

3 tablespoons brown rice flour

1 to 2 eggs or ¼ cup (60 ml) aquafaba from 1 (15-ounce/425-g) can chickpeas (see Notes)

1 cup (80 g) whole-wheat or gluten-free panko breadcrumbs (see Notes)

1 heaping teaspoon finely chopped fresh flat-leaf parsley leaves (optional)

1½ teaspoons kosher sea salt

1 teaspoon ground turmeric

¼ teaspoon ground coriander

¼ teaspoon garlic powder

¼ teaspoon paprika

⅛ teaspoon black pepper

Refined coconut oil or olive oil for pan-frying

### COCONUT CREAM

1 (5.3-ounce/150-g) container unsweetened coconut milk yogurt (see Notes)

½ teaspoon lime zest

2 tablespoons fresh lime juice (from 1 large lime)

¼ teaspoon salt

¼ teaspoon garlic powder

1 teaspoon chopped fresh mint leaves

1 teaspoon chopped fresh cilantro leaves

*Abbie: This is a unique creation of Jacq's that is full of flavor and surprisingly filling. The crispy tofu's warm, earthy flavor pairs perfectly with the coconut cream, which adds a bright note to every bite. Serve it with steamed rice and a side of sautéed greens to make it a meal.*

**MAKE THE TOFU** Drain the tofu and wrap it in a dish towel. Squeeze gently to remove excess moisture. Remove the towel and wrap the tofu in another towel and place it on a dinner plate. Use paper towels if dish towels are unavailable. Lay a plate on top of the tofu and place a can or a sweet potato on top to help press the tofu and remove extra moisture.

Allow the tofu to sit while you set up a breading station using three shallow bowls. Place the flour in the first bowl. In the second, lightly beat the egg or aquafaba with a whisk. In the third, mix the breadcrumbs, parsley, if using, salt, turmeric, coriander, garlic powder, paprika, and black pepper.

Unwrap the tofu and give it a final pat to dry off as much moisture as possible, then slice it into ½-inch- (12-mm-) thick tiles. Dip and turn each piece of tofu to coat lightly first in the flour, then in the egg, shaking off any excess as you go. Next, gently press the tofu into the breadcrumbs to coat well, and transfer to a plate.

In a large skillet, heat ¼ inch (6 mm) oil over medium-high heat until shimmering. If you drop in a breadcrumb, it should sizzle. Lower the heat to medium and use a slotted spatula to carefully lay the tofu in the pan in a single layer, without crowding. Working in batches, cook for 2 to 3 minutes per side, until golden brown and crispy. Transfer the cooked tofu to a paper towel-lined plate or cooling rack.

**MAKE THE COCONUT CREAM** In a small bowl, whisk the yogurt with the lime zest and juice, salt, and garlic powder, then fold in the mint and cilantro. Serve it spread under the crispy tofu or as a topping or dipping sauce.

**CHEF'S NOTES** Note whole-wheat panko breadcrumbs are not gluten-free.

If using eggs, start with one egg, and if you need more, use a second egg. Alternatively, you can use the liquid from canned chickpeas. This liquid is known as aquafaba and works well as an egg replacer in this recipe.

Look for thick yogurt such as Coyo or Anita's brands.

PREP // **1 hour, plus sweet potato (see page 26) and Red Quinoa with Herbes (page 32)**

COOK // **55 minutes**

MAKES // **8 burgers**

# CALIFORNIA DREAM BURGERS

1 cup (200 g) mashed baked sweet potato (from 1 large sweet potato; see page 26)

2 cups (260 g) Red Quinoa with Herbes (page 32)

1½ cups (280 g) cooked black beans plus ⅓ cup (75 ml) bean cooking liquid or 1 (15-ounce/425-g) can drained, liquid reserved, and rinsed

3 tablespoons chia seeds (see Notes)

3 garlic cloves, peeled

½ onion, cut into wedges (about 1 cup/110 g)

1 shallot, quartered

1½ teaspoons smoked salt

1 teaspoon black pepper

1 teaspoon chili powder

2 tablespoons barbecue sauce

1 teaspoon liquid smoke (optional)

¼ cup (20 g) old-fashioned or gluten-free rolled oats

2 tablespoons tapioca flour

¾ cup (75 g) raw walnuts

½ cup (35 g) loosely packed fresh flat-leaf parsley leaves and tender stems

8 hamburger buns

### TOPPINGS

Dijon mustard

⅓ cup (75 ml) Kale-Walnut Pesto (page 161) or store-bought pesto

½ cup (55 g) oil-packed sun-dried tomatoes, drained and sliced

2 tomatoes, sliced

2 cups (40 g) baby arugula

*Jacq: Of all of the recipes in this book, this one took me the longest to perfect. I was tweaking it for years and was only satisfied when I saw my most carnivorous friend hold back tears one Fourth of July when he found out that the burgers had run out. Yep, they're that good. They take a while to make, but freeze beautifully. Now I always make a double batch and freeze any leftovers.*

Preheat the oven to 375°F (190°C) and line a baking sheet with parchment paper.

In a large bowl, combine the sweet potato, quinoa, and black beans. Lightly mash the black beans with a fork and set aside.

In a small bowl, mix the ⅓ cup (75 ml) reserved liquid from the beans and the chia seeds with a fork. Set aside to thicken into a gel.

Place the garlic in a food processor and process until roughly chopped. Add the onion and shallot and process until finely chopped. Remove the blade, then transfer the mixture to the bowl with the black beans, leaving behind any excess liquid.

Give the chia seeds a stir with a fork to mix in the seeds that have floated to the top.

Add the smoked salt, pepper, chili powder, barbecue sauce, and liquid smoke, if using, to the black bean mixture. Add the chia seed gel, the oats, and tapioca flour and stir with a fork until they are mixed well and the beans are mostly mashed. It's OK to leave a few beans whole for texture.

Wipe out the bowl of the food processor with a paper towel. Replace the blade, add the walnuts and parsley, and process until finely chopped but not ground. Add the walnuts and parsley to the burger mixture and combine with a fork.

Make your patties with a slightly rounded ½ cup (160 g) measure of the burger mixture. Flip the cup so the mixture falls into your hand and slightly flatten to form a ¾-inch-(2-cm-) thick patty. Set on a baking sheet and repeat to make 8 burgers. Bake for 25 minutes, flip using a spatula, and bake for 10 to 15 minutes more, until lightly browned.

Spread a thin layer of mustard on the tops of the hamburger buns. Arrange the bottom buns and the burger patties on a serving platter. Top each burger with a layer of pesto, a few sun-dried tomato slices, a slice of fresh tomato, and a handful of arugula. Add the top bun and serve. Refrigerate leftovers in an airtight container for up to 3 days. (See Notes for freezing directions.)

**CHEF'S NOTES**  To freeze, layer the patties in an airtight container with parchment paper between each layer. Alternatively, freeze them on a baking sheet and when solid, transfer them to zip-top freezer bags. Reheat in a preheated 375°F (190°C) oven on a baking sheet for 20 to 30 minutes, until warmed through. If you are reheating just a couple of patties, you can stick them in the toaster for 2 to 3 toast cycles. Use tongs to remove them from the toaster to avoid breakage.

Use 1 large beaten egg in place of the chia seeds and bean liquid, if preferred.

**FEEL GOOD INGREDIENT  //  ARUGULA**  In Roman times, arugula was believed to be an aphrodisiac. Virgil even wrote that it "excites the sexual desire of drowsy people." Not surprising, really, since this highly antioxidant and nutrient-dense cruciferous vegetable can help improve the functioning of almost every system in the body. Full of vitamin K, folate, and beta carotene, arugula helps to improve circulation, block toxins in the environment that can lower libido, and has stimulating, energizing qualities.

PREP // **15 minutes, plus Creamy Cashew Sour Cream (page 138) and/or The Savory Everything Spread (page 121)**

COOK // **30 minutes**

SERVES // **12**

# TOP-SECRET VEGGIE CHILI

1 shot espresso or ½ cup (120 ml) dark roast coffee

2 tablespoons olive oil

1 onion, diced

1 shallot

4 garlic cloves, peeled

1 green bell pepper

3 carrots

2 (14.5-ounce/411-g) cans stewed tomatoes, preferably Italian style

3 ears corn or 1 (15-ounce/425-g) can of corn, drained

3 zucchini

1 (15-ounce/425-g) can black beans

1 (15-ounce/425-g) can kidney beans

1 (15-ounce/425-g) can garbanzo beans

1 (15-ounce/425-g) can cannellini beans

1 (15-ounce/425-g) can pinto beans

2 teaspoons kosher sea salt

1 teaspoon black pepper

Chili Seasoning Mix (page 138) or any store-bought chili seasoning packet of your choice

1 teaspoon raw cacao powder

¾ teaspoon maple syrup

¼ teaspoon chipotle chile powder (see Note)

Pinch ground cinnamon

2 teaspoons sriracha

8 ounces (225 g) sliced cremini mushrooms

8 ounces (1 pint/225 g) cherry or grape tomatoes

½ cup (20 g) fresh cilantro leaves, plus more for garnish

### TOPPINGS

Creamy Cashew Sour Cream (page 138) and/or The Savory Everything Spread (page 121)

Avocado Ranch Dressing (page 196; optional)

*Abbie: This is one of my favorites. It's so warm, comforting, and homey, and is packed full of healthy veggies. The chili cooks at a low temperature, so rather than prep everything ahead of time, you can chop as you go, which saves time. There are a few secret ingredients—coffee, cacao, and sriracha—that make it extra special. People invariably ask for this recipe. It's up to you whether you reveal your secret.*

If you don't have any on hand, brew coffee or make a shot of espresso and set aside.

In a large pot (5-quart/5-L minimum), heat the oil over medium-low heat, add the onion, and stir to coat the onion in the oil. Thinly slice the shallot and add it to the onion. Mince the garlic, add it to the pot, and give it a good stir.

Dice the bell pepper and throw it in with the onion. Slice the carrots into ¼-inch- (6-mm-) thick coins and stir them in. Drain the liquid from the canned stewed tomatoes into the pot, then roughly chop the stewed tomatoes and add them in.

Cut the kernels off of the corn cobs and add the kernels to the pot (or add the canned corn). Slice the zucchini into ¼-inch- (6-mm-) thick coins, add them to the pot, and gently stir.

Place all of the beans in a colander. Rinse, drain, then add them to the pot and sprinkle with the salt, pepper, and chili seasoning. Pour the coffee or espresso over the beans and stir until the seasonings dissolve. Add the cacao powder, maple syrup, chipotle chile powder, cinnamon, and sriracha and stir again.

Add the mushrooms to the beans and cover. Simmer while you cut the fresh tomatoes in half and roughly chop the cilantro. Add the tomatoes and cilantro to the pot and stir. Cover and simmer for 3 minutes more, or until the mushrooms are tender.

Serve the chili in bowls and top with sour cream or The Everything Spread and garnish with fresh cilantro leaves.

**CHEF'S NOTE** If you don't have chipotle chile powder, you can substitute a pinch of cayenne pepper.

**FEEL GOOD INGREDIENT // BEANS** Author Dan Buettner, who has been researching Blue Zones, areas with the highest concentrations of healthy centenarians, found that in all of the areas he studied, beans and/or legumes are a cornerstone of the population's diet.

# CHILI SEASONING MIX

*Store-bought chili seasoning packets can be pricey and sometimes include strange additives. Make this tasty mix at home to save money and know exactly what's going into your chili.*

**2 tablespoons dried onion flakes**

**2 teaspoons chili powder**

**1 teaspoon masa harina or brown rice flour**

**1 teaspoon seasoned salt**

**½ teaspoon smoked paprika**

**½ teaspoon garlic powder**

**¾ teaspoon ground cumin**

**Pinch ground dried oregano**

In a small bowl, combine all the ingredients and mix with a fork. Keep in a small jar with a lid in your spice cabinet for up to 1 year.

# CREAMY CASHEW SOUR CREAM

*Here's a simple, plant-based alternative to traditional sour cream. The ingredients are natural and nutritious, filled with enzymes and essential minerals. It complements Mexican food, wraps, or bowls, adding a cooling richness. We like to make it during our weekly food prep to use throughout the week.*

**1 cup (120 g) raw cashews, preferably soaked for 2 to 4 hours, drained, and rinsed**

**¼ cup (60 ml) filtered water**

**1½ tablespoons raw apple cider vinegar**

**¼ plus ⅛ teaspoon kosher sea salt**

In a high-speed blender, combine all the ingredients and blend until smooth, about 1 minute. Transfer the sour cream to a jar with a lid and store in the refrigerator. Enjoy within 5 days.

**CHEF'S NOTE** Use a couple of tablespoons in smoothies to add a little tang and extra creaminess.

# STUFFED MAPLE-GLAZED ACORN SQUASH

ROASTED ACORN SQUASH

**2 acorn squash**

**2 tablespoons melted coconut oil or olive oil**

**2 tablespoons maple syrup**

**Kosher sea salt and black pepper**

**Cinnamon**

**Nutmeg**

**2 garlic cloves, peeled**

FILLING

**3 tablespoons coconut or olive oil**

**1 small onion, thinly sliced (about 1½ cups/ 165 g)**

**Pinch kosher sea salt**

**1 teaspoon balsamic vinegar**

**2 cups (375 g) cooked or canned garbanzo beans, drained (rinse if using canned)**

**⅓ cup (40 g) chopped pecans, plus 4 halves for garnish**

**1 (12-ounce/340-g) package soy chorizo**

**⅓ cup (17 g) fresh flat-leaf parsley leaves, chopped, plus 2 teaspoons for garnish**

**¼ cup (35 g) dried cranberries, plus 2 teaspoons for garnish**

**Pinch smoked salt (optional)**

*This is our favorite meat-free main dish to serve during the holiday season. Using the acorn squash as bowls makes for a beautiful presentation. It's flavorful, hearty, and super satisfying thanks to a combination of protein, fiber, and healthy fats. Pecans, cranberries, and warming spices like cinnamon and nutmeg make it the perfect dish for your fall and winter celebrations. Serve it with Spiced Sweet Potato Puree (page 141).*

**MAKE THE SQUASH** Preheat the oven to 400°F (205°C) and line a baking sheet with parchment paper. Cut the squash in half lengthwise, avoiding the stem. Scrape out the seeds and strings using a spoon. Score the flesh of the squash with a knife, cutting ½ inch (12 mm) deep on the diagonal to make a crisscross pattern. Poke the flesh several times with a fork, without piercing through the skin, and place the squash on a baking sheet skin side up.

In a small bowl, mix the oil and maple syrup, and using your hands or a basting brush, rub some of it over the skin of the squash. Sprinkle generously with salt and pepper. Flip the squash, cavity-side up, and divide the remaining oil and maple mixture among the pieces. Sprinkle the flesh generously with salt, pepper, cinnamon, and nutmeg (about ⅛ teaspoon each per piece of squash). Spread the oil and spices around on the flesh of the squash with a brush or spoon. (It's OK if it pools a bit in the middle.)

Cut the garlic cloves in half and put ½ clove inside each piece of squash. Roast in the oven for about 45 minutes, until browned and the flesh is easily pierced with a fork.

**MEANWHILE, MAKE THE FILLING** Heat the oil in a large sauté pan over medium heat. Add the onion and salt and cook, stirring occasionally, until the onion becomes translucent, about 2 minutes. Lower the heat to medium-low and cook, stirring every 5 minutes or so, until it is soft and caramelized, about 25 minutes. If the onion starts to blacken at all, lower the heat. Sprinkle the vinegar over the onion and stir. Add the beans and pecans, raise the heat to medium, and sauté for 2 minutes. Add the chorizo and stir gently to incorporate; heat until everything is heated through. Do not smash the garbanzo beans. Fold in the parsley and cranberries and mix until the ingredients are evenly distributed, then remove from the heat.

CONTINUES

**TO ASSEMBLE** When the squash is browned and tender, remove it from the oven. Using a fork, remove the garlic cloves from the squash, slice them, and fold them into the filling. Heap the filling into each squash half. Place 1 pecan half on top and sprinkle with chopped parsley and a few more cranberries. Finish with the smoked salt, if desired.

**FEEL GOOD INGREDIENT // ACORN SQUASH** This sweet, dense squash is the most nutritious of all of the squashes. Its high potassium content can have a positive effect on blood pressure, and a single serving of acorn squash contains 9 grams of fiber, more than a third of your daily requirement. A diet rich in high-fiber foods may help lower "bad" cholesterol levels and help control blood-sugar levels.

PREP // **2 minutes**
COOK // **1 hour**
SERVES // **4**

# SPICED SWEET POTATO PUREE

1 large sweet potato (about 1 pound, 3 ounces/600 g)

½ cup (120 ml) unsweetened almond or cashew milk

¼ cup (60 ml) vegetable broth

2 teaspoons maple syrup

1 small garlic clove, peeled

¼ teaspoon kosher sea salt

¼ teaspoon black pepper

1 tablespoon fresh orange or tangerine juice

1 teaspoon berbere spice (see Note)

*The consistency of this dish is thinner and smoother than a traditional mashed sweet potato, but thicker and creamier than a sauce. We love it with our Stuffed Maple-Glazed Acorn Squash (page 139), but it also makes a wonderful base layer under sautéed veggies, tofu, or fish. It adds a beautiful pop of color, a ton of flavor, and a boost of fiber and antioxidants to any meal.*

Preheat the oven to 400°F (205°C) and line a baking sheet with parchment paper.

Prick the sweet potato several times with a fork and bake until it is easily pierced with a fork, 45 minutes to 1 hour. Once cool enough to handle, peel the skin and chop the flesh into chunks. Add to a food processor or high-speed blender along with the remaining ingredients and blend until smooth. Refrigerate any leftovers in an airtight container for up to 5 days.

**CHEF'S NOTE** Berbere is a delicious Ethiopian spice blend sold at specialty and ethnic food markets and online. If unavailable, substitute: ¼ teaspoon plus ⅛ teaspoon chili powder, ⅛ teaspoon ground cinnamon, ⅛ teaspoon ground ginger, and a pinch of ground nutmeg.

**FEEL GOOD INGREDIENT // MAPLE SYRUP** Pure maple syrup is made from the boiled-down sap of maple trees without the addition of chemical agents or preservatives. While all sweeteners should be used in moderation, maple syrup is a natural food that contains important antioxidants and minerals like zinc and manganese. It also has a lower glycemic index than table sugar, so it impacts your blood sugar levels less dramatically.

PREP // **10 minutes**

COOK // **25 minutes**

SERVES // **6**

# CREAMY WHITE WINE RISOTTO WITH ROASTED MUSHROOMS AND THYME

### RISOTTO

**4 cups (960 ml) vegetable broth**

**2 cups (480 ml) warm filtered water**

**¼ cup (60 ml) extra-virgin olive oil**

**1 yellow onion, finely diced (about 1½ cups/ 125 g)**

**Kosher sea salt**

**4 garlic cloves, minced**

**1 heaping teaspoon fresh thyme leaves, plus 6 small sprigs for garnish**

**2 cups (380 g) arborio rice**

**¾ cup (180 ml) dry white wine**

**2 tablespoons chickpea miso**

**2 tablespoons nutritional yeast**

**¼ teaspoon white pepper**

**Truffle oil**

**3 tablespoons fresh flat-leaf parsley leaves, minced, for garnish**

### MUSHROOMS

**1 pound (455 g) mixed mushrooms (such as cremini, chanterelles, hen of the woods, oyster, or shiitake), cut or torn into bite-size chunks**

**3 tablespoons olive oil**

**2 teaspoons fresh thyme leaves**

**4 garlic cloves, roughly chopped**

**¼ teaspoon kosher sea salt**

**¼ teaspoon freshly ground black pepper**

*Risotto must be the world's most elegant comfort food. It's so satisfying and warming, but also feels like a special occasion dish. The creaminess is achieved by coaxing the starch out the of the grains of arborio rice. You do this by adding hot broth little by little and by stirring often. To get the umami boost that Parmesan traditionally provides, we add a little miso paste and nutritional yeast. It's all topped off with meaty roasted mushrooms.*

Preheat the oven to 450°F (230°C) and line a baking sheet with parchment paper. Set aside.

**MAKE THE RISOTTO** In a large pot, combine the broth and water and bring to a simmer.

Heat the oil in a large, heavy-bottomed pan over medium heat. Add the onion and a pinch of salt and sauté, stirring frequently with a wooden spoon, until the onion softens and starts to become translucent, about 3 minutes.

Add the garlic and thyme leaves to the pan, stir, then add the rice. Continue to stir frequently to coat the rice in the oil and to prevent sticking. Toast the rice for 2 to 3 minutes, until it smells nutty and the edges of the grains look translucent. Pour the wine into the rice and stir until it is completely absorbed.

Ladle in 1 cup (240 ml) of the broth. Continue cooking the rice and gently stirring until most of the liquid has been absorbed before adding another cup. Adjust the heat as needed to keep both pots at a simmer. Continue to add and incorporate the broth 1 cup (240 ml) at a time. Cook the rice until it is tender, about 20 minutes. You do not need to stir continuously, but stirring frequently will help your risotto cook evenly and achieve the desirable creamy consistency. You may have a little leftover broth. If you run out of liquid before the rice is tender, add more water.

**MEANWHILE, MAKE THE MUSHROOMS** Gently toss the mushrooms with the oil, thyme, garlic, salt, and pepper on a baking sheet then spread out the mushrooms in a single layer. Roast until the mushrooms are browned, about 14 minutes, turning once midway.

Once the risotto is done, stir in the miso, nutritional yeast, and white pepper. Just before serving, stir in a splash of the broth to loosen the consistency, if necessary. Plate and drizzle the risotto with a bit of truffle oil, about 1 teaspoon per serving. Top with the roasted mushrooms and garnish each dish with the parsley and a sprig of thyme. Enjoy immediately.

**CHEF'S NOTES**  The risotto should be loose enough that if you put a scoop in the middle of the plate and shake it, it will spread out. If it holds its form, it is too dry; stir in a bit more hot broth or water to loosen it.

Make a champagne risotto with truffles using this recipe! Simply use champagne instead of wine and freshly shaved Burgundy truffles in place of the mushrooms.

**FEEL GOOD INGREDIENT  //  ARBORIO RICE**  Arborio rice undergoes less milling than ordinary long-grain rice, so it retains more of its natural starch content and fiber. Though it's not the most nutritious grain, its unique ability to develop into a creamy risotto makes people happy, a valuable quality in any ingredient.

# LEMON-PEA RISOTTO WITH MINT

4 cups (960 ml) vegetable broth

2 cups (480 ml) warm filtered water

¼ cup (60 ml) extra-virgin olive oil

1 yellow onion, finely diced (about 1½ cups/ 125 g)

Kosher sea salt

4 garlic cloves, minced

2 cups (380 g) arborio rice

¾ cup (180 ml) dry white wine

2 tablespoons chickpea miso

1 tablespoon nutritional yeast

1 tablespoon nondairy butter (preferably Miyoko's Vegan Butter)

3 tablespoons fresh lemon juice (from 1 lemon)

1 cup (135 g) frozen peas, thawed

¼ cup (13 g) lightly packed fresh mint leaves, chopped, plus more for garnish

Handful sugar snap peas for garnish (optional)

Lemon slices for garnish (optional)

*Peas and mint come together again in this beautiful risotto that tastes rich and creamy but leaves you feeling light. We've served this the last couple of years at our Easter luncheon to rave reviews. Try it with pesto grilled shrimp on top (see Note) or match it with our colorful Spring Salad with Green Goddess Dressing (page 107).*

Combine the broth and water in a medium pot and bring to a simmer.

In a large heavy-bottomed pot, heat the oil over medium heat. Add the onion and a pinch of salt and sauté, stirring frequently with a wooden spoon, until the onion softens and starts to become translucent, about 3 minutes. Avoid browning the onion.

Add the garlic to the pan, stir, then add the rice. Continue to stir frequently to coat the rice in the oil and to prevent sticking. Toast the rice for 2 to 3 minutes, until it smells nutty and the edges of the grains look translucent. Pour the wine into the rice and stir until it is completely absorbed.

Ladle in 1 cup (240 ml) of the broth. Continue cooking and gently stirring until most of the liquid has been absorbed before adding another cup. Adjust the heat as needed to keep both pots at a simmer. Continue to add and incorporate the broth 1 cup (240 ml) at a time. Cook the rice until it is tender, about 20 minutes. You do not need to stir continuously, but stirring frequently will help your risotto cook evenly and achieve the desirable creamy consistency. You may have a little leftover broth. If you run out of liquid before the rice is tender, add more water.

Once the risotto is done, stir in the miso, nutritional yeast, butter, and lemon juice until well incorporated. Fold in the peas and mint and turn off the heat. Just before serving, stir in a splash of hot liquid to loosen the consistency, if necessary (see Notes, page 143). Garnish with the mint leaves, snap peas, and lemon slices, if desired. Enjoy immediately.

**CHEF'S NOTE** To serve with shrimp, toss 1 pound (455 g) shrimp with 3 tablespoons pesto. Grill them over medium-high heat until they turn pink, about 2 minutes per side.

**FEEL GOOD INGREDIENT // LEMON** Iron from animal sources (heme-iron) is more readily absorbed by your body than iron from plant sources (non-heme iron). Pairing plant foods, such as rice, with foods rich in vitamin C and citric acid, like lemons, can help you absorb as much iron as possible.

# FIESTA VEGGIE RICE

2 tablespoons olive oil

½ onion, diced

1 cup (185 g) brown basmati rice, rinsed in a fine-mesh strainer and drained well

½ (14.5-ounce/411-g) can diced tomatoes (preferably fire-roasted)

1 carrot, thinly sliced into coins

2 celery stalks, thinly sliced

1¾ cups (420 ml) vegetable broth

¾ teaspoon kosher sea salt

¾ teaspoon black pepper

½ teaspoon ground cumin

½ teaspoon oregano (preferably Mexican)

¼ teaspoon smoked paprika

1 bay leaf

1 cup (135 g) frozen peas

½ cup (20 g) fresh cilantro leaves, chopped

*This colorful and fragrant pilaf is another great dish for family get-togethers. Serve it with Fiesta Black Beans (page 38) and Calabacitas con Elote (page 50) for a trifecta of side dishes. It goes great with Broiled Fish Tacos with Smoky Salsa Verde (page 177) and Tilapia al Mojo de Ajo (page 188), or it can be used as a flavorful base for veggie bowls or burritos.*

In a large pot with a tight-fitting lid, heat the oil over medium heat until hot, about 1 minute, then add the onion. Sauté until soft and translucent, about 2 minutes. Add the rice and stir continuously until the grains smell nutty and appear translucent and lightly toasted on the tips, about 3 minutes. Add the diced tomatoes and cook, stirring, until most of the liquid from the tomatoes evaporates, about 3 minutes more. Add the carrot and celery and stir.

Pour in the vegetable broth and add the salt, pepper, cumin, oregano, and paprika. Stir to dissolve the spices. Add the bay leaf and bring to a boil over medium-high heat, then lower the heat to maintain a simmer. Cover and cook for 45 minutes, or until the grains are tender and most of the water is absorbed. If there is excess water at 45 minutes, leave the lid off and cook for an additional 5 to 10 minutes. Turn off the heat and allow the rice to rest, covered, for 10 minutes.

While the rice cooks, place the peas in a small bowl and cover with boiling water. Stir once and allow the water to cool. When the rice is done resting, drain the peas and fold them into the rice, fluffing the rice with a fork as needed. Remove the bay leaf. Garnish with the cilantro and serve immediately, or cool completely and store in an airtight container in the refrigerator for up to 5 days or 3 months in the freezer.

**FEEL GOOD INGREDIENT // OREGANO** Oregano is closely related to mint, so it has many of the same health benefits. It is a common digestive aid, and the essential oils in oregano have antibacterial and antifungal properties. As with most herbs, it is extremely rich in antioxidants.

*"Everything you see I owe to spaghetti."*

—SOPHIA LOREN

# Pizza and Pasta

# LINGUINE CARBONARA WITH PEAS, ARTICHOKES, AND SHIITAKE BACON

Kosher sea salt

10 ounces (280 g) whole-wheat or gluten-free linguine (see Notes) or zucchini noodles (see page 158)

1 tablespoon olive oil

½ cup (70 g) minced shallot

⅓ cup (80 ml) dry white wine (see Notes)

1 recipe Creamy White Sauce (page 152)

¼ cup (60 ml) vegetable broth

1 recipe Shiitake Mushroom Bacon (page 153) or ½ cup (40 g) chopped tempeh bacon

1 cup (135 g) frozen petite peas

1 cup (170 g) frozen artichoke hearts

¼ cup (30 g) sliced oil-packed sun-dried tomatoes

¼ cup (10 g) fresh basil leaves, coarsely chopped

Freshly ground black pepper

*Both of us love the flavor of a good creamy pasta dish, but not so much the brick-in-the-belly feeling afterward. With this recipe, you can enjoy the creamy, decadent taste of carbonara while getting the nutrients your body craves. Instead of feeling like you need to take a nap afterward, you'll actually feel more energized! Pair it with a salad of slightly bitter greens, such as arugula or baby kale, dressed simply with extra-virgin olive oil and balsamic vinegar, and you've got yourself an exquisite meal.*

Bring a large pot of salted water (the water should be salty like the ocean) to a boil and cook the linguine according to the package directions.

Meanwhile, heat the oil in a large sauté pan over medium-high heat. Add the shallot and cook, stirring, until it begins to brown, 3 to 5 minutes. Add the wine and cook, stirring, for 1 to 2 minutes until mostly absorbed, scraping up any browned bits from the bottom of the pan. Pour in the cream sauce and vegetable broth and stir well. Add the bacon, peas, artichoke hearts, and sun-dried tomatoes and mix thoroughly. Adjust the heat as needed to maintain a gentle simmer and cook, stirring occasionally, until the vegetables are heated through, 7 to 8 minutes. Taste and add a pinch or two of salt if needed.

When the pasta is al dente, reserve ½ cup (120 ml) of the pasta cooking water. Drain the pasta and add it to the sauce. Toss well to fully coat the pasta. Add a splash of the pasta water, if needed, to thin the sauce. Remove from the heat and toss in the basil, reserving a bit to use as garnish. Finish with a sprinkle of pepper. Serve immediately.

**CHEF'S NOTES** Please note that whole-wheat pasta is not gluten-free.

Much of the flavor in this dish comes from the wine, so be sure to use one that you really enjoy.

**FEEL GOOD INGREDIENT // ARTICHOKES** Artichokes have been recommended for liver health since ancient times, and now modern science is backing it up. Two antioxidants found in artichokes, cynarin and silymarin, have been shown to boost the production of digestive bile and can help facilitate the elimination of toxins from the liver and body.

PREP // **5 minutes, plus 2 to 4 hours soaking time**
COOK // **10 minutes**
MAKES // **4 cups (960 ml)**

# CREAMY WHITE SAUCE

1 tablespoon extra-virgin olive oil

½ medium onion, diced (about 1 cup/125 g)

2 cloves garlic, thinly sliced

1 cup (120 g) raw cashews, soaked for 2 to 4 hours and rinsed

1 (12-ounce/340-g) package soft silken tofu, drained (see Note)

1 cup (240 ml) vegetable broth

¼ cup (60 ml) dry white wine

1 tablespoon plus 1 teaspoon nutritional yeast

1 tablespoon chickpea miso

½ teaspoon kosher sea salt

⅛ teaspoon freshly ground nutmeg

⅛ teaspoon white pepper

*We wanted to create a rich, indulgent-tasting sauce that leaves you feeling light, nourished, and satisfied, and we found the perfect balance by using cashews for creaminess and soft silken tofu to lighten things up. Both deliver a generous amount of cell-rejuvenating, lean-muscle-building plant protein in the most delicious way possible. Use this feel-good version of white sauce in place of any béchamel or Alfredo sauce.*

Heat a small skillet over medium-low heat and add the oil. Add the onion and sweat for 5 to 8 minutes, until fragrant and translucent. Avoid browning to keep the sauce a nice light color. Add the garlic and sweat for 2 minutes more.

Transfer the cooked onion and garlic to a blender. Add the cashews, tofu, broth, wine, nutritional yeast, miso, salt, nutmeg, and pepper and blend, starting on low and bringing it up to high speed, until smooth. Store in an airtight container in the refrigerator for up to 3 days or freeze for up to 6 months. After thawing, blend again briefly before using.

**CHEF'S NOTE** If time does not permit soaking the cashews, place them in a small pot and cover them with plenty of water. Bring to a boil, simmer for 10 minutes before draining them, then proceed with the recipe.

**FEEL GOOD INGREDIENT // SILKEN TOFU** A staple in Asian cooking, tofu is rumored to have been a happy accident when thousands of years ago a Chinese cook inadvertently curdled his soy milk by adding nigari seaweed to it. Silken tofu is soft and moist and has fewer calories than the firmer varieties. It can add body and creaminess to sauces, desserts, smoothies, and dressings in place of dairy while providing protein, vitamins, and minerals.

PREP // **5 minutes**

COOK // **30 minutes**

MAKES // **about ⅔ cup (40 g)**

# SHIITAKE MUSHROOM BACON

**4 ounces (115 g) shiitake mushrooms, woody stems trimmed, thinly sliced**

**2 tablespoons Bragg Liquid Aminos or tamari**

**1 tablespoon olive oil**

**1 teaspoon maple syrup**

**¼ teaspoon smoked paprika**

**Generous pinch black pepper**

*In this recipe, shiitake mushrooms are transformed into a crispy, crunchy, savory, salty treat that can stand in for pork bacon in all of your favorite dishes. Try this mushroom bacon as a topping for salads or scrambled eggs, let it shine as the star ingredient in a shiitake BLT, or use it as a flavorful garnish in bowls and soups like our Creamy Truffle Mushroom Soup (page 108).*

Preheat the oven to 375°F (190°C) and line a baking sheet with parchment paper. Set aside.

In a medium bowl, gently toss the mushrooms with the liquid aminos, oil, maple syrup, paprika, and pepper. Allow the mushrooms to marinate for 10 minutes.

Transfer the mushrooms to the baking sheet and bake for about 30 minutes, turning with a spatula every 10 minutes, until browned and slightly crisp. Remove from the oven and transfer to a paper towel–lined plate. The shiitake bacon will continue to crisp as it cools. Store in an airtight container in the refrigerator for up to 1 week.

**FEEL GOOD INGREDIENT // SHIITAKE MUSHROOMS**

Shiitake mushrooms have a meaty, earthy flavor and have been used in traditional herbal medicine for thousands of years. They contain a compound unique to shiitakes called lentinan, which has been shown to strengthen the immune system's ability to fight infection and disease.

PREP // 10 minutes, plus Tastes Like
Summer Pesto (page 160) or Kale-Walnut
Pesto (page 161), and Gooey Cashew Mozzarella
(page 165)

COOK // 1 hour 15 minutes

SERVES // 4 to 6

# THE FEEL GOOD PIZZA

### CRUST

2 tablespoons chia seeds (see Notes)

⅓ cup (75 ml) room-temperature filtered water

1 small or ½ large cauliflower (about 1½ pounds/750 g), cut into florets, leaves and core discarded

½ cup (100 g) mashed baked sweet potato (about half of a sweet potato; see page 26)

1 cup (125 g) whole-wheat flour (substitute brown rice or buckwheat flour, if preferred)

2 tablespoons fresh lemon juice

1 tablespoon Bragg Liquid Aminos

2 tablespoons olive oil

¾ teaspoon kosher sea salt

½ teaspoon Italian herbs

Pinch garlic powder

### TOPPINGS

½ head radicchio (about 5 ounces/140 g), cut into 4 wedges, core trimmed but still attached

½ bunch asparagus (about 7 ounces/200 g), woody ends trimmed

2 tablespoons olive oil

1 tablespoon balsamic vinegar

1 tablespoon honey

⅓ to ½ cup (75 to 120 ml) Tastes Like Summer Pesto (page 160) or Kale-Walnut Pesto (page 161)

¾ cup (100 g) frozen peas, thawed

¼ cup (35 g) kalamata olives, pitted and halved

1 recipe Gooey Cashew Mozzarella (page 165) or 4 ounces (115 g) nondairy Mozzarella (preferably Miyoko's)

Pinch herbes de Provence

Kosher sea salt and freshly cracked black pepper

*Abbie: I fell head over heels for this pizza after the very first bite. The toppings are full of interesting flavors— bitter, earthy, salty, and sweet—making every bite a new experience. The sweet potato and lemon juice in the crust add a delightful sweetness and a little tang to this savory creation. We love it for lunch, dinner, or for a healthy snack.*

**MAKE THE CRUST** Preheat the oven to 400°F (205°C). Line the base of a 12-inch (30.5-cm) pizza baking dish (or a baking sheet) with parchment paper and set aside.

In a small bowl, mix the chia seeds and water with a fork. Set aside to form a gel while you prepare the remaining ingredients. After a few minutes, stir in any chia seeds that have floated to the top.

Run the cauliflower through a centrifugal juicer and discard the cauliflower juice (see Notes). Remove the cauliflower pulp from the juicer and place it in a large bowl. Add the sweet potato and mix well with a fork. Add the flour, lemon juice, liquid aminos, 1 tablespoon of the oil, the salt, Italian herbs, and garlic powder. Once the chia seeds have formed a gel, add them to the bowl and knead the ingredients together with your hands until a moist dough ball forms.

Spread the remaining 1 tablespoon oil on the parchment. Place the dough in the middle of the pan and flatten it by pressing out toward the edges until the dough is spread evenly into a round disk about ¼-inch (6-mm) thick. Bake for 30 minutes, or until the base is firm, holds together, and is lightly browned at the edges.

If the underside of the crust feels moist, which is more common if using gluten-free flour, flip the crust. To do so, wear oven mitts and place a large plate on top of the crust, then carefully flip the crust onto the plate. Discard the parchment paper and slide the crust back onto the baking sheet. Bake an additional 5 to 10 minutes until the top of the crust is mostly dry and firm.

**MEANWHILE, PREPARE THE TOPPINGS** Line another baking sheet with parchment paper. Place the radicchio on one half of the baking sheet and the asparagus on the other half.

Drizzle 1 tablespoon of the oil over the radicchio and gently toss to coat. Toss the asparagus with the remaining tablespoon oil. Place the vegetables in the oven to roast. Roast the asparagus until just bright green, 5 minutes for very thin asparagus or 10 minutes for medium asparagus, then remove to a plate and set aside. Roast the radicchio for 15 minutes total, turning halfway, until charred and tender. Remove from the oven, drizzle the radicchio with the vinegar and honey, and toss. Set aside. Prepare the Gooey Cashew Mozzarella, if using.

**ASSEMBLE THE PIZZA** When the crust is ready, use a spatula to lift it up and slide the parchment out from underneath, if necessary. Spread a thin layer of the pesto on the crust using the back of a spoon. Arrange the roasted vegetables, peas, olives, and cheese on top. Season well with the herbes de Provence, salt, and pepper. Bake about 5 minutes more until the vegetables are warmed through and the cheese is melted.

**CHEF'S NOTES** Substitute 1 large beaten egg for the chia seed gel, if preferred.

If you do not have a juicer, process the cauliflower in a food processor for about 1 minute, until it looks like couscous. Transfer to a nut milk bag and knead out excess water until most has been removed and proceed.

**FEEL GOOD INGREDIENT** // **RADICCHIO** Radicchio has a slightly bitter, peppery taste that mellows and sweetens with cooking. It is one of the best sources of vitamin K, helping your body maintain strong bones.

PREP // **20 minutes**
COOK // **20 minutes**
SERVES // **4**

# SPAGHETTI ALLE VONGOLE

2 pounds (910 g) Manila clams (see below)

Kosher sea salt

12 ounces (340 g) whole-grain or gluten-free spaghetti

1 cup (135 g) frozen petite peas

½ cup (120 ml) extra-virgin olive oil

1 shallot, thinly sliced

8 garlic cloves, thinly sliced

¼ teaspoon red pepper flakes

¾ cup (40 g) chopped fresh flat-leaf parsley leaves, divided

½ cup (120 ml) white wine

½ cup (120 ml) fresh lemon juice (from 2 to 3 lemons), divided

½ teaspoon lemon zest

## HOW TO BUY AND STORE LIVE MUSSELS AND CLAMS

*Fresh bivalves smell like the ocean, not fishy. Toss any that are open or cracked. If an open clam or mussel closes when you tap on its shell with your fingernail, it is still safe to eat.*

*Be sure that the fishmonger does not pack live shellfish in an airtight plastic bag, as this will cause them to suffocate. You want to keep them cold until you are ready to cook. Ask for a bag of ice to place next to your purchase for the trip home.*

*Store live clams and mussels in a colander set over a shallow dish and cover with a damp towel. Keep them in the coldest part of your fridge; between 33°F and 35°F (0.5°C and 1.6°C) is ideal. Do not store them in water or on ice and eat within a day of purchase.*

*This is one of the great Italian dishes, but few restaurants do it justice. That's why spaghetti and clams are best eaten at home! This recipe is very easy to make, and the final dish is gorgeous. It's as perfect for a weeknight meal as it is for a fancy dinner party. The fresh clams and brothy sauce are a treat.*

Rinse the clams well under cool tap water, then place them in a bowl of cool water to soak for 20 minutes. When you remove the clams from the water, lift them out instead of pouring them into a strainer, allowing any sand to settle to the bottom of the bowl. Use a firm brush or steel wool to brush off any additional sand or barnacles, if necessary. Rinse the clams again and set aside.

Make the pasta: Place a colander in the sink. Bring a large pot of salted water to a boil. The water should be salty like the ocean. Add the pasta to the boiling water right before you start cooking your clams, so that they will be ready at about the same time. Cook the pasta according to the package directions until al dente. Stir in the peas and immediately drain the pasta and peas into the colander. Do not rinse.

Meanwhile, in a 12-inch (30.5-cm) skillet, heat the oil and shallot over medium-high heat. Sauté until the shallot softens, 1 to 2 minutes. Add the garlic and continue to sauté until the garlic becomes fragrant, about 1 minute more. Add the red pepper flakes and half of the parsley and stir.

Pour in the wine and half of the lemon juice. Add the clams and cook, uncovered, until they open, 6 to 8 minutes. If any clams stay closed after most of them have opened, move them to the center of the pan, making sure they have direct contact with the pan, and cook for 1 to 2 minutes more. If any remain closed, discard them. Turn off the heat.

Transfer the pasta and peas to a large bowl. Pour the clams and sauce on top and sprinkle with the lemon zest, the remaining parsley, and the remaining lemon juice. Gently toss and serve immediately.

**FEEL GOOD INGREDIENT** // **CLAMS** Clams are one of the best sources of vitamin $B_{12}$ and are also high in iron and protein. They're a date-night favorite in Italy and thought to be an aphrodisiac.

PREP // 5 minutes, plus Tastes Like Summer Pesto (page 160) and Cashew–Pine Nut Parmesan (page 167; optional)

COOK // 5 minutes

SERVES // 2

# PESTO ZUCCHINI NOODLES WITH CANNELLINI BEANS AND SUN-DRIED TOMATOES

2 zucchini, spiralized or peeled into noodles (see below)

¼ cup (60 ml) Tastes Like Summer Pesto (page 160) or store-bought pesto of your choice

1½ cups (220 g) cherry tomatoes, halved

¼ cup (40 g) pitted Kalamata olives (optional)

Olive oil, if needed

¼ cup (30 g) sun-dried tomatoes, drained if in oil, sliced

1½ cups (280 g) cooked cannellini beans, or 1 (15-ounce/425-g) can cannellini beans, drained and rinsed

1 handful (about ¼ cup/15 g) baby arugula

1 handful (about ¼ cup/30 g) walnut pieces

Fresh basil leaves, for garnish

Kosher sea salt and freshly ground black pepper

Cashew–Pine Nut Parmesan (page 167; optional)

*Jacq: This is one of the recipes that falls into a category I like to call Real Food Fast. It takes less than ten minutes to make, is light and nourishing, and makes you feel great after you eat it. It gives you a wonderful balance of vitamins, plant protein, fiber, and healthy fats, and, perhaps most important, is super tasty!*

Heat a large skillet or sauté pan over medium heat. Add the zucchini noodles, pesto, cherry tomatoes, and olives, if using, and gently toss. If the pesto is too thick to coat the noodles, add a splash of oil. Cook for 2 minutes, then add the sun-dried tomatoes and beans and lightly toss again. Once the beans are heated through, about 1 minute more, turn off the heat. Throw in the arugula and toss again to wilt.

Serve immediately using tongs or a slotted spoon. Sprinkle the noodles with the walnuts and garnish with basil. Top with salt, pepper, and Parmesan, if desired.

**CHEF'S NOTE** You can also serve this as a raw salad. Toss the raw zucchini noodles with the pesto and top with the remaining ingredients.

**FEEL GOOD INGREDIENT // SUN-DRIED TOMATOES** Drying tomatoes concentrates their sweetness and deepens their flavor. Both fresh and sun-dried tomatoes contain lycopene, but it is more readily available for absorption when the tomatoes are eaten with oil or heated. Sun-dried tomatoes contain approximately 20 percent more bioavailable lycopene than raw tomatoes.

**HOW TO MAKE ZUCCHINI NOODLES //** *Zucchini noodles are a nutritious, hydrating, fiber-filled alternative to traditional pasta. Zucchini also happens to be one of the lowest calorie vegetables around, so they can be really helpful for maintaining a healthy weight. A spiralizer turns zucchini and other vegetables into noodles quickly, but if you don't have one, simply use a julienne peeler to cut the zucchini into spaghetti-like strands or use a Y-shaped vegetable peeler to create flat wide noodles like pappardelle. These noodles are best served raw or sautéed for only a short time—2 to 3 minutes. Overcooked noodles will become limp and soggy.*

# TASTES LIKE SUMMER PESTO

4 ounces (115 g) fresh basil leaves (3 cups lightly packed)

½ cup (70 g) raw pine nuts

2 garlic cloves, peeled

3 tablespoons fresh lemon juice (from 1 lemon)

1 teaspoon kosher sea salt

¼ teaspoon black pepper

¾ cup (180 ml) extra-virgin olive oil, plus more for storing

*Sometimes the best things in life are the simplest. It's certainly true in the case of this classic basil and pine nut pesto. Whether on pasta or in our White Bean and Celery Salad with Pesto Grilled Shrimp (page 122), it makes the meal. It also makes an amazing salad dressing or dip when tossed with balsamic vinegar.*

In a food processor, combine the basil, pine nuts, garlic, lemon juice, salt, and pepper and pulse until chopped. Then, with the machine running on low, slowly pour the olive oil into the bowl through the feed tube and process until the pesto reaches your desired consistency. Alternatively, add the ingredients to a blender and briefly puree.

Store in a glass jar and drizzle a layer of olive oil over the top. Cover and refrigerate for up to 2 weeks. Pesto also freezes nicely for up to 6 months.

**FEEL GOOD INGREDIENT // BASIL** Basil is one of the most beneficial herbs. It contains an impressive list of nutrients: vitamin K, which is essential for blood clotting, plus vitamin A, iron, calcium, manganese, magnesium, vitamin C, and potassium. Basil also has antibacterial properties and contains DNA-protecting flavonoids.

PREP // **10 minutes**

MAKES // **1 cup (240 ml)**

# KALE-WALNUT PESTO

**Kosher sea salt**

**4 ounces (115 g) dinosaur kale, stems and center ribs removed**

**2 ounces (55 g) fresh basil leaves (2 cups lightly packed)**

**½ cup (55 g) raw chopped walnuts**

**2 garlic cloves, peeled**

**2 teaspoons chickpea miso**

**1 tablespoon umeboshi vinegar (also called ume plum vinegar)**

**1 tablespoon plus 1 teaspoon fresh lemon juice**

**1 teaspoon nutritional yeast**

**¾ cup (180 ml) extra-virgin olive oil, plus more for storing**

*Some dairy-free pestos are left a little flat without the addition of Parmesan, but we've made up for it here with umami-rich plant-based ingredients. The nutritional yeast adds a cheesy nuttiness, the chickpea miso deepens and rounds out the flavor, and umeboshi vinegar gives it the needed saltiness and tang. Try it with our California Dream Burgers (page 134) or Sweet Potato Pizzette with Roasted Radishes and Fried Sage (page 209).*

Set a pasta strainer in a bowl next to where you are working on the stove.

Bring a pot of water to a boil and add a generous pinch of salt. Blanch the kale for 10 seconds. Using tongs or a slotted spoon, remove the kale and set it in the strainer. Blanch the basil for 2 to 3 seconds, remove it, and add it to the strainer with the kale. Immediately rinse the kale and basil in cool water to stop the cooking. Form the kale and basil into a ball with your hands. Squeeze repeatedly to remove all excess moisture.

Add the kale, basil, walnuts, garlic, miso, vinegar, lemon juice, and nutritional yeast to a food processor and pulse to chop 10 to 15 times. Scrape down the sides of the bowl. With the processor running on low, slowly pour the olive oil into the bowl through the feed tube and process until the pesto reaches your desired consistency.

Store in a glass jar and drizzle a layer of olive oil over the top. Taste and add a pinch of salt if desired. Cover and refrigerate for up to 2 weeks. The pesto also freezes nicely for up to 6 months.

**FEEL GOOD INGREDIENT // CHICKPEA MISO** This salty, savory paste is made using garbanzo beans (chickpeas), which are one of the most easily digestible beans. Because it's fermented, chickpea miso is brimming with beneficial, live probiotic cultures, which provide a multitude of benefits, including promoting digestive health.

PREP // **10 minutes, plus Creamy White Sauce (page 152), Kale-Walnut Pesto (page 161), and Gooey Cashew Mozzarella (page 165)**

COOK // **1 hour**

SERVES // **12**

# CREAMY MUSHROOM LASAGNA WITH PESTO

**Creamy White Sauce (page 152; see Notes)**

MUSHROOMS

**2 tablespoons olive oil**

**1 shallot, finely chopped**

**1½ pounds (680 g) mixed mushrooms (such as shiitake, cremini, oyster, chanterelle, and maitake), stems trimmed, and cut into ¼-inch-(6-mm-) thick slices no more than 1-inch (2.5 cm) long**

**2 garlic cloves, finely chopped**

**½ teaspoon kosher sea salt**

**½ teaspoon black pepper**

**1 tablespoon thyme leaves, divided**

**3 tablespoons red wine**

**½ teaspoon kosher sea salt**

**½ teaspoon black pepper**

LASAGNA

**Kosher sea salt**

**6 to 8 fresh or dried lasagna noodles (see Notes)**

**Olive oil for greasing the pan**

**1 cup (240 ml) Kale-Walnut Pesto (page 161) or store-bought dairy-free pesto, plus more for serving**

**1 recipe Gooey Cashew Mozzarella (page 165; see Notes)**

*Jacq: This is one of my favorite dishes to make on holidays because I can put it together in the morning and pop it in the oven just before guests arrive. It's so rich and creamy that people cannot believe that it's completely dairy free! This is phenomenal with a simple salad or a side of Roasted Brussels Sprouts, Dried Cherries, and Walnuts (page 42).*

Preheat the oven to 375°F (190°C) and spread a thin layer of oil on the bottom and sides of a 9 by 13-inch (23 by 33-cm) baking dish. Set aside.

**MAKE THE CREAMY WHITE SAUCE** and transfer it to a pitcher or bowl. Set aside. There is no need to rinse the blender you used for the sauce, as you will use it to make the cashew mozzarella.

**MAKE THE MUSHROOMS** Heat the oil in a large sauté pan over medium heat. Add the shallot and cook for about 2 minutes, stirring occasionally, until translucent. Add the mushrooms, garlic, salt, pepper, and half of the thyme leaves and gently toss. After a few minutes, the mushrooms will begin to release liquid. When most of the water has evaporated, after about 8 minutes total, add the wine, toss, scraping the bottom of the pan, and cook for 2 to 3 minutes more, until the wine is absorbed. Remove from the heat and set aside.

**PUT TOGETHER THE LASAGNA** Put a large pot of water to boil for the pasta, adding enough salt to make it salty like the ocean. When the water comes to a rolling boil, add the pasta and gently stir to separate the noodles. Boil for 2 minutes if using fresh pasta or according to package directions for dried. It's best if the pasta remains slightly undercooked. Drain and rinse the pasta with cool water and gently separate the sheets, laying them out in a single layer on a baking sheet so they don't stick together.

In the baking dish, lay a single layer of pasta on the bottom, then spread out half of the mushrooms and cover with half of the white sauce. Add another layer of pasta, cover with the remaining mushrooms, then spoon the pesto on top. Cover with the remainder of the white sauce and sprinkle with half of the remaining thyme leaves.

**MAKE THE CASHEW MOZZARELLA** according to the recipe and top the lasagna with dollops of the mozzarella.

Bake for about 30 minutes, until the top just begins to brown. Sprinkle with the remaining thyme leaves. Serve with additional pesto on the side, if desired. Cover and refrigerate leftovers for up to 3 days. To reheat, cover the lasagna dish with foil and bake in a preheated 350°F (175°C) oven until heated through, about 25 minutes.

**CHEF'S NOTES** "No boil" lasagna noodles also work in this recipe and do not need to be cooked ahead of time. Be sure to choose noodles marked gluten-free if you are avoiding gluten.

The white sauce can be made a day ahead of time, but the cashew mozzarella is best made fresh, just before it is placed on top of the lasagna.

**FEEL GOOD INGREDIENT // MUSHROOMS** For thousands of years, Eastern cultures have revered mushrooms for their health benefits. Beta-glucans, found in mushrooms, have shown immunity-stimulating effects and can help contribute to resistance against allergies and the common cold.

PREP // **2 to 4 hours soaking time**
COOK // **5 minutes**
MAKES // **about 1 cup (260 g)**

# GOOEY CASHEW MOZZARELLA

¼ cup (30 g) raw cashews, soaked for 2 to 4 hours, drained, and rinsed (see Note)

1 cup (240 ml) filtered water

2 tablespoons tapioca flour

1 tablespoon nutritional yeast

1 garlic clove, peeled

1½ teaspoons apple cider vinegar

½ teaspoon kosher sea salt

*We both lived in Italy for a time when we were in our twenties, so all things Italian have a special place in our hearts. We put our own spin on the Italian staple mozzarella by creating a versatile plant-based version. The tapioca flour gives it a creamy, melted texture, and nutritional yeast adds a cheesy, nutty flavor. Serve it in dollops on toasted bread with sautéed mushrooms as an appetizer, or on grilled eggplant with tomato sauce for an easy main dish. Buon appetito!*

Combine all the ingredients in a high-speed blender and blend until very smooth, 1 to 2 minutes. If using a regular blender, blend 2 to 3 minutes, then strain through a sieve.

Pour the liquid into a medium skillet and heat over medium heat. Stir continuously with a large spoon, scraping the sides and bottom of the pan. First, curdles will begin to appear. Continue stirring until the sauce is thick and smooth like melted cheese and pulls away from the edges of the pan as you stir, about 3 minutes.

Serve immediately in dollops on your favorite dishes, or use it as a lasagna, casserole, or pizza topping. Leftovers will keep in the fridge up to 5 days. To reheat, pour the cheese into a small pan over medium heat and add a splash of water. Stir continuously until melted. The texture of the cheese will be somewhat less smooth when reheated.

**CHEF'S NOTE** If time does not permit soaking the cashews, place them in a small pot and cover them with plenty of water. Bring to a boil, simmer for 10 minutes before draining them, then proceed with the recipe.

**FEEL GOOD INGREDIENT // NUTRITIONAL YEAST** This deactivated yeast is appropriately named because it provides a significant dose of more than a dozen minerals, like iron, selenium, and zinc, along with fiber, B vitamins, and complete protein that keep you feeling satisfied and ready for action. There's a reason it's a favorite food of marathon runners and other endurance athletes.

PREP // **5 minutes, plus Cashew–Pine Nut Parmesan (recipe follows)**

COOK // **35 minutes**

SERVES // **4**

# VEGGIE TEMPEH BOLOGNESE

**3 tablespoons extra-virgin olive oil**

**1 small onion, diced**

**1 carrot, thinly sliced**

**1 celery rib, thinly sliced**

**2 tablespoons tomato paste**

**4 cloves garlic, minced**

**8 ounces (225 g) tempeh, crumbled**

**¼ teaspoon kosher sea salt, plus more to taste**

**¼ teaspoon black pepper, plus more to taste**

**¼ cup (60 ml) red wine**

**1 (28-ounce/795-g) can crushed tomatoes**

**¼ cup (60 ml) unsweetened cashew or almond milk**

**1 teaspoon dried oregano**

**1 bay leaf**

**Pinch ground nutmeg**

**Pinch red pepper flakes**

**½ cup (10 g) baby spinach or other baby greens**

TO SERVE

**Cooked pasta, zucchini noodles, or rice**

**Cashew–Pine Nut Parmesan (recipe follows)**

## CASHEW-PINE NUT PARMESAN

*This Parmesan takes just a couple of minutes to make, but adds a wonderfully cheesy, delicious flavor to any soup, pasta, or pizza.*

PREP // **5 minutes**

MAKES // **¾ cup (70 g)**

**¼ cup (35 g) plus 2 tablespoons raw pine nuts**

**¼ cup (30 g) plus 2 tablespoons raw cashews**

**3 tablespoons nutritional yeast**

**1 teaspoon dried onion flakes**

**½ teaspoon kosher sea salt**

*Abbie: Even though this veggie bolognese is made to serve over rice or pasta, I often eat a little bowl of it on its own as a tasty snack. The tempeh is the perfect protein substitute, adding just the right density and texture to the sauce that leaves you feeling totally satisfied. The veggies lighten up the dish, and the oregano and nutmeg add extra flavor to every bite. It's an absolute winner.*

Heat the oil in a large saucepan over medium heat. Add the onion and cook, stirring frequently with a wooden spoon, until soft and translucent but not browned, about 3 minutes. Add the carrot and celery and continue cooking, stirring, for 3 minutes more. Stir in the tomato paste, garlic, tempeh, salt, and pepper and continue cooking for about 5 minutes more, until the tempeh begins to brown. Add the wine and deglaze the pan to remove any stuck browned bits, then add the tomatoes, milk, oregano, bay leaf, nutmeg, and red pepper flakes. Season with more salt and black pepper. Lower the heat to medium-low and simmer until the sauce thickens, 10 to 15 minutes. Add the spinach and stir until wilted, about 1 minute more.

Serve over cooked pasta, zucchini noodles, or rice. Allow leftovers to cool, then store in an airtight container and refrigerate for up to 5 days.

**FEEL GOOD INGREDIENT // TEMPEH** Tempeh is a traditional Indonesian food made from fermented soybeans. It's similar to tofu in its culinary uses but is even more nutritious, containing more protein, vitamins, fiber, and probiotics. Many people find tempeh easier to digest than tofu.

Combine the pine nuts and cashews in a food processor, then add the nutritional yeast, onion flakes, and salt and pulse until the mixture is coarsely ground. (Do not overprocess, or you will make nut butter.) Refrigerate in an airtight container for up to 3 weeks.

**FEEL GOOD INGREDIENT // PINE NUTS** Pine nuts are an excellent source of vitamins and minerals and a natural appetite suppressor. They were also one of the earliest aphrodisiacs, likely because they are rich in zinc, which can help improve male sperm production, energy, and fertility.

*"One cannot think well, love well, sleep well, if one has not dined well."*

—VIRGINIA WOOLF

# Seafood

# THAI GREEN CURRY MUSSELS

2 pounds (910 g) mussels (see page 157)

1 lemongrass stalk

2 tablespoons coconut oil

1 onion, thinly sliced

1 shallot, thinly sliced

4 garlic cloves, thinly sliced

3 tablespoons thinly sliced peeled ginger

2 tablespoons green curry paste

1 (13.5-ounce/398-ml) can coconut milk

2 tablespoons fish sauce

1 teaspoon sambal oelek or other hot sauce

3 carrots, thinly sliced on the bias

3 celery ribs, thinly sliced on the bias

2 limes, one halved and one quartered

1 cup (155 g) frozen shelled edamame (soybeans), thawed

¾ cup (30 g) fresh torn cilantro leaves and tender stems

4 cups (720 g) cooked rice, or 1 loaf crusty bread

*Abbie: I really love Thai food, so it was no surprise to me that I swooned over this flavorful and light green curry right from the get-go. I don't usually go wild for mussels, but this dish made me fall in love. The smell, the taste, and the look of this dish is a culinary delight that works wonders on your taste buds and sends your senses flying high.*

Rinse the mussels well under cool tap water, then place them in a bowl of cool water to soak for 20 minutes. When you remove the mussels from the water, lift them out instead of pouring them into a strainer, allowing any sand to settle to the bottom of the bowl. Remove any beards by grabbing them between your thumb and forefinger and pulling toward the hinge end of the mussels. Use a firm brush or steel wool to brush off any additional sand or barnacles, if necessary. Rinse the mussels again and set aside.

Remove the rough outer layers of the lemongrass, cut the top off the stalk, leaving 5 inches (12 cm) at the root end, and discard the top. Cut the remaining stalk into 1-inch (2.5-cm) pieces and smash them with the flat side of your knife as if you were smashing garlic (see page 36).

Heat the oil in a large pot or 12-inch (30.5-cm) sauté pan over medium-high heat. Add the onion and shallot and sauté until softened and just beginning to brown, about 3 minutes. Add the garlic, lemongrass, ginger, and curry paste and cook, stirring frequently, until the garlic just begins to brown, about 2 minutes. Add the coconut milk, fish sauce, and sambal oelek and stir. Add the mussels, carrots, and celery. Squeeze the juice from the lime halves over the mussels, then add the rinds.

Cook, stirring occasionally, until the mussels open, about 8 minutes. If any mussels stay closed after most of the mussels have opened, move them to the center of the pan, making sure they have direct contact with the pan, and cook for 1 to 2 minutes more. If any remain closed, discard them. Turn off the heat. Stir in the edamame. Sprinkle with the cilantro. Serve over rice or with crusty bread on the side.

**FEEL GOOD INGREDIENT // MUSSELS** Mussels are a relatively inexpensive, nutritious, and sustainable shellfish. Farmed mussels can even have beneficial effects on marine ecosystems. They contain high levels of $B_{12}$ and long-chain omega-3 fatty acids EPA and DHA. Mussels also have levels of iron and folic acid similar to those found in red meat.

PREP // **10 minutes**

COOK // **40 minutes**

SERVES // **4 as an entree or 6 as an appetizer**

# SHRIMP WITH MOLE SAUCE

MOLE

½ cup (75 g) raisins

1 tablespoon olive oil

1 onion, roughly chopped

1 jalapeño, trimmed, halved, and seeded

2 garlic cloves, peeled

1 cup (180 g) chopped tomatoes

1 cup (240 ml) vegetable broth

3 tomatillos, husked, rinsed, and roughly chopped

¼ cup (60 ml) tahini

¼ cup (35 g) pumpkin seeds, plus more for garnish

3 tablespoons cacao nibs

2 tablespoons cacao powder

2 teaspoons chili powder

1 teaspoon smoked salt

1 teaspoon kosher sea salt

½ teaspoon black pepper

¼ teaspoon ground cinnamon

¼ teaspoon ground anise seed (substitute fennel seed, if unavailable)

¼ teaspoon ground cumin

¼ teaspoon dried oregano

¼ teaspoon cayenne pepper

1 cup (240 ml) warm filtered water

Sesame seeds and pumpkin seeds for garnish

SHRIMP

½ lime

¼ cup (30 g) thinly sliced red onion

Kosher sea salt and black pepper

1¼ pounds (570 g) large shrimp, peeled and deveined (see page 176)

3 tablespoons olive oil or melted refined coconut oil

¼ cup (10 g) fresh cilantro leaves and tender stems for garnish

*Jacq: Mole evokes images of old Mexican women grinding spices and simmering chiles for days. While the chef in me loves the idea of cooking up an old family recipe for hours on end, the busy working girl was looking for a simpler process. This version allows the aromatics to cook and mellow slowly while you throw everything else into a blender. What you end up with is a sauce with all of the complexity and warmth of the traditional recipes in a fraction of the time. It's wonderful on shrimp, but also try it on baked tofu, roasted carrots, and fried eggs.*

**MAKE THE MOLE** In a small bowl, cover the raisins with warm water and set aside.

Heat the oil in a large sauté pan over medium-low heat. Add the onion, jalapeño, and garlic and stir to coat in the oil. Cook, stirring occasionally, for 15 to 20 minutes, until softened and browned. If they begin to blacken, lower the heat to low. It's OK if there is a bit of charring.

Meanwhile, in a blender, combine the tomatoes, broth, tomatillos, tahini, pumpkin seeds, cacao nibs, cacao powder, chili powder, smoked salt, kosher sea salt, black pepper, cinnamon, anise seed, cumin, oregano, and cayenne. Drain the raisins and add them to the blender. Then add the softened onion, garlic, jalapeño, and the water. Blend, starting on low and bringing up to high speed, until smooth. You may need to scrape down the sides once or twice as you blend. If you are not using a high-speed blender, you may need to add a splash more broth. Pour the mole into the sauté pan and warm over low heat, stirring occasionally, while you prepare the shrimp, up to 20 minutes.

**PREPARE THE SHRIMP** In a small bowl, squeeze the juice from the lime over the onion. Sprinkle with a pinch of salt and pepper and toss. Set aside.

Heat a grill or grill pan to medium-high heat. In a large bowl, toss the shrimp with the oil and season with salt and pepper. Add ½ cup (120 ml) of the mole sauce and toss. Grill the shrimp until light grill marks appear and the shrimp is just opaque all the way through, 1 to 2 minutes per side.

To serve, pour ⅓ cup (75 ml) of the mole sauce onto the middle of each serving plate. Spread the mole into a circle with the bottom of the measuring cup. Divide the shrimp among the plates and arrange them nicely. Lightly sprinkle with sesame and pumpkin seeds, about ½ teaspoon each per plate. Top with the sliced onion and a scattering of fresh cilantro. Serve immediately.

PREP // **5 minutes, plus Citrus-Herb Wild Rice (page 33)**

COOK // **1 hour 15 minutes**

SERVES // **6**

# HONEY-HARISSA GRILLED SHRIMP WITH ROASTED VEGETABLES, CHARRED GRAPEFRUIT, AND WILD RICE

**Citrus-Herb Wild Rice (page 33)**

ROASTED VEGETABLES

**1 red cabbage (about 2½ pounds/1.2 kg)**

**3 beets (about 1 pound/455 g)**

**1 large fennel bulb (about 1 pound/455 g, including stalks and fronds)**

**½ cup (120 ml) olive oil**

**¼ cup (60 ml) balsamic vinegar**

**1 tablespoon whole-grain mustard**

**½ teaspoon kosher sea salt**

**½ teaspoon black pepper**

**1 tablespoon honey**

CHARRED GRAPEFRUIT

**¾ large ruby red grapefruit**

**1 tablespoon coconut sugar**

*We both agree that this is our most visually stunning dish. Of course, good looks only take you only so far, so we made sure that it has the flavor to back up its alluring appearance. Earthy, savory, spicy, sweet, and bitter elements come together in perfect harmony. It also happens to be a nutritional powerhouse. Beauty and substance—what's not to love?*

Preheat the oven to 400°F (205°C) and line two baking sheets with parchment paper. Set aside.

**MAKE THE CITRUS-HERB WILD RICE** according to the recipe, using dill as the herb and grapefruit for the juice and zest. Use one-quarter grapefruit for the wild rice recipe and reserve the remaining three-quarter grapefruit to make the charred grapefruit.

**MAKE THE ROASTED VEGETABLES** Cut the cabbage into quarters. Cut out the white core, then slice into 2-inch- (5-cm-) thick wedges. Peel the beets and cut into ½-inch- (12 mm-) thick wedges. Trim the stalks off of the fennel and set aside (You will use the fronds for garnish). Trim the bottom of the fennel and remove any battered or woody outer leaves. Cut the fennel into ½-inch- (12 mm-) thick wedges.

Arrange the vegetables in a single layer on the baking sheets. Cover one sheet with cabbage, and the other sheet with half fennel and half beets. Leave a little space between each piece so air can circulate.

In a small bowl, whisk the oil, vinegar, mustard, salt, and pepper. Drizzle the mixture over the vegetables and turn the vegetables once or twice to make sure they are well coated.

Roast the vegetables in the oven for 40 minutes, then remove the baking sheet with the beets. Drizzle the honey over the beets and toss to coat. Remove any well-done fennel to a plate and set aside. Return the baking sheet to the oven and roast until all of the vegetables are charred and tender, 5 to 15 minutes more.

**MAKE THE CHARRED GRAPEFRUIT** Preheat the broiler. Cut the remaining grapefruit into 1-inch- (2.5-cm-) thick wedges. Lay the slices on a baking sheet and sprinkle with the coconut sugar. Broil for about 3 minutes, until the rind just begins to char.

CONTINUES

2 tablespoons harissa paste

2 tablespoons honey

2 tablespoons olive oil

1 pound (455 g) large white shrimp, shells on (see below)

⅓ cup (17 g) loosely packed dill fronds for garnish

**MAKE THE SHRIMP** Heat a grill or grill pan over medium-high heat. In a large bowl, whisk the harissa, honey, and oil. Add the shrimp and toss to coat. Grill the shrimp until pink and opaque, about 2 minutes per side.

**TO SERVE** Spread the wild rice on a serving platter and lay the roasted vegetables on top. Scatter half of the dill fronds over the vegetables. Arrange the grapefruit slices and shrimp on top of the vegetables and garnish with the remaining dill fronds and a few fennel fronds.

**CHEF'S NOTE** Source wild-caught shrimp from sustainable US fisheries or farmed shrimp from recirculating aquaculture farms in the United States and Canada. Imported shrimp, both wild and farmed, should be avoided due to concerns about sustainability, contamination, and unethical labor practices.

**FEEL GOOD INGREDIENT // GRAPEFRUIT** Grapefruit has long been considered a food that can help with weight loss and glowing skin. It's low-calorie and loaded with nutrients. Though all types of grapefruit provide health benefits, red grapefruit is the most nutritious. Its blend of vitamins and carotenoids, including lycopene and beta-carotene, which gives it its color, stimulate tremendous antioxidant activity in the bloodstream.

## HOW TO PREPARE SHRIMP FOR COOKING

*You can find shrimp that has already been peeled and deveined at the market, but you can save money by doing it yourself with these easy steps. Many people prefer the flavor of freshly peeled shrimp to those that have been pre-peeled. Most shrimp at the seafood counter has been previously frozen anyway, so shrimp is a great protein to keep ready-to-go in your freezer for an easy main.*

*RINSE // When working with fresh or previously thawed shrimp, simply place the shrimp in a colander, rinse, drain, and pat dry. If using frozen shrimp, allow it to thaw overnight in the fridge. For a quicker thaw, place the shrimp in a colander set inside a large bowl of cold tap water. Let sit for ten minutes, then lift the colander out of the water. Smaller shrimp may be defrosted. If not, change the water and re-submerge the shrimp. Let sit for an additional five to ten minutes, until they are completely defrosted and pliable but still cool to the touch, then drain for two to three minutes and pat dry with paper towels.*

*PEEL (OPTIONAL) // Gently twist and pull to remove the head if it is still attached. Next, remove the shell by using your thumb to peel it, starting at the underside by the legs. Most chefs prefer to keep the tail on for aesthetic reasons, but you can pull it off gently if you like.*

*DEVEIN // For peeled shrimp, make a shallow incision along the back curve of the shrimp, starting at the head end and cutting toward the tail, stopping about two-thirds of the way down. Use the tip of your knife to remove the black sand vein that runs along the center of the back and discard. Not every shrimp will have one, so if you don't see a black line running down the back, move along. If you are working with shrimp with the shell on, use scissors to snip the shells down the middle of the back where you will be making the incision before you devein the shrimp.*

PREP // **10 minutes, plus Avocado-Lime Cream (page 179)**

COOK // **15 minutes**

MAKES // **8 tacos**

# BROILED FISH TACOS WITH SMOKY SALSA VERDE

### TORTILLAS AND TOPPINGS

**8 (6-inch/15-cm) corn, whole-grain, or cassava-coconut flour tortillas**

**1 recipe Avocado-Lime Cream (page 179)**

**1 cup (78 g) shredded red cabbage**

**3 radishes, thinly sliced**

**¼ cup (13 g) fresh cilantro leaves**

**2 limes, cut into wedges**

**Plain coconut milk yogurt or Creamy Cashew Sour Cream (page 138; optional)**

### FISH

**1 pound (450 g) flaky white fish fillets, such as tilapia, cod, halibut, or Chilean sea bass**

**1 tablespoon coconut oil, melted**

**¼ teaspoon New Mexico or ancho chili powder**

**¼ teaspoon ground cumin**

**¼ teaspoon kosher sea salt**

**¼ teaspoon black pepper**

### SALSA VERDE

**12 ounces (340 g) fresh tomatillos, husks removed and rinsed (see Note)**

**2 fresh serrano or jalapeño chiles**

**½ onion, cut into 3 wedges**

**2 unpeeled garlic cloves**

**¼ cup (13 g) fresh cilantro, thick stems removed**

**1 teaspoon kosher sea salt**

*Abbie: Eating seafood, let alone cooking it, is still a relatively new experience for me. One of the things I've loved about working on this book is recipe testing Jacq's creations in my own home. The first fish taco I ever ate was from this recipe, and boy, was it awesome! There's something about the taste of the sea in the flaky fish and the crunchy lightness of the cabbage and radishes with the Avocado-Lime Cream that make you instantly feel like you're on vacation by the ocean.*

Prep all of your toppings, then preheat the broiler.

**MAKE THE FISH** Brush the flesh of the fish with the oil and sprinkle with the chili powder, cumin, salt, and pepper. Place the fish on a small rimmed baking sheet skin side down, if applicable. Place the tomatillos, chiles, onion, and garlic in a cast-iron pan or other small baking dish in a single layer.

Broil the fish and the salsa verde ingredients 4 inches (10 cm) from the heat source (usually on the top rack of the oven) for 4 minutes. Quickly turn the vegetables with tongs (do not turn the fish) and broil for an additional 3 minutes, until the tomatillos are softened and slightly charred and the fish is opaque but still moist. (Thin fillets may take less time; thick cuts of fish may take a minute or two longer.) Remove both pans from the oven. Turn off the broiler and place the tortillas in a stack in the oven directly on the top rack.

**MAKE THE SALSA VERDE** Peel the garlic and remove the tops and seeds from the chiles. (If you like your salsa extra-hot, leave the seeds in.) Add to a blender, along with the charred tomatillos and onion, the cilantro, and salt, and blend to a coarse puree.

**TO SERVE** Remove the tortillas from the oven and wrap in a dish towel to keep warm. Flake the fish with a fork and serve with the warm tortillas, salsa verde, and toppings.

**CHEF'S NOTE** Fresh tomatillos have a papery outer husk that needs to be removed before cooking. Underneath, you'll feel a sticky coating on the outside, which can easily be rinsed off with water. If fresh tomatillos are not available, use 2 (11-ounce/312-g) cans of tomatillos and drain and measure out 1 cup (240 ml). Do not broil the canned tomatillos.

**FEEL GOOD INGREDIENT // TOMATILLOS** Tomatillos originated in Mexico and taste like a tomato crossed with citrus. According to the USDA, one medium tomatillo contains only 11 calories! They're a good source of vitamin C, fiber, and niacin and help you feel full and satisfied.

# AVOCADO-LIME CREAM

**1 cup (155 g) mashed avocado (about 2 avocados)**

**½ cup (120 ml) unsweetened cashew or almond milk**

**1 tablespoon plus 1 teaspoon fresh lime juice (from ½ lime)**

**1 to 2 teaspoons hot sauce, preferably sriracha**

**¼ teaspoon kosher sea salt, or to taste**

**Generous pinch white pepper (see Note)**

*This is a regular at our Sunday meal-prep sessions. It's so simple, but as a topping it adds an incredible amount of flavor and richness to everything from your basic Buddha bowls to your favorite Mexican dishes. It can also be used as a quick party dip served with chips or crudités, or as a creamy and nutritious mayo substitute on sandwiches.*

In a blender, combine all the ingredients and blend on high speed until smooth and creamy. Taste for seasoning and add more salt and pepper if desired; blend again briefly.

To store leftovers, place the avocado cream in a small bowl or ramekin and lay plastic wrap directly onto the surface of the cream to avoid browning. Gently press down to remove any air bubbles and refrigerate for up to 3 days.

**CHEF'S NOTE** White pepper has a slightly mellower flavor than black pepper, but really, it just looks nicer in light colored foods. Substitute black pepper, if necessary.

**FEEL GOOD INGREDIENT // AVOCADO** Avocado is one of the most nutrient-dense foods and has amazing anti-inflammatory properties. Not only is it good for your heart but it's full of omega-9 fatty acids that do fabulous things for your skin.

# PAN-SEARED BRANZINO WITH LIMA BEAN-AVOCADO PUREE AND TARRAGON-MINT SAUCE

### TARRAGON-MINT SAUCE

¼ **cup (13 g) lightly packed fresh tarragon**

¼ **cup (13 g) lightly packed fresh mint leaves**

**2 tablespoons chopped fresh chives**

¼ **cup (60 ml) unsweetened almond milk**

**3 tablespoons olive oil**

1½ **tablespoons fresh lemon juice**

¼ **teaspoon kosher sea salt**

### LIMA BEAN-AVOCADO PUREE

**2 cups (310 g) frozen baby lima beans**

½ **avocado (about ⅓ cup/50 g mashed)**

¼ **cup (10 g) lightly packed fresh basil leaves**

**3 garlic cloves, thinly sliced**

¾ **cup (180 ml) vegetable broth, plus more as needed**

½ **cup (120 ml) olive oil**

½ **teaspoon kosher sea salt**

### ROASTED VEGETABLES

**1 bunch French breakfast, red, or mixed radishes, cut into quarters lengthwise**

**1 tablespoon plus 2 teaspoons olive oil**

**Kosher sea salt and freshly ground black pepper**

**1 bunch asparagus (1 pound/455 g), 1 to 1½ inches (2.5 to 4 cm) trimmed off the bottom**

*In this recipe, branzino, a firm white fish prized for its delicate flavor, is paired with a creamy lima bean puree, a lemony herb sauce, and colorful roasted spring vegetables. It makes a wonderful dinner-party or special-occasion meal, and with a little artful plating, you have a dish that would fit right in at any fine-dining restaurant.*

Preheat the oven to 400°F (205°C) and line two baking sheets with parchment paper. Set aside.

**MAKE THE TARRAGON-MINT SAUCE** In a blender, combine the tarragon, mint, chives, milk, oil, lemon juice, and salt and blend until the herbs are very finely chopped and the sauce is nearly smooth. Transfer to a small bowl and set aside.

**MAKE THE LIMA BEAN-AVOCADO PUREE** Cook the lima beans according to package directions, but do not add salt. Drain the beans and blend with the avocado, basil, garlic, broth, oil, and salt in a high-speed blender or food processor until smooth. Add a splash more broth, if needed, to get the blades to turn. Set aside.

**MAKE THE ROASTED VEGETABLES** Toss the radishes with 2 teaspoons of the oil, season with salt and pepper, and spread in a single layer on one of the prepared baking sheets. Toss the asparagus with the remaining 1 tablespoon oil, season with salt and pepper, and spread in a single layer on the second prepared baking sheet. Roast the vegetables until bright and tender but still slightly crisp in the center. For the asparagus, roast thin spears for 7 to 8 minutes; thick spears, 12 to 15 minutes. Roast the radishes for 15 to 18 minutes.

CONTINUES

## BRANZINO

**4 boneless, skin-on branzino fillets**

**Kosher sea salt and black pepper**

**1 to 2 tablespoons olive oil**

**MAKE THE BRANZINO** Pat the fillets dry with paper towels and sprinkle both sides with salt and pepper. Place one large or two smaller skillets on the front burner(s) of your stovetop over medium-high heat. There should be enough room in the skillet for the fish to cook without overlapping. Swirl 1 tablespoon oil in each skillet to coat the bottom of the pan and heat until the oil is shimmering, 60 to 90 seconds. Add the fillets, skin side down, being sure to lay the fish away from you to avoid splatters. Lightly press on each fillet with a spatula to make sure the skin has full contact with the pan and cooks for 3 minutes. Gently flip the fillets away from you and cook for 1 minute more. Transfer the branzino, skin side up, to a platter lined with paper towels to remove any excess oil.

**TO SERVE** Divide the lima bean puree among four plates, and use the back of a large spoon to spread it in a circle. When the vegetables are cool enough to handle, cut 1-inch (2.5-cm) pieces off the bottom of the asparagus and toss them with the radishes. Place a pile of radishes and asparagus stems on top of the puree on each plate. Drizzle each with 1 tablespoon of the herb sauce.

Place a branzino fillet, skin side up, on top of each radish pile. Arrange the remaining asparagus stalks on top and drizzle with the remaining herb sauce.

**CHEF'S NOTE** Warm plates are always a nice touch, but particularly so with this dish. To heat plates, place them in the oven on its lowest temperature setting. To heat plates in the microwave, sprinkle each plate with water and stack them up. Heat on high for 1 minute and wipe dry with a dish towel. Be sure to use plates that do not have any metal edges or decorations and are microwave- and oven-safe.

**FEEL GOOD INGREDIENT // BRANZINO** Branzino is a type of Mediterranean sea bass also known as *loup de mer* in French cooking. Considered one of the healthiest fish, it's high in omega-3s, low in mercury, and rated "Best Choice" on the Monterey Bay Aquarium's Seafood Watch list.

# HOW TO FILLET A FISH

*Use a sharp thin-bladed knife, and starting just behind the head, cut along the backbone toward the tail.*

*Using a thin spatula, gently lift the top fillet away from the spine and set aside. Starting from the tail, slowly lift up the spine, using the knife as needed to separate it from the bottom fillet. Discard the head, tail, spine, and any aromatics.*

*Use the knife to scrape away any remaining rib bones from the bottom fillet, or if you want to get really fancy, you can use tweezers.*

PREP // **10 minutes**

COOK // **25 to 30 minutes**

SERVES // **4**

# ISLAND-STYLE WHOLE-ROASTED FISH WITH PICKLED VEGETABLES

**1 red bell pepper, cut into ¼- by 2-inch (6-mm by 5-cm) strips**

**3 carrots, cut into ¼- by 2-inch (6-mm by 5-cm) strips**

**1 small red onion, thinly sliced**

**½ lime, cut into 3 wedges, plus additional lime wedges for serving**

**Generous pinch red pepper flakes**

**Kosher sea salt and black pepper**

**Olive oil**

**3 tablespoons red wine vinegar**

**1 whole firm white fish (3 pounds/1.4 kg), such as snapper or sea bass, gutted and scaled (see Note)**

**1 lemon**

**1 small bunch thyme**

**Handful of fresh cilantro, chopped**

*Jacq: I learned this recipe from my dear friend Faith, who is from Jamaica. She told me this is how they do it down in the islands, and oh, man, do they do it right! The fish comes out tender and flaky and the vegetables add the perfect balance of acidity, sweetness, and heat. Serve this with Red Quinoa with Herbes (page 32) or The Happy Hippy Quinoa Salad (page 118) and a side of Roasted Curried Cauliflower with Raisins and Pine Nuts (page 44).*

Preheat the oven to 450°F (230°C) and line a baking sheet with parchment paper. Set aside.

In a loaf pan or small baking dish, combine the bell pepper, carrots, and half the onion. Squeeze the juice from the 3 lime wedges over the vegetables and toss. Add the spent rinds to the vegetables. Sprinkle with the red pepper flakes, ¼ teaspoon salt, and ¼ teaspoon black pepper. Add 3 tablespoons oil and the vinegar and toss again to coat.

Working on the baking sheet, rub the fish with oil and season both sides generously with salt and pepper. Score the fish by cutting three deep diagonal lines along each side. Cut the lemon in half lengthwise and thinly slice it into half-moon shapes. Stuff each cut in the fish with slices of lemon and a branch of thyme. Fill the cavity of the fish with the remaining lemon, thyme, and red onion.

Put the fish and vegetables in the oven. Roast until the flesh of the fish is opaque and the vegetables are tender-crisp, 25 to 30 minutes.

Before serving, add the cilantro to the vegetables. You can serve the fish whole on a platter for a dramatic presentation and allow people to lift the fish away from the bones at the table, or you can go the more traditional route and cut the fish into fillets (see page 183). Enjoy with the pickled vegetables and a wedge of lime.

**CHEF'S NOTE** You can use two smaller white fish such as branzino in place of the large fish. They will cook more quickly, in about 20 minutes.

**FEEL GOOD INGREDIENT // BELL PEPPER** As bell peppers mature, their sugar and nutritional content increase. Although green peppers are tasty, your dishes will be both sweeter and healthier with red, yellow, orange, and even purple bell peppers. Full of essential vitamins, just one of these bright peppers provides more than twice the daily recommended amount of vitamin C. Plus, they have other antioxidants like lutein and zeaxanthin, which are must-haves when it comes to keeping your eyes healthy.

# SALMON WITH MANGO CHUTNEY AND CRUSHED PECANS

**1 skin-on salmon fillet or side (2 pounds/910 g)**

PER POUND (455 G) OF FISH, USE

**⅛ teaspoon kosher sea salt**

**Pinch black pepper**

**Pinch paprika**

**2 tablespoons mango chutney**

**⅓ cup (40 g) finely chopped pecans**

**1 teaspoon cold nondairy butter (preferably Miyoko's Vegan Butter; optional)**

*Jacq: This is one of the most popular recipes on my blog, which is no surprise since it's one of the easiest dishes to make! It's quick enough for a weeknight meal, but the complex flavors also make it a great choice for a dinner party. The sweet nuttiness of the pecans works beautifully with the spicy mango chutney and the rich salmon. It's also perfect for a brunch buffet since it's equally tasty hot out of the oven as it is after it's cooled. Cook a side of salmon for a striking presentation and allow people to serve themselves as much as they like, or cook a small fillet for an easy date night dish.*

Preheat the oven to 350°F (175°C) and line a baking sheet with parchment paper. Place the fish, skin side down on the sheet, and season it lightly with the salt, pepper, and paprika.

Spread a layer of the chutney on the flesh of the fish as if you were spreading jam on toast. Next, cover the fish completely in the pecans and press gently to create a crust. If using butter, use a vegetable peeler or paring knife to cut the butter into slivers, then dot the crust with the butter.

Bake until the fish is just opaque and flaky, about 15 minutes for a small fillet, or 25 to 30 minutes for a side of salmon. To check your fish for doneness, poke with a paring knife. If you feel very little resistance, the fish is done. If there is significant resistance, bake it for a few more minutes. If you have a meat thermometer, the thickest part of the fish should read between 120°F and 125°F (49°C and 52°C).

**CHEF'S NOTE**  Fresh salmon is brightly colored, plump, and shiny rather than dull or dried out. Look for wild Alaskan salmon or farmed salmon listed as a "best choice" on the Seafood Watch app. Salmon with the blue ASC or MSC labels are also great choices.

**FEEL GOOD INGREDIENT  //  PECANS**  Native to the southern United States and Mexico, wild pecans were used by many Native American tribes as a major food source during autumn. They're high in "good fats" and also have significant amounts of protein and fiber. Some of the nutrients found in pecans, like manganese, copper, and zinc, play an important role in reducing inflammation and supporting brain health.

# TILAPIA AL MOJO DE AJO

2 limes, halved

2 tilapia fillets (about 6 ounces/170 g each)

Kosher sea salt and black pepper

¼ teaspoon ground cumin

¼ cup (60 ml) olive oil

4 garlic cloves, thinly sliced

¼ cup (40 g) whole-wheat or brown rice flour

2 tablespoons fresh cilantro leaves

*Jacq: This was one of the recipes my mom taught me how to make before I moved out of the house, and I still make it regularly twenty years later. It cooks up in a flash and gives you maximum flavor with minimum effort. Try it with Fiesta Veggie Rice (page 146), Calabacitas con Elote (page 50), and a little lettuce or shredded cabbage on the side.*

Squeeze the juice of 1 lime over the fish. Sprinkle both sides of the fish with salt, pepper, and the cumin. Set aside.

Line a small plate with paper towels and set aside. In a large frying pan, heat the oil and garlic over medium heat until the oil begins to bubble around the garlic, about 1 minute, then lower to medium-low heat. Cook the garlic slices for 2 to 4 minutes until they are just golden, being careful not to let them burn. Remove them with a slotted spatula as they are ready and place them on the lined plate. Leave the garlic oil in the pan. You will use it to pan-fry the fish.

Spread the flour on a large plate. Lift a tilapia fillet up by one end and shake off any excess lime juice, then lightly dredge in flour and shake off any excess. Repeat with the second fillet.

Turn the heat under the skillet up to medium-high, and when the oil is shimmering, after about 30 seconds, add the fish. Be sure to lay the fish away from you to avoid splatters. Cook until it is golden brown and easily flaked with a fork, 2 to 3 minutes per side. Use a slotted spatula to remove the fillets from the oil. Transfer to serving plates and squeeze the juice of the remaining lime on top. Scatter the golden garlic slices over the fillets and garnish with the cilantro leaves.

**CHEF'S NOTE** Look for tilapia from recirculating aquaculture farms in the United States and Canada. The next best are those raised in ponds in Ecuador or raceways in Peru.

**FEEL GOOD INGREDIENT // TILAPIA** Tilapia is believed to be the first farmed fish, with tilapia-pond farms dating back to ancient Egypt. Rich in protein, this fish provides more than 34 grams in a 6-ounce (170-g) serving. The protein found in tilapia is a complete protein that contains all of the essential amino acids. And, along with canned salmon and sardines, it contains one of the lowest mercury levels of any fish.

PREP // **5 minutes**

COOK // **30 minutes**

SERVES // **4**

# ITALIAN-STYLE GRILLED HALIBUT

### SAUCE

**3 tablespoons olive oil**

**4 cloves garlic, minced**

**1 pint (275 g) cherry tomatoes, halved**

**1 cup (240 ml) jarred marinated artichoke hearts, drained**

**¼ cup (40 g) Kalamata olives**

**⅓ cup (17 g) chopped fresh flat-leaf parsley leaves and tender stems**

**Kosher sea salt and black pepper**

**Pinch crushed red pepper flakes**

**½ cup (120 ml) dry white wine**

### HALIBUT

**4 halibut steaks (6 ounces/170 g each, about 1 inch/2.5 cm thick; see Notes)**

**Olive oil**

**Kosher sea salt and black pepper**

**½ lemon**

**¼ cup (10 g) fresh basil leaves, cut into chiffonade**

*Pour yourself a glass of pinot grigio, put on some music, turn on the barbecue, and get ready to take a mini-vacation. Nothing tastes more like summertime at the Italian seaside than grilled fish in a fresh tomato, olive, and artichoke sauce with sweet basil sprinkled on top. Use the juiciest tomatoes and the freshest fish you can find and take a moment to enjoy* la dolce vita.

**MAKE THE SAUCE**  Heat a large skillet or sauté pan over medium heat, and add the oil and garlic. Cook, stirring frequently, until the garlic becomes fragrant, about 1 minute. Add the tomatoes, artichoke hearts, olives, and half of the parsley. Sprinkle with a generous pinch of salt and black pepper and the red pepper flakes and gently stir.

Pour in the white wine and simmer for about 9 minutes, stirring occasionally, until the tomatoes soften. Remove from the heat and stir in the remaining parsley leaves just before serving. The sauce can be made a day ahead and stored in a jar in the refrigerator. Reheat in a saucepan over medium heat until warmed through.

**MAKE THE HALIBUT**  Preheat a grill to medium-high heat. Using a basting brush or your clean hands, coat the halibut well in oil. Season the fish on all sides with salt and pepper and place it on the grill. Cook undisturbed until the fish releases from the grill, 4 to 5 minutes, then flip with a fish spatula and cook for about 4 minutes more, until the flesh is opaque and flaky.

Serve the halibut steaks with the sauce. Finish with a squeeze of lemon juice and the basil. Cool, cover, and refrigerate leftovers immediately and enjoy within 24 hours.

**CHEF'S NOTES**  Halibut has been plagued by overfishing. Look for domestic wild-caught halibut from Marine Stewardship Council–certified fisheries to ensure your halibut is from a sustainable source.

If halibut is not available, another meaty fish such as tuna or mahi mahi may be substituted.

**FEEL GOOD INGREDIENT // HALIBUT**  Halibut is a firm white fish with a meaty texture and delicate flavor. Halibut provides loads of protein, selenium, niacin, magnesium, vitamins $B_{12}$ and $B_6$, potassium, and omega-3 fatty acids. It can have anti-inflammatory effects on your body to help fight disease.

PREP // **5 minutes, plus overnight marinade**
COOK // **20 minutes**
SERVES // **2**

# MISO-GINGER GLAZED BLACK COD

2 tablespoons tamari

2 tablespoons warm filtered water

1 tablespoon fresh lemon juice

1 tablespoon roughly chopped fresh ginger

2 tablespoons honey

½ teaspoon Dijon mustard

½ teaspoon sweet white miso

2 skin-on black cod (also called sablefish or butterfish) fillets (6 to 8 ounces/170 to 225 g)

½ teaspoon arrowroot

**CHEF'S NOTE** If your broiler element is separate from your oven, preheat your oven to 350°F (175°C).

**FEEL GOOD INGREDIENT // BLACK COD** Black cod has a rich buttery flavor and succulent texture from its high fat content. It contains as much heart-healthy omega-3 EPA and DHA and vital $B_{12}$ as salmon. Currently the Monterey Bay Aquarium's Seafood Watch ranks black cod from Alaska as a "Best Choice."

*It might seem a little crazy to marinate a fish for up to 2 days, but it is so worth it! You end up with flaky, buttery fish with mind-blowing flavor. It's like something that would be served at the fanciest Japanese restaurant, straight out of your oven. The rich umami flavors of the miso and black cod are complemented by the citrus and spice in our Bok Choy with Spicy Lime Dressing (page 46) and a side of steamed rice.*

**MAKE THE MARINADE** In a small pot, combine the tamari, water, lemon juice, ginger, honey, mustard, and miso and heat over medium-high heat, whisking until the miso dissolves. Bring the sauce to a boil, then pour it into a small bowl and allow it to cool to room temperature. You can speed up this process by placing the small bowl into a larger bowl filled with ice.

Place the fish in a heavy-duty zip-top bag and pour the marinade over it. Make sure the entire surface of the fish is in contact with the marinade. Marinate in the refrigerator overnight or for up to 2 days.

**COOK THE FISH** Preheat the oven to 200°F (90°C; see Note). Place a fine-mesh sieve over a small saucepan and strain the excess marinade from the bag into the saucepan. Add the arrowroot and stir until it dissolves. Heat the sauce over medium-high heat, stirring constantly, until it comes to a boil, then lower the heat and simmer for about 1 minute, until the sauce thickens and bubbles. Turn off the heat.

Turn on the broiler. Remove the fish from the bag and transfer to a small plate. Scrape any ginger pieces off the fish. Shake any excess liquid off the fillets and place them on a broiler pan or cast-iron skillet. Broil skin side up 4 inches (10 cm) from the heat source (usually on the top rack of the oven) until the skin crisps and begins to bubble, about 3 minutes. Carefully flip with a spatula and broil until the fish begins to flake, about 2½ minutes more.

Remove the fish from the oven and brush each fillet with 1 tablespoon of the sauce. Turn off the broiler and bake at 350°F (175°C) until the fish is flaky and opaque throughout, 3 to 7 minutes depending on the thickness. (It's OK if the oven is not immediately up to temperature.)

Carefully check for pin bones along the middle of the fillet and remove any with tweezers. When the fish is cooked through, the bones come out with no resistance. Enjoy immediately.

*"People who love to eat are always the best people."*
—JULIA CHILD

# Party Food

PREP // **5 minutes**

COOK // **45 minutes**

SERVES // **4**

# SPICY BUFFALO TOFU FINGERS WITH AVOCADO RANCH DRESSING

TOFU FINGERS

**2 (16-ounce/455-g) packages super-firm tofu (see Notes on page 72)**

**¼ cup (60 ml) virgin coconut oil**

**¼ cup (60 ml) hot sauce (see Notes)**

**¼ cup (60 ml) sriracha**

**3 tablespoons honey**

**2 tablespoons fresh cilantro leaves**

AVOCADO RANCH DRESSING

**1 cup (155 g) mashed avocado (about 2 avocados)**

**½ cup (120 ml) unsweetened almond or cashew milk, plus more as needed**

**2 garlic cloves, peeled**

**2 tablespoons chopped onion**

**2 tablespoons apple cider vinegar**

**1 teaspoon Dijon mustard**

**2 teaspoons nutritional yeast**

**½ teaspoon black pepper**

**¼ teaspoon kosher sea salt**

**¼ cup (11 g) lightly packed fresh chives**

**¼ cup (13 g) lightly packed fresh flat-leaf parsley leaves and tender stems**

**¼ cup (13 g) lightly packed fresh dill fronds**

*We make these for the Super Bowl every year and they're a big hit with everyone from the vegans to the meat-and-potato guys. You don't have to be watching a sporting event to enjoy these, but they do have a little kick that stands up nicely to a cold beer and a loud television. Serve them with our creamy Avocado Ranch Dressing. It's the perfect cooling complement to these fiery treats.*

**MAKE THE TOFU** Preheat the oven to 400°F (205°C) and line a baking sheet with parchment paper. Cut the tofu into fingers about ¾ inch (2 cm) wide on all sides and 3 inches (7.5 cm) long. Lay the fingers on the baking sheet so there is a little space between each one and bake for 15 minutes.

Meanwhile, in a small pot, melt the oil over medium-low heat. Add the hot sauce, sriracha, and honey and whisk to combine. Turn off the heat. Remove the tofu from the oven and brush with the sauce on all sides. Bake for 15 minutes more.

Turn the tofu fingers in the oven and brush with any remaining sauce. Bake for a final 15 minutes, or until lightly browned (see Notes).

**MEANWHILE, MAKE THE DRESSING** Using a large spoon, scoop the avocado flesh into a blender. Add the milk, garlic, onion, vinegar, mustard, nutritional yeast, pepper, and salt and blend until smooth. Scrape the sides and add milk to thin the dressing, if needed. Add the herbs and pulse until finely chopped. Taste and add a pinch of salt, if desired, and pulse again.

**TO SERVE** Garnish the tofu with cilantro and serve hot with the dressing on the side. Refrigerate any leftovers in an airtight container for up to 3 days.

**CHEF'S NOTES** Use any hot sauce that lists vinegar as an ingredient.

If the tofu has not browned after 45 minutes, you can place it under the broiler for 2 to 4 minutes before serving. Keep a close eye so that it doesn't burn.

This recipe can easily be multiplied to feed a crowd. You can also cut the tofu into cubes before you bake it and use as a topping for salads, Buddha bowls, or stir-fries.

**FEEL GOOD INGREDIENT // HOT SAUCE** Studies have shown that eating spicy food can help your body burn more calories by raising your metabolic rate by 8 percent. This means you can eat 8 percent more tofu fingers, making you 8 percent happier. That's science.

PREP // **20 minutes, plus Spicy Black Beans (page 128), Quick Pico de Gallo (page 200) and Creamy Cashew Sour Cream (page 138)**

COOK // **55 minutes**

SERVES // **6**

# SUPER NACHOS WITH GOOEY SWEET POTATO CHEESE SAUCE

CHEESE SAUCE

**1 garnet sweet potato (about 1 pound/455 g)**

**¼ cup (30 g) raw cashews, soaked for 2 to 4 hours, drained, and rinsed**

**1¼ cups (300 ml) hot water**

**2 tablespoons nutritional yeast**

**2 tablespoons tapioca flour**

**1½ teaspoons apple cider vinegar**

**1 teaspoon Dijon mustard**

**1 garlic clove, peeled**

**¾ teaspoon kosher sea salt**

**1 to 2 teaspoons sriracha or other hot sauce**

**Pinch ground cumin or taco seasoning**

GUACAMOLE

**1 garlic clove, peeled**

**1 large or 2 small avocados**

**Juice of ½ lime**

**Pinch kosher sea salt**

**Pinch ground cumin**

**½ cup (90 g) chopped tomato**

**¼ jalapeño, seeded and minced**

**1½ tablespoons finely diced onion**

**¼ cup (10 g) torn fresh cilantro leaves**

TO SERVE

**3 to 4 cups (75 to 100 g) organic corn chips**

**1 small jicama, peeled and sliced into chips**

**½ recipe Spicy Black Beans (page 128)**

**Quick Pico de Gallo (page 200)**

**Creamy Cashew Sour Cream (page 138)**

**2 radishes, thinly sliced**

**2 tablespoons pickled jalapeños (optional)**

**Fresh cilantro for garnish**

*Abbie: I have seen these nachos devoured more times than I've seen the Lakers win a basketball game. They not only look colorful and beautiful but are a healthy and delicious party snack the whole crowd will enjoy. I love the mix of crunchy jicama and corn chips and the gooey cheese sauce with a hint of sweetness and spice.*

**MAKE THE CHEESE SAUCE** Preheat the oven to 450°F (230°C). Prick the sweet potato several times with a fork, place on a baking sheet, and bake until easily pierced through with a knife, about 50 minutes.

Meanwhile, in a high-speed blender or food processor, combine the cashews, hot water, nutritional yeast, tapioca flour, vinegar, mustard, garlic, salt, hot sauce, and cumin and blend until smooth, 1 to 2 minutes.

When the sweet potato is ready, cut it in half and scoop the flesh from half of the sweet potato into the blender or food processor and puree again. (Reserve the other half for another use.) Pour the mixture into a small saucepan and set aside.

**MAKE THE GUACAMOLE** Mash the garlic into a paste in a molcajete or mince it with a knife and transfer it to a medium bowl. Add the avocado, lime juice, salt, and cumin to the garlic and mash together using the pestle or a fork. Make it as chunky or smooth as you prefer, then fold in the tomato, jalapeño, onion, and cilantro.

**TO SERVE** Cover a small platter with half corn chips and half raw jicama chips. Heat the beans in a small pot over medium-low heat, stirring occasionally, until warmed through. Heat the cheese sauce over medium heat for 2 to 3 minutes, stirring gently but continuously with a wooden or silicone spoon, until it thickens. Be sure to scrape the sides and bottom of the saucepan as you stir to avoid scorching.

Pour half of the beans onto the chips. Top with the cheese sauce, pico de gallo, and guacamole, followed by the remaining beans. Add a big dollop of cashew sour cream. Dot with the radish slices and pickled jalapeños, if using, and garnish with cilantro.

**FEEL GOOD INGREDIENT // JICAMA** Jicama has a starchy crunchy texture similar to raw potato but with a mild, slightly sweet flavor. It contains inulin, a special type of plant fiber that plays a prebiotic role in the intestines. That means that it promotes the growth of "good" bacteria, which help contribute to a healthy gut microbiome.

# QUICK PICO DE GALLO

**1 cup (135 g) chopped tomato or halved grape tomatoes**

**1½ tablespoons finely chopped onion**

**¼ jalapeño, seeded and minced**

**1 handful torn fresh cilantro leaves**

**½ lime**

**Kosher sea salt and black pepper**

*As with most things in life, when it comes to food, boring is never better! With this pico de gallo, you can add freshness, beautiful color, and a little heat to all of your favorite bowls, wraps, and Mexican dishes. If you like things extra spicy, leave in a few of the jalapeño seeds.*

In a small bowl, mix the tomatoes, onion, jalapeño, and cilantro. Squeeze the juice from the lime over top. Sprinkle with a pinch of salt and pepper and toss. Use immediately, or store in a container in the refrigerator for up to 5 days.

**FEEL GOOD INGREDIENT // TOMATOES** Considered a health food since ancient times, a single tomato can provide about a quarter of your daily vitamin C and vitamin A requirements. Tomatoes are also one of the best sources of the phytonutrient lycopene, which has been shown to be closely tied to enhanced immunity and cancer risk reduction.

## PRETTY PARTY PLATTERS

*Whenever we host a party or dinner together, we always make sure there are a couple of party platters on the table when guests arrive. This allows people to serve themselves and gives us time to play hostess or prepare the rest of the meal. The key is to create a look of abundance. We fill one tray with delicious vegan cheeses (see Stocking your Kitchen on page 18), and piles of crackers, nuts, chocolates, and seasonal fresh and dried fruits. On the other tray, we create a mezze plate (opposite), which is a typical Mediterranean/Middle Eastern party platter with hummus, baba ghanoush, and our feel-good versions of feta and tabouli (recipes follow). Served with warm pita and the freshest veggies from the farmers' market, it makes an impressive display without breaking the bank. For casual occasions, a big tray piled with corn chips and served with little bowls of our Quick Pico de Gallo, Avocado-Lime Cream (page 179), and Creamy Cashew Sour Cream (page 138) fits the bill.*

*If you don't have a big party tray, you'll need to invest in a couple. We found a few fancy ones at estate sales for the same price you'd pay for plastic platters at a discount store, so keep your eyes peeled at yard sales and vintage shops. Large wooden cutting boards also work well.*

PREP // **10 minutes**

MAKES // **2 cups (480 g)**

SERVES // **8**

# ARTICHOKE HUMMUS WITH ZA'ATAR

1 (14-ounce/400-g) can baby artichoke hearts, drained (see Note)

1½ cups (280 g) cooked or 1 (15-ounce/425-g) can garbanzo beans, drained, liquid reserved

¼ cup (60 ml) extra-virgin olive oil

¼ cup (60 g) tahini

2 garlic cloves, peeled

2 tablespoons fresh lemon juice

½ teaspoon kosher sea salt

½ teaspoon freshly ground white pepper

½ teaspoon paprika

½ teaspoon ground cumin

TOPPINGS

2 teaspoons za'atar spice

Small handful (about 2 tablespoons) fresh cilantro leaves and tender stems

1 tablespoon extra-virgin olive oil (optional)

*This creamy, garlicky hummus is totally addictive and so much better than anything you can buy premade at the grocery store. It's always a hit on any mezze or crudités platter, and is a delicious way to add protein and flavor to sandwiches, wraps, and bowls.*

Chop 3 artichoke hearts and place them in a small bowl with 1 tablespoon of the garbanzo beans. Set aside.

Place the remaining beans and artichokes in a blender or food processor and add the oil, tahini, garlic, lemon juice, salt, pepper, paprika, and cumin. Add 2 tablespoons of the bean cooking water or drained liquid from the canned beans. Blend until smooth, scraping down the sides as necessary, about 2 minutes. If the blades stick, add an additional tablespoon of bean liquid.

Spoon the hummus into a serving dish and top with the cut artichoke chunks and whole garbanzo beans or fold them in. Finish with the za'atar and garnish with the cilantro. Drizzle with a bit of oil, if desired. Store in an airtight container in the refrigerator for up to 5 days.

**CHEF'S NOTE** If you can't find baby artichokes, use quartered artichoke hearts instead.

**FEEL GOOD INGREDIENT // GARBANZO BEANS** Garbanzo beans, also known as chickpeas or ceci beans, are one of the world's oldest cultivated crops. Like all legumes, garbanzo beans contain a beneficial combination of complex carbohydrates, fiber, protein, vitamins, and minerals that the body is able to slowly digest and use for sustained energy.

Get your savory, salty feta fix with this scrumptious baked tofu feta. It instantly adds tons of umami-packed flavor to a mezze plate, but can also be added to sandwiches, salads, pizza, and wraps. Toss it with romaine lettuce, red onion, and cucumber to make a quick Greek salad or with bow-tie pasta and baby spinach for a protein-rich pasta salad.

PREP // **5 minutes**

COOK // **45 minutes**

MAKES // **2 cups (480 g)**

# MEDITERRANEAN TOFU FETA

1 (14-ounce/400-g) package extra-firm tofu, drained

2 tablespoons chickpea miso

2 tablespoons umeboshi vinegar (also called ume plum vinegar)

2 tablespoons fresh lemon juice

2 tablespoons extra-virgin olive oil

1 teaspoon nutritional yeast

½ teaspoon dried rosemary

½ teaspoon dried oregano

½ teaspoon dried basil

2 tablespoons warm water

¼ cup (60 g) marinated artichoke hearts, drained

3 tablespoons pitted Kalamata olives

3 tablespoons oil-packed sun-dried tomatoes

Preheat the oven to 300°F (150°C) and line a baking sheet with parchment paper.

Cut the tofu into ¾-inch (2-cm) cubes and place on the prepared baking sheet. Bake for about 45 minutes, turning every 15 minutes, until lightly golden.

Meanwhile, in a medium bowl, whisk the miso, vinegar, lemon juice, oil, nutritional yeast, rosemary, oregano, basil, and water. Set aside.

Chop the artichoke hearts, olives, and sun-dried tomatoes and set aside.

When the tofu is done baking and cool enough to handle, add it to the marinade and gently toss to coat. Fold in the artichoke hearts, olives, and sun-dried tomatoes. Allow to marinate for at least 4 hours in the refrigerator before using. Store covered in the refrigerator for up to 5 days, or place in an airtight jar and cover in olive oil to keep for up to 10 days in the refrigerator.

**FEEL GOOD INGREDIENT** // **TOFU** Tofu is a wonderful source of protein and one of the few plant proteins that contains all nine essential amino acids needed to build and repair muscle and tissue. It's also filled with iron, calcium, and other micronutrients.

**Party Food** // **203**

PREP // **20 minutes**

MAKES // **about 3½ cups (650 g)**

# CAULIFLOWER TABOULI SALAD

**2 cups (5.5 ounces/156 g) cauliflower florets (about ⅓ head cauliflower)**

**1 cup (50 g) lightly packed chopped fresh flat-leaf parsley leaves**

**1 cup (180 g) diced tomato**

**4 scallions, thinly sliced**

**½ cup (24 g) lightly packed chopped fresh mint**

**2 celery ribs, cut in half lengthwise and thinly sliced**

**½ cup (120 ml) fresh lemon juice (from 3 to 4 lemons)**

**¼ cup (60 ml) extra-virgin olive oil**

**1 teaspoon kosher sea salt**

*This recipe has all of the bright lemony and herbal flavors of the classic Middle Eastern salad with an extra dose of cruciferous magic. We've swapped out the traditional bulgur wheat for cauliflower, which adds an impressive array of phytonutrients without sacrificing taste. A traditional component of the mezze plate, tabouli also makes a vibrant addition to bowls, wraps, and salads.*

Pulse the florets in a food processor or high-speed blender until they resemble rice. Alternatively, use a box grater to grate the cauliflower into rice-size pieces. You should have 1 cup (100 g) cauliflower rice.

In a large bowl, combine the 1 cup (100 g) cauliflower rice, parsley, tomato, scallions, mint, and celery. Drizzle with the lemon juice and oil. Sprinkle with half of the salt and toss, then sprinkle in the remaining salt and toss again. Chill in the refrigerator until ready to serve. The tomatoes will release water as the tabouli sits, so tilt the bowl over the sink to drain off the excess liquid and toss the salad again just before serving. Refrigerate any leftovers in an airtight container for up to 3 days.

**FEEL GOOD INGREDIENT // SCALLIONS** Though often used only as a garnish, scallions are an immune-boosting, disease-fighting vegetable that boasts some serious health benefits. Along with cruciferous vegetables, leafy greens, and berries, scallions are considered to be a cancer-fighting food. They are extremely low in calories yet rich in vitamins K, A, C, and folate, and the minerals calcium, iron, potassium, and manganese.

COOK // **15 minutes**
MAKES // **2 cups (480 g)**
SERVES // **8**

# FIRE-ROASTED BABA GHANOUSH

2 eggplants (about 1 pound/455 g each)

½ cup (120 ml) tahini

¼ cup (60 ml) plus 2 tablespoons fresh Meyer lemon juice (from 2 Meyer lemons; substitute regular lemons, if necessary)

2 garlic cloves, peeled

1 teaspoon kosher sea salt

1 teaspoon black pepper

Generous pinch paprika

1 teaspoon za'atar spice

*Abbie: The fun part about making this baba ghanoush is cooking the eggplant on your stovetop directly over the flame. The smell that comes off the eggplant as the raw flame licks around its skin is absolutely delightful. It's aromatherapy in the kitchen. This particular method creates an earthy, smoky, barbecue-like flavor. It's great on its own as a dip for chips, veggies, or crostini and is also a nice addition to a mezze.*

Working on two burners on your stovetop, turn the flame to medium. (If you do not have a gas stove, see Note.) Place one eggplant directly on each burner, in contact with the flame. As the skin chars, turn the eggplants with tongs so that the entire skin chars uniformly. After about 10 minutes, when the outside of the eggplants are completely blackened and the center of the flesh is easily pierced with a paring knife, transfer the eggplant to a large plate to cool.

Once the eggplants are cool enough to handle, cut the tops off. Using your fingers, peel off the skin, then scrape off any remaining skin with a paring knife. If you'd like, you can leave a few black flakes attached for an extra smoky flavor.

Transfer the peeled eggplants to a food processor, leaving behind the liquid that has seeped onto the plate. Add the tahini, lemon juice, garlic, salt, and pepper and process on high speed until well blended. Pour the dip into a small bowl and serve with the paprika and the za'atar spice. Refrigerate any leftovers in an airtight container for up to 5 days.

**CHEF'S NOTE** If you do not have a gas burner, you can cook the eggplant on a hot grill or in the oven. To cook in the oven, place the eggplants in a roasting pan and roast in a 450°F (230°C) oven until the skin has charred and the interior is tender, about 20 minutes. Let cool, then proceed to step 2.

**FEEL GOOD INGREDIENT // EGGPLANT** These deep purple glossy beauties are full of phytonutrients and antioxidants. Eggplants, or aubergine, contain a somewhat rare and extremely beneficial type of antioxidant known as nasunin, which is a potent fighter of inflammation and protects DNA and cell membranes from oxidative stress. Cooking eggplant increases the bioavailability of their antioxidant content and disease-fighting compounds.

PREP // **10 minutes**
MAKES // **24 stuffed dates**
SERVES // **12**

# HAZELNUT-STUFFED MEDJOOL DATES

½ cup (120 ml) cashew butter (see Note)

**Pinch ground cinnamon**

**Pinch kosher sea salt**

**Small pinch ground cardamom**

**24 Medjool dates**

**¼ cup (35 g) raw or toasted hazelnuts**

**¼ cup (30 g) cacao nibs or chocolate chips**

**¼ cup (35 g) pomegranate seeds**

**1 tablespoon shredded coconut**

*Abbie: These little delicacies are packed full of flavor and are a healthy alternative to the other candies, cookies, and chips, served at parties that may not be so good for you. The richness of the nut butter, the hint of spice, and the sweetness of the dates make them a hit with all ages. The serving plate always comes back to the kitchen empty. Feel free to make them your own and take creative license with the toppings.*

Place the nut butter in a small bowl and sprinkle with the cinnamon, salt, and cardamom. Mix well with a fork. Split the dates with your thumb and remove the pits. Fill each date with a teaspoon of the nut butter. Decorate the dates with the hazelnuts, cacao nibs, pomegranate seeds, and shredded coconut.

**CHEF'S NOTE** Almond or pecan butter can be substituted for the cashew butter.

**FEEL GOOD INGREDIENT // HAZELNUTS** Hazelnuts (also called filberts) are nutrient dense, filling, and used in both sweet and savory recipes. The nuts are rich in dietary fiber, vitamins, and minerals and packed with health-promoting phytochemicals. Hazelnuts contain vitamins E and B$_6$, and folate, as well as minerals including manganese, potassium, copper, iron, magnesium, zinc, and selenium.

# WATERMELON RADISH AND SMOKED SALMON CANAPÉS

½ cup (120 g) nondairy cream cheese (preferably Kite Hill)

4 to 5 watermelon radishes, thinly sliced into 24 rounds

8 ounces (225 g) smoked salmon

⅓ cup (45 g) thinly sliced grape tomatoes

1 small carrot, thinly sliced

¼ cup (35 g) finely diced red onion

¼ cup (30 g) capers, drained

¼ cup (60 ml) fresh lemon juice (from 2 lemons)

Flaky sea salt and freshly cracked black pepper

1 bunch fresh dill

*Abbie: These tasty canapés look beautiful and make for a light, colorful, and fun addition to any party. The flavor is similar to that of a well-made smoked salmon bagel, only here, the delicious combo of cream cheese, onion, smoked salmon, and capers sit on top of a thinly cut slice of peppery, colorful radish. Your guests will surely enjoy these sophisticated bite-size treats, as they'll light up and appeal to all of their senses.*

Spread 1 teaspoon of the cream cheese onto each radish round. Top each radish round with a small piece of salmon. Add a slice of grape tomato and a slice of carrot to each piece. Sprinkle each canapé with ¼ teaspoon red onion, 3 to 4 capers, and ½ teaspoon lemon juice. Season lightly with salt and pepper. Garnish with dill fronds and arrange the canapés nicely on a serving platter.

**FEEL GOOD INGREDIENT // WATERMELON RADISHES**

Watermelon radishes are an heirloom variety of daikon radish and a member of the mustard family, which includes arugula and turnips. They have a sweeter, milder taste than most other radishes. They are a rich source of vitamins, including vitamins A, C, and folate, and also contain ten minerals, including calcium, potassium, and phosphorus, all important for bone health.

PREP // **5 minutes, plus Kale-Walnut Pesto (page 161) and Gooey Cashew Mozzarella (page 165)**

COOK // **40 minutes**

MAKES // **about 20 pizzette**

# SWEET POTATO PIZZETTE WITH ROASTED RADISHES AND FRIED SAGE

**2 medium to large sweet potatoes (about 1½ pounds/680 g each)**

**Olive oil**

**Kosher sea salt**

**Freshly ground black pepper**

**5 red or Easter egg radishes, quartered, or 10 French breakfast radishes, halved**

**1 bunch sage leaves**

**1 recipe Kale-Walnut Pesto (page 161) or 1 cup (240 g) store-bought pesto of your choice**

**1 recipe Gooey Cashew Mozzarella (page 165)**

**About 20 walnut halves**

*Whenever we are plating food, we always keep in mind that people eat with their eyes first. These adorable little pizzette may be small in size, but they provide a feast for the eyes and have a bold and beautiful fall flavor to match. They are a perfect hors d'oeuvre to serve at holiday cocktail parties to keep people feeling festive all night long.*

Preheat the oven to 425°F (220°C) and line a baking sheet with parchment paper. Cut the sweet potatoes into ¼-inch- (6-mm-) thick rounds, leaving the skin on. Place them in a large bowl and drizzle with just enough oil to coat and toss. Lay the slices on the baking sheet in a single layer and season with a generous pinch of salt and pepper. Flip the slices and season the other side. Bake for 12 minutes.

Meanwhile, in a medium bowl, drizzle the radishes with a bit of oil to coat and season with salt and pepper. Remove the sweet potato slices from the oven, turn them over, and add the radishes to the baking sheet. Bake until the sweet potatoes and radishes are lightly browned and tender, 12 to 17 minutes more.

To make the fried sage, line a plate with paper towels and set aside. In a small skillet, heat ¼ inch (6 mm) olive oil over medium-high heat until shimmering. Working in batches, add the sage leaves and fry for 5 to 10 seconds, until their color brightens and they are lightly crisp. Remove with a fork or tongs and drain on the paper towels (see Notes). They will continue to crisp as they dry. Sage leaves can be fried up to 3 days ahead. Allow them to cool completely, then keep in an airtight container at room temperature.

Top each sweet potato round with a heaping teaspoon of pesto and cashew mozzarella. Add a half or quarter radish, a walnut half, and a fried sage leaf.

**FEEL GOOD INGREDIENT // SWEET POTATO** Sweet potatoes might taste like candy, but their natural sugars release slowly into the bloodstream. This means they provide a steady stream of energy without the blood-sugar spikes, linked to fatigue and weight gain, that other sweet food can give you.

**CHEF'S NOTES** An alternative sage-frying method: Line a soup skimmer with sage leaves, lower it into the oil, and lift them out when crisp. You may need to use slightly more oil with this method.

Adjust the recipe based on the seasons. In spring, you may want to swap fresh asparagus for the radish; in summer, try zucchini. When sweet tomatoes are in season, we recommend using fresh tomato sauce in place of the pesto and garnish with toasted pine nuts instead of the walnut.

# PEEWEE POTATOES AND CAVIAR

Kosher sea salt

2 pounds (910 g) peewee potatoes

2 tablespoons olive oil

⅔ cup (165 g) nondairy cream cheese (preferably Kite Hill)

1½ teaspoons fresh lemon juice

½ cup (25 g) finely snipped fresh chives

½ cup (65 g) minced red onion

4 hard-boiled eggs, whites and yolks separated and minced

3 ounces (85 g) caviar (see Notes)

*Abbie: I'm crazy about caviar; it's one of my favorite delicacies. This is a really fun, fast, and fancy recipe to serve for a cocktail party, brunch, or as an hors d'oeuvre before your guests sit down to eat. You don't have to go all out on buying expensive caviar, as these little guys taste just as good with an affordable caviar. The peewee potatoes are adorably cute and make for a perfect bite-size treat filled with a little pop of sophisticated yumminess inside.*

Bring a large pot of salted water to a boil over medium-high heat. The water should be salty like the ocean. Add the potatoes and boil until tender and easily pierced with a fork, 10 to 15 minutes. Drain and toss in the oil to lightly coat.

Place the cream cheese in a small serving bowl; add the lemon juice and whisk with a fork until well blended. Place the chives, onion, egg whites, and egg yolks into four separate small serving bowls.

Cut a lengthwise slit into each potato, cutting halfway through so the potato remains intact. Squeeze the sides of each potato with gentle pressure so the potato opens slightly and looks ready to be stuffed. (Alternatively, you can skip this step and place a paring knife on the serving platter so your guests can make their own incisions.)

Place the caviar tin in a small bowl surrounded by ice and place the bowl on a platter. Arrange the potatoes on the platter and serve with the cream cheese, chives, onion, egg whites, and egg yolks. Serve with very cold Champagne.

**CHEF'S NOTES**  Look for farmed American sturgeon or Servuga caviar for a special treat. More affordable trout and salmon caviar (aka roe) are good alternatives.

Metal adversely affects the flavor of caviar. Use traditional spoons made from mother of pearl or plastic spoons instead.

**FEEL GOOD INGREDIENT** // **CAVIAR**  Caviar are fish eggs that contain immune-boosting vitamins, minerals, and essential fats, including vitamins A, E, and B$_{12}$, zinc, selenium, and EPA and DHA omega-3 fatty acids. They are also a guaranteed mood enhancer, not due to any one nutrient, but thanks to their rich buttery flavor. It's hard to be grumpy when you have caviar in your mouth. That's a fact!

*"All you need is love. But a little chocolate now and then doesn't hurt."*

—CHARLES M. SCHULZ

# Dessert

PREP // **10 minutes**

COOK // **35 minutes plus chilling time**

SERVES // **12**

# CHOCOLATE TAHINI TART WITH FRESH ORANGES

### CRUST

**1 heaping teaspoon coconut oil, plus more for greasing the pan**

**1 cup (100 g) raw pecan halves**

**½ cup (55 g) old-fashioned or gluten-free rolled oats**

**½ cup (110 g) pitted and packed Medjool dates**

**1 tablespoon coconut butter**

**½ teaspoon smoked salt**

**Pinch cayenne pepper**

### FILLING

**¾ cup (180 ml) plus 2 tablespoons filtered water**

**⅓ cup (80 ml) maple syrup**

**1 tablespoon Bragg Liquid Aminos**

**1 teaspoon vanilla extract**

**⅓ cup (80 ml) tahini**

**1 cup (85 g) raw cacao powder**

**⅓ cup (73 g) raw almond butter**

**⅓ cup (40 g) Medjool dates, pitted and packed**

**⅓ cup (73 g) coconut butter**

**1½ teaspoons spirulina (optional)**

### TOPPING

**1 to 2 oranges, cut into ¼-inch- (6-mm-) thick rounds (see Notes)**

**Edible flowers such as pansies, borage, violets, or calendula (optional)**

**FEEL GOOD INGREDIENT // TAHINI** Tahini is a paste made out of ground sesame seeds. Rich in protein and healthy oils, it's a good source of amino acids, vitamins E and B, fatty acids, and zinc which contribute to skin-cell rejuvenation and help to prevent early signs of aging.

*This rich chocolate tart topped with bright orange slices on a nutty crust is impossible to resist. Show someone you care by making this their birthday cake, or make your friends happy by serving it up at your next dinner party.*

Preheat the oven to 350°F (175°C) and grease a 10-inch (25-cm) fluted tart pan with a removeable bottom with coconut oil.

**MAKE THE CRUST** In a food processor, combine the coconut oil, pecans, oats, dates, coconut butter, salt, and cayenne and pulse until coarsely ground. The ingredients should stick together when pressed. Scrape the mixture into the prepared tart pan. Using wet hands, press the crust into an even layer over the bottom and up the sides of the pan. If any areas are too crumbly, wet your hands again and press firmly to smooth. Bake for about 15 minutes, until lightly browned. Remove from the oven and set aside.

**MAKE THE FILLING** In a high-speed blender or food processor, combine the water, maple syrup, liquid aminos, vanilla, tahini, cacao powder, almond butter, dates, coconut butter, and spirulina, if using, and process until smooth. Scrape the sides occasionally with a rubber spatula, if needed. If it's very difficult to blend, add more water, 1 tablespoon at a time, until it blends smoothly. Pour the chocolate filling into the tart crust and smooth into an even layer with the back of a serving spoon.

**TO SERVE** Carefully cut the peel away from the orange slices using a paring knife. Arrange the slices on top of the chocolate filling. Place the tart in the freezer for 20 minutes or in the refrigerator for at least 45 minutes to fully set. Keep refrigerated until ready to serve. Unmold the tart and garnish with a few edible flowers, if desired, just before serving. Cover any leftovers with plastic wrap and refrigerate. This pie is best when eaten within a day, or frozen and served slightly thawed.

**CHEF'S NOTES** We like to use one blood orange and one Cara Cara orange when available.

In spring or summer, try this recipe with fresh berries or cherries instead of the orange slices.

The best way to slice the tart is to place your knife into a tall cup of hot water for a few seconds, then remove the knife, wipe away the water, and cut with the hot knife. Repeat this step for every time you slice to get a clean cut.

PREP // **5 minutes**

COOK // **35 minutes**

SERVES // **4**

# CARDAMOM-ROSE PEACH MELBA

2 cups (480 ml) warm filtered water

1 cup (240 ml) dry white wine

4 tablespoons fresh lemon juice, divided

6 tablespoons honey

½ teaspoon ground cardamom

4 medium to large peaches

2 cups (250 g) raspberries

1 tablespoon maple syrup

⅛ teaspoon rosewater

FOR SERVING

2 tablespoons toasted pistachios

1 pint (480 ml) nondairy vanilla ice cream, slightly softened, or 2 (5.3-ounce/150-g) containers vanilla-flavored coconut milk yogurt

Ground cinnamon

Dried rose petals for garnish

*Jacq: The peach melba was created by famed French chef Auguste Escoffier in the late 1800s to honor the Australian opera singer Nellie Melba. I created this slightly more exotic version to celebrate my own favorite Australian. Beautiful floral notes and spice are added to the heavenly match of peaches and raspberries. Traditionally, this dessert is served with ice cream, but it's also wonderful with creamy coconut milk yogurt.*

In a medium saucepan, bring the water and wine to a boil over medium-high heat. Add 2 tablespoons of the lemon juice, the honey, and cardamom and stir until dissolved. Score the bottom of the peaches with a large X. Place the peaches in the saucepan scored side down. Lower the heat to a simmer and cook until the peaches begin to soften, 5 to 15 minutes (the riper the peach, the less time it will need to soften), then remove from the heat and carefully turn the peaches over, letting them cool in the cooking syrup.

In a blender, combine the raspberries, the remaining 2 tablespoons lemon juice, the maple syrup, rosewater, and ¼ cup (60 ml) of the peach cooking liquid. Place a fine-mesh sieve over a small bowl and strain the sauce to remove the seeds. Refrigerate to chill.

Once the peaches are cool enough to handle, peel each carefully with your fingertips or a paring knife. Place the peaches into a bowl and drizzle each with 1 tablespoon of the cooking syrup. Place in the refrigerator to chill for a minimum of 15 minutes. Reserve the cooking liquid for another use (see Note).

In a small dry skillet, lightly toast the pistachios over medium heat, for about 2 minutes, stirring constantly so they don't burn. Divide the ice cream or yogurt among four serving dishes and sprinkle each with a pinch of cinnamon. Roll each peach in the raspberry sauce until well coated. Place a peach on each dish and spoon a little more sauce on top. Garnish with the pistachios and a few rose petals.

**CHEF'S NOTE** Save the leftover peach cooking liquid to add to sparkling water and serve over ice for a lightly sweet summer soda.

**FEEL GOOD INGREDIENT // PEACHES** Peaches have been cultivated for thousands of years and were a favorite food of the ancient Romans. They're now one of the largest crops grown in the United States. Their sweet, juicy flesh provides ten different vitamins including A, C, K, and E, and each medium peach is only about 50 calories.

# HIGH-PROTEIN BLACK BEAN BROWNIES

½ cup (120 ml) coconut oil, plus more for greasing

1 tablespoon ground chia seeds

1 (15-ounce/425-g) can black beans, including their liquid

⅓ cup (75 ml) maple syrup

½ cup (120 ml) unsweetened applesauce

2½ teaspoons vanilla extract

1 shot (2 tablespoons) espresso or strong coffee

5 Medjool dates, pitted

¾ cup (60 g) natural cocoa or cacao powder

½ teaspoon baking soda

¼ teaspoon kosher sea salt

¾ cup (118 g) brown rice flour (see Note)

⅓ cup (40 g) chopped pecans, plus 12 pecan halves for topping

½ cup (79 g) dairy-free chocolate chunks or chips, plus 1 heaping tablespoon for topping

Flaky sea salt (optional)

*These brownies have the perfect balance of ingredients to satisfy your sweet tooth and are packed with nutrients. They're full of chocolatey goodness but also protein-filled beans! No one will ever guess what they are made of. The brownies give you a nice little energy kick from the natural sugars and leave you feeling satisfied thanks to the fiber in the beans.*

Preheat the oven to 350°F (175°C) and grease a cupcake pan or an 8-inch (20-cm) square baking pan with coconut oil. Set aside.

In a high-speed blender or food processor, combine the chia seeds, beans and their liquid, maple syrup, applesauce, vanilla, coffee, dates, coconut oil, cocoa powder, baking soda, and salt. Blend, starting on low and turning it up to high speed, until smooth, scraping down the sides if necessary. Pour into a large bowl.

Slowly sprinkle or sift the flour into the wet ingredients a little at a time. Stir to incorporate before adding more flour to avoid lumps. Once all of the flour is added, fold in the pecan pieces and chocolate chunks.

Fill the pan evenly with the batter. Press a pecan half and a few chocolate chunks onto the top. Sprinkle with flaky salt, if desired. Bake for 30 minutes, or until a cake tester comes out dry. Cool completely in the pan and cut into rectangles if using a baking pan. To remove the brownies from the pan, gently loosen them with a butter knife and pop them out. Store leftovers in an airtight container for up to 1 week.

**CHEF'S NOTE** You can substitute whole-wheat flour, if necessary, but please note that whole-wheat flour contains gluten.

**FEEL GOOD INGREDIENT // BROWN RICE FLOUR** As the name might suggest, brown rice flour is a nutritious flour made from ground rice. It's gluten-free and a good source of protein and fiber. It's also extremely high in the trace mineral manganese, which is needed to help with nutrient absorption, production of digestive enzymes, bone development, and immune system function.

PREP // **5 minutes**
COOK // **5 minutes**
MAKES // **4 full portions, or 12 minis**

# CHOCOLATE-ORANGE BLOSSOM AVOCADO MOUSSE

*This sophisticated, sweet, and creamy mousse packs a superfood punch. Avocado, spirulina, and cacao are some of the most nutrient-dense ingredients on the planet, but they come together in a treat that tastes of pure chocolate decadence. The orange blossom water adds a delicate floral note, and spirulina balances the sweetness of this dessert with its earthy flavor. It's topped with toasted coconut chips and pomegranate seeds for a deliciously crunchy final touch.*

3 large avocados, mashed (about 2 cups/310 g)

1½ cups (360 ml) almond milk

¾ cup (60 g) raw cacao powder

½ cup (120 ml) orange blossom honey

1 tablespoon vanilla extract

½ teaspoon spirulina powder

½ teaspoon orange blossom water

Pinch ground cinnamon

Pinch ground cardamom

Pinch kosher sea salt

1 cup (150 g) ice cubes

TOPPINGS

⅓ cup (30 g) toasted coconut chips

4 tablespoons pomegranate seeds

1 orange, sliced

In a blender, combine the avocado, milk, cacao powder, honey, vanilla, spirulina, orange blossom water, cinnamon, cardamom, and salt, and blend on high speed until smooth. Add the ice cubes and blend again until smooth, 30 seconds to 1 minute.

Divide the mousse into small bowls or shot glasses for minis. Top with the coconut chips and pomegranate seeds and garnish each with an orange slice. Keep leftovers refrigerated in an airtight container and enjoy within 3 days.

**CHEF'S NOTE** Orange blossom water can be found next to rose water in the baking aisle or Middle Eastern section of the supermarket.

**FEEL GOOD INGREDIENT // SPIRULINA** Spirulina is a blue-green algae that may be the most nutrient-dense food on the planet. It's super high in protein, more than 60 percent by weight, which is far more than in beef! In fact, a single tablespoon of spirulina powder contains 4 grams of complete protein, as well as significant amounts of B vitamins, copper, iron, and manganese.

PREP // **5 minutes**
COOK // **45 minutes**
SERVES // **8 to 10**

# LEMON-THYME BLACKBERRY CRUMBLE

### TOPPING

¾ cup (65 g) old-fashioned, gluten-free, or extra-thick rolled oats

½ cup (55 g) slivered almonds

½ cup (65 g) whole wheat or gluten-free flour

½ cup (95 g) coconut sugar

¼ teaspoon kosher sea salt

⅛ teaspoon ground cinnamon

⅛ teaspoon powdered ginger

½ cup (120 g) coconut oil

### FILLING

2 pounds (910 g, about 3 pints) blackberries, divided

2 teaspoons fresh lemon juice

2 teaspoons fresh thyme leaves

1 teaspoon vanilla extract

Pinch kosher sea salt

3 tablespoons maple syrup (use ¼ cup/60 ml if the berries are not sweet)

1 tablespoon arrowroot

Coconut yogurt or nondairy vanilla ice cream for serving

*Jacq: Blackberries are so delicious in the summer, and they're even better when baked with a crunchy crumble topping. This recipe adds a touch of maple sweetness to the berries without covering up their natural goodness with piles of white sugar. A little lemon adds brightness, and the thyme gives it a subtle herbal flavor that makes it a step above your ordinary crumble. It's a match made in heaven with nondairy vanilla ice cream.*

Preheat the oven to 350°F (175°C).

**MAKE THE TOPPING** In a large bowl, whisk together the oats, almonds, flour, sugar, salt, cinnamon, and ginger with a fork. Add the coconut oil and mix with a fork or your fingers, until it is incorporated and has a crumbly appearance. Set aside.

**MAKE THE FILLING** In a large oven-safe skillet, heat half of the berries over medium heat until they begin to release their liquid, about 6 minutes. Add the lemon juice, thyme, vanilla, salt, and maple syrup and gently stir to combine.

In a small bowl, whisk the arrowroot and 1 tablespoon water with a fork to dissolve, then stir the mixture into the pan. Cook for 1 to 2 minutes more, until the liquid thickens and some of the berries begin to lose their shape. The total time on the stove should be 10 to 11 minutes. Turn off the heat.

Stir in the remaining berries and sprinkle with the crumble topping. Bake in the oven for 25 minutes, until bubbling and golden. Allow to cool slightly, then serve with yogurt or ice cream. Once cooled completely, cover and refrigerate any leftovers for up to 3 days.

**FEEL GOOD INGREDIENT // BLACKBERRIES** Though blueberries get more attention, blackberries have many of the same nutrients and health benefits. They are an anti-inflammatory, antioxidant, and antibacterial food that can support your body in fighting everything from premature aging to serious diseases. They're also one of the most energy-boosting fruits, so they put a little pep in your step when you eat them.

PREP // **10 minutes**

COOK // **25 minutes**

SERVES // **8 to 12**

# ALMOND BUTTER MOUSSE FRUIT PIE WITH ROSEMARY COOKIE CRUST

### CRUST

¼ cup (60 ml) melted coconut oil, plus more for greasing

¾ cup (65 g) old-fashioned or gluten-free rolled oats

½ cup (65 g) whole-wheat pastry flour, or Bob's Red Mill Gluten-Free 1-to-1 baking flour

½ cup (70 g) toasted white or black sesame seeds

¼ teaspoon kosher sea salt

1½ teaspoons finely chopped fresh rosemary or ¾ teaspoon dried

2 tablespoons warm water, plus more as needed

1 tablespoon maple syrup

### FILLING

2 (13.5-ounce/398-ml) cans full-fat coconut milk

1 cup (240 g) unsalted almond or peanut butter

¼ cup (60 ml) maple syrup

½ teaspoon vanilla extract

½ teaspoon kosher sea salt

Pinch cinnamon

1 (5.3-ounce/150-g) container plain cashew or coconut milk yogurt

### TOPPING

1½ pounds (680 g) your choice of fruit

1 tablespoon fruit jam or preserves

2 tablespoons toasted almond slivers or pomegranate seeds

*Abbie: This pie is a uniquely delicious dessert. I love its smooth texture and beautiful sandy color. It's sweet but not too sweet, and the rich mousse pairs so nicely with fresh fruit. Share with friends at a lunch or dinner party.*

Preheat the oven to 350°F (175°C) and grease a 9-inch (23-cm) pie or 10-inch (25-cm) tart pan with oil. Set aside.

**MAKE THE CRUST** In a high-speed blender or food processor, process the oats to create a coarse flour. Transfer the oats to a medium bowl and add the pastry flour, sesame seeds, salt, and rosemary. Mix with a fork, then add the oil, water, and maple syrup and mix again until well combined. The mixture should look crumbly but hold together when you squeeze a ball of it in your hand. If it is too dry, add more water 1 teaspoon at a time.

With wet fingers, press the mixture into the pan to create an even layer. If using a pie pan, the crust will reach only about halfway up the sides. Bake for 20 to 25 minutes, until golden. Allow to cool completely.

**MEANWHILE, MAKE THE FILLING** Chill the coconut milk overnight in the fridge or for 1 hour in the freezer. Without shaking or tipping, remove the lid from both cans and scoop out the solid cream from the top into a chilled mixing bowl. Refrigerate the remaining liquid to use later in smoothies.

In a mixer, beat the coconut cream until light and fluffy, about 1 minute, then add the nut butter, ½ cup (120 g) at a time, and continue beating to incorporate. Add the maple syrup, vanilla, salt, cinnamon, and yogurt and beat again.

Spread the filling evenly onto the cooled crust and place in the freezer while preparing your fruit.

**MAKE THE TOPPING** Slice the fruit into ¼-inch- (6-mm-) thick slices, or if using small berries, leave whole. Remove the pie from the freezer and arrange the fruit in overlapping concentric circles starting around the outside edge and working toward the middle. Brush the fruit with a thin coating of jam. We like to use the same flavor as the fruit topping—for, example fig jam on figs—but apricot jam also works well with any fruit.

Top with the toasted almond slivers or pomegranate seeds. Serve immediately, or refrigerate until ready to eat. Alternatively, you can freeze the base and filling for up to 2 weeks and let thaw slightly before adding the fruit topping and serving. Leftovers will keep for 2 days covered in the refrigerator or several weeks in the freezer.

**CHEF'S NOTE**  You can make the crust and mousse a day ahead. The crust can be left out, covered with a kitchen towel; the mousse should be refrigerated in a covered container until just before assembling the tart.

**FEEL GOOD INGREDIENT // ALMONDS**  Not so long ago, nuts were feared for containing too much fat (oh, the nineties were dark days!). It's now been shown that the fats and dietary fiber in nuts can actually help you maintain a healthy weight. Almonds and other nuts give you a long-lasting feeling of satiety, which can help prevent overeating.

PREP // **10 minutes**

COOK // **1 hour**

SERVES // **8**

# GRILLED PINEAPPLE WITH VANILLA ICE CREAM AND COCONUT DULCE DE LECHE

2 (13.5-ounce/398-ml) cans coconut milk

¼ cup (50 g) plus 2 tablespoons coconut sugar

¼ teaspoon kosher sea salt

½ teaspoon vanilla extract

¼ teaspoon ground cinnamon

¼ teaspoon ground cardamom

1 large pineapple

Olive oil

1 pint (480 ml) nondairy vanilla ice cream

1 heaping tablespoon fresh mint, cut into chiffonade, plus whole leaves for garnish

Flaky sea salt

1 large or 2 small limes, cut into 8 wedges

**FEEL GOOD INGREDIENT // PINEAPPLE** Pineapple is a particularly beneficial food to enjoy at the end of a meal. It's rich in fiber and contains a digestive enzyme called bromelain, which helps your digestive system break down and absorb proteins from the foods you eat.

*Jacq: This recipe holds a special place in my heart because I first made it for my culinary school graduation barbecue. It takes me right back to that New York City rooftop. We had run out of cutlery and everybody was eating this dessert with sticky hands and giant smiles. There's nothing more summery than smoky grilled fruit. Topped with ice cream and a warm, spiced dulce de leche sauce, it's irresistible and lick-your-fingers good!*

Combine the coconut milk and coconut sugar in a medium saucepan. Place over medium heat and bring to a boil, then lower the heat and simmer for 25 to 35 minutes. Using a wooden spoon, stir occasionally as it simmers, until the sauce begins to thicken and bubble, then stir frequently, scraping the bottom and sides as you stir. If the bubbles begin to splatter or boil over, lower the heat. When your spoon leaves a trail as you stir and the sauce coats the back of your spoon, stir in the salt and vanilla. Sprinkle in the cinnamon and cardamom little by little while stirring vigorously to prevent clumping. The sauce should be a nice amber color at this stage. Turn off the heat.

If you have a pineapple corer, cut the pineapple into rings. Otherwise, cut off the crown and the bottom of the pineapple and discard. Stand the pineapple upright, then cut away the peel from top to bottom with a serrated knife. Remove any remaining eyes with a paring knife. Cut the pineapple into 8 slices, about ¾- to 1-inch- (2- to 2.5-cm-) thick, then cut the core out of each slice with an apple corer, small round cookie cutter, or the pairing knife (see Note).

Heat an outdoor grill or grill pan to medium-high heat. Lightly brush the pineapple rings with olive oil. Grill the pineapple rings until dark grill marks appear, 4 to 5 minutes. Flip the slices with a fish spatula or other flat spatula and cook for about 4 minutes more to achieve grill marks on the other side.

If the dulce de leche has cooled, reheat it over medium-low heat, stirring occasionally, until warm. Top each pineapple slice with a ¼-cup (33-g) scoop of ice cream, a drizzle of dulce de leche, and a sprinkle of mint chiffonade. Garnish with mint leaves. Finish each with a tiny pinch of flaky sea salt and serve with a lime wedge.

**CHEF'S NOTE** This preparation makes it easier to eat the pineapple slices, but you can also leave the rind on and allow people to trim the slices themselves.

# SPICED ROSÉ POACHED PEARS WITH VANILLA-PINE NUT CREAM CHEESE

POACHED PEARS

**4 Bosc pears, peeled**

**2 cups (480 ml) warm filtered water**

**2 cups (480 ml) dry rosé wine**

**1 cinnamon stick**

**4 cardamom pods, lightly crushed (see Note)**

**¾-inch (2-cm) piece ginger, thinly sliced**

**1 star anise**

**6 tablespoons (90 ml) honey**

**¾ teaspoon ground turmeric**

PINE NUT CREAM CHEESE

**1 cup (140 g) plus 3 tablespoons pine nuts, divided**

**1 tablespoon plus 1 teaspoon fresh lemon juice**

**3 tablespoons cool filtered water**

**1 teaspoon sweet white miso**

**2 teaspoons maple syrup**

**Pinch kosher sea salt**

**Pinch black pepper**

**½ vanilla bean, split in half lengthwise (see Note)**

**3 tablespoons golden raisins**

**2 tablespoons pomegranate seeds (optional)**

*No dessert is quite as elegant as the poached pear. In this recipe, the beautifully shaped pears are enhanced with a delicate infusion of color and flavor from rosé wine, honey, turmeric, and other warming spices. Inside, there is a luscious surprise in the form of a tempting pine nut cream cheese. This treat makes a rich and memorable end to any meal without leaving you feeling heavy.*

**MAKE THE PEARS** Using a small melon baller or small thin-edged spoon, core the pears by cutting into the bottom end and scooping out the base and core, leaving the stem end intact.

In a medium saucepan, combine the water, wine, cinnamon, cardamom, ginger, and star anise. Bring to a boil over medium-high heat, then add the honey and turmeric and stir until dissolved. Place the pears in the saucepan so that they are lying on their sides and lower the heat to maintain a simmer. Cook for 10 minutes, turn the pears, and cook for 5 to 10 minutes more, until the pears are tender and easily pierced with the tip of a paring knife.

**MAKE THE CREAM CHEESE** In a high-speed blender, combine 1 cup (135 g) of the pine nuts, the lemon juice, water, miso, maple syrup, salt, and pepper and blend, starting on low and brigning it up to medium-high speed, until smooth, scraping the sides as necessary. Transfer to a small bowl. Scrape the seeds from the vanilla bean using a paring knife and stir them into the cream. Fold the raisins and the remaining 3 tablespoons pine nuts into the cream.

**TO SERVE** Remove the pears from the cooking liquid when they are cool enough to handle and set aside. Bring the cooking liquid to a boil and reduce to about ½ cup (60 ml) until syrupy, 15 to 20 minutes.

Using a teaspoon, completely fill the cavity of each pear with the pine nut mixture. Transfer to a serving plate and drizzle each with a few spoonfuls of the syrup. Garnish with the pomegranate seeds, if desired.

**CHEF'S NOTE** If you don't have whole cardamom pods, you can substitute ¼ teaspoon ground cardamom. If you do not have a vanilla bean, blend ½ teaspoon vanilla extract into the cream.

**FEEL GOOD INGREDIENT // PEARS** Pears are super high in fiber and packed with vitamin C. They contain significant levels of vitamin K and potassium and are great for your immune system, heart health, skin, and hair.

# GATHERINGS

We've talked a lot about cooking in this book, but now we come to the best part—enjoying a meal with friends and family! Here are some menu ideas for all of your special occasions—the dinners and parties where memories are made. We've included starters, main dishes, sides, and desserts for most; you may choose to make all of the dishes or just a few, depending on how elaborate you want your meal to be. Don't be afraid to ask guests if they want to come over early to help you prepare. You may be surprised to find that people are usually happy to lend a hand. At our dinner parties, making the food is always half the fun.

## Spring Celebration

Poached Salmon with French Green Beans and Strawberry Salad (page 113)

Lemon-Pea Risotto with Mint (page 145)

Almond Butter Mousse Fruit Pie with Rosemary Cookie Crust (page 224)

## Summer BBQ Celebration

Mezze Platter (see pages 200–205)

Italian-Style Grilled Halibut (page 191)

White Bean and Celery Salad with Pesto Grilled Shrimp (page 122)

Grilled Pineapple with Vanilla Ice Cream and Coconut Dulce de Leche (page 226)

## Fall Celebration

The Happy Hippy Quinoa Salad (page 118)

Stuffed Maple-Glazed Acorn Squash (page 139) and/or Salmon with Mango Chutney and Crushed Pecans (page 187)

Spiced Sweet Potato Puree (page 141)

Spinach sautéed with garlic and olive oil (see Cooking School Sautéed Veggie Basics on page 49)

Almond Butter Mousse Fruit Pie with Rosemary Cookie Crust with fresh sliced persimmon (page 224)

## Winter Celebration

Roasted Acorn Squash Soup with Rosemary-Spice Candied Pecans (page 111)

Creamy Mushroom Lasagna with Pesto (page 162)

Whole Roasted Maple-Ginger Carrots (page 42)

Roasted Brussels Sprouts, Dried Cherries, and Walnuts (page 42)

Chocolate Tahini Tart with Fresh Oranges (page 214)

## New Year's Eve Celebration

Peewee Potatoes and Caviar (page 210)

Creamy Truffle Mushroom Soup (page 108)

Champagne Risotto with Truffles (see Note on page 143)

Spiced Rosé Poached Pears with Vanilla-Pine Nut Cream Cheese (page 229)

## Fancy Dinner Party

Spring Salad with Green Goddess Dressing (page 107) and/or English Pea Soup with Mint (page 104)

Pan-Seared Branzino with Lima Bean-Avocado Puree and Tarragon-Mint Sauce (page 180)

Cardamom-Rose Peach Melba (page 217)

## Casual Dinner Party

The Happy Hippy Quinoa Salad (page 118)

Linguine Carbonara with Peas, Artichokes, and Shiitake Bacon (page 151) or Spaghetti with Veggie Tempeh Bolognese (page 167)

High-Protein Black Bean Brownies (page 218) with nondairy vanilla ice cream

## Fancy Cocktail Party

Creamy Truffle Mushroom Soup served in shot glasses (page 108)

Peewee Potatoes and Caviar (page 210)

Watermelon Radish and Smoked Salmon Canapés (page 207)

Sweet Potato Pizzette with Roasted Radishes and Fried Sage (page 209)

Chocolate-Orange Blossom Avocado Mousse minis (page 221)

## Casual Cocktail Party

Mezze Platter (page 201)

Hazelnut-Stuffed Medjool Dates (page 206)

Sweet Potato Pizzette with Roasted Radishes and Fried Sage (page 209)

High-Protein Black Bean Brownies (page 218)

*"Laughter is brightest where food is best."*
—IRISH PROVERB

**CHEF'S NOTE** Check the serving size on each recipe. You may have to double the recipe depending on the number of guests that you are serving. This is usually not a problem as long as you use cookware that is large enough to hold the doubled amount. Alternatively, you can split the doubled recipe between two pots, pans, or baking sheets.

**FEEL GOOD INGREDIENT //
FRIENDS** Researchers at the University of Oxford found in a study that the more people eat with others, the more likely they are to feel satisfied and happy in their lives. They also found that people who eat socially are more likely to feel better about themselves and have wider emotional support networks, a key contributor to psychological health.

# KITCHEN EQUIPMENT

**BLENDER** No other piece of kitchen equipment will change your life quite as much as a high-speed blender. We've both grown to love our Vitamix blenders so much that we often lug them around when we travel. That might sound a bit crazy, but when something makes your daily life so much easier, it's worth it. They're pricey, but they can last a lifetime. In the long run, you will save money by making your own creamy soups, nut milks, purees, dips, dressings, nut butters, and the smoothest smoothies in town.

**FISH SPATULA** This long, thin, slotted spatula is specially designed for slipping under and turning delicate fish fillets. It's also ideal for shimmying loose sticky vegetables from a baking sheet or transferring fresh-baked goodies from the oven to the cooling rack. Look for one that has a nice balance of strength and flexibility.

**FOOD PROCESSOR** This kitchen helper can chop, shred, mix, mince, and puree faster than the best sous chef. You'll use it for making chunky sauces like salsa and pesto, nondairy cheeses, dips, energy balls, and about a million other recipes. It will also save you some tears when a recipe calls for a pile of chopped onion. Some newer models even have an attachment to make spiralized veggies.

**JUICER** Unless you're opening up a juice shop, you don't need to spend thousands of dollars on a juicer. For everyday juicing needs, we like the compact Breville juicer, which is super easy to clean and small enough to live on your counter. If you're really into juicing, you may want to look into a higher-end masticating juicer like the Champion juicer.

**VEGETABLE AND JULIENNE PEELER** Y-shaped OXO Good Grips peelers are the best. The julienne peeler works like a vegetable peeler, but turns veggies into pretty julienne strips to use as garnishes, salad toppings, and in stir-fries. It works well on firm fruits and vegetables such as zucchini, carrots, potatoes, apples, and citrus peels, and can be used to make zucchini noodles.

**KITCHEN SCALE** You can purchase a decent kitchen scale for around twenty dollars. It's so worth it! An average scale is small and lightweight and has multiple weighing modes including grams (g), kilograms (kg), ounces (oz), and pounds (lbs). They usually measure up to 5 kg.

**KNIVES** Sharp knives save you time and make your prep work so much more fun as you bring out your inner ninja. You can do almost anything with one good chef's knife, but it's nice to have a small paring knife for detail work and a serrated knife for cutting bread and soft fruits. If you're looking to add one more knife to your collection, we recommend a 5-inch (12-cm) Santoku knife, which looks like a cross between a chef's knife and a small cleaver. Its shape makes it ideal for chopping fresh herbs and slicing hard vegetables like sweet potatoes.

**MANDOLINE** This low-tech tool might be our favorite. It gives you beautiful, even, thin vegetable slices to use in sauces or frittatas—no knife skills required! We love the simple single-blade versions over the fancy French-style mandolines with multiple parts. The only cleanup required is a quick rinse. It's also useful for making raw lasagna noodles out of zucchini. We're all for having a glass of wine (or two) while we're cooking, but we like to warn people (only half-jokingly) that this tool is hungry for human flesh. It's best to be super mindful and, more important, sober when you're working with it!

**MEASURING CUPS AND SPOONS** Having a nice set of measuring cups and spoons is essential. We prefer ones in stainless steel. Look for narrow rectangular spoons that can fit inside spice jars.

**MICROPLANE** Use this fine handheld grater to make citrus zest, grated ginger, or grated garlic. If you ever get your hands on a fresh truffle, a Microplane will help you make the most of it by creating thin wisps of pungent flavor. This is particularly helpful if you are using it in sauces.

**MORTAR AND PESTLE/MOLCAJETE** A molcajete is a Mexican version of a mortar and pestle. It's a small three-legged bowl carved out of volcanic rock and is perfect for preparing salsa, guacamole, and pesto. The molcajete is one of the world's oldest culinary tools and a must-have in the kitchen. A small mortar and pestle with grooves on the inside is ideal for grinding spices and small seeds such as sesame seeds.

**NUT MILK BAG** Use this finely woven bag to make nut milks that are smoother and even creamier than store-bought nut milks.

**POTS AND PANS** Even though we have cupboards full of cookware, we find ourselves using the same few pieces over and over. A 12-inch (30.5-cm) cast-iron pan, once seasoned, is naturally nonstick, and can add iron to your food. Lodge has been making reasonably priced, nearly indestructible cast iron pans in Tennessee since 1896. They also make enameled cast iron that we love along with our classic Le Creuset. Enameled cast iron is more expensive, but one 10-inch (25-cm) skillet and one 4½-quart (4-L) or larger Dutch oven will last a lifetime and take care of most of your cooking needs. An 8-inch (20-cm) nontoxic, nonstick Green Pan ceramic omelette pan is also a must. Heavy-bottomed stainless-steel pans, such as All-Clad, are also outstanding but require a bit more oil to keep things from sticking. Avoid inexpensive aluminum cookware that can heat unevenly and leach aluminum into your food.

**SALAD SPINNER** Nobody likes a soggy salad! Watch the centripetal force in action as the spinning motion whisks away excess water from your squeaky-clean greens.

**SPIRALIZER** If you don't have a food processor with a spiralizer attachment, you'll want to get a stand-alone unit to turn your veggies into spaghetti-like strands. This allows you to create gorgeous, nutrient-dense dishes with sweet potato, carrot, parsnip, beet, or zucchini noodles as the star.

**STRAINER** Get an extra-large strainer, or colander, for washing veggies and draining pasta in the sink. Use a smaller fine-mesh sieve for straining liquids like broths, oil infusions, and sauces.

**STAND MIXER** A good stand mixer is like having an extra set of fast-working hands in the kitchen. You can use it to make smooth and creamy mashed potatoes or to beat eggs. They are especially useful if you love to bake since they are often called for in recipes for bread, cakes, frostings, pie crusts, and fillings. KitchenAid sets the standard in the category.

**TIMER** A timer, cell phone, or smart speaker with an alarm is key in the kitchen. This allows you the freedom to take your eyes off the clock and focus on the task at hand. Plus, an alarm will ensure an accurate cooking time. We use a vocally operated smart speaker to keep our hands free while cooking.

**WATER FILTER** We hear a lot about clean eating, but how about clean drinking? Bottled water is expensive, and in most cases, no better for you than tap water. Filtered water is a much better and environmentally friendly alternative. Filters can remove many impurities and toxins like mercury and chlorine. Water-filter pitchers are a good start, but if you plan to be in your home for a long time, you might want to invest in a more thorough under-sink water filtration system.

**WOODEN SPOON** This is one of the most versatile and durable kitchen items you'll ever own. Wooden spoons are very tolerant of high temperatures without transferring the heat to the handle. They won't chemically react with acidic foods or scratch pots and pans, as metal spoons can, and you don't have to worry about them melting or leaching chemicals into hot foods the way plastic does. Plus, like a quality chef's knife, a nice wooden spoon just feels good in your hand, and feeling good is what we're all about.

# ACKNOWLEDGMENTS

*Thank you to our incredible team who made this book as beautiful as we'd imagined it would be: Kari Stuart and Catherine Shook at ICM; Holly Dolce, Sarah Massey, Deb Wood, Danielle Youngsmith, and Connor Leonard at Abrams; Laura Palese, our amazing book designer; our dear friend George Cawood at Framework Studio; and our talented photographers, Ren Fuller, Jennifer Rovero, Andrew Herrold, Pete Halvorsen, and Pasha Poosh. Much love and thanks to all of the people who have supported us along our journey; this book is for you.*

## From Jacq

All my love to Zack for letting me feed him black cod fifteen times in a row while recipe testing, and generally being the best husband ever. Thanks to Adele and TJ for being rock stars in the kitchen, Shannon and Alice for making research fun when fun was needed, and to Denise Lopez for handmaking our gorgeous ceramics. To my friends and family who became volunteer taste testers, you're welcome.

I'm grateful to all of my teachers, especially Chef Elliott Prag and Chef Rich LaMarita at the Natural Gourmet Institute for responding to my queries while writing this book, Chef Chad Sarno and Chef Ken Rubin at Rouxbe Cooking School, and Chef Diego Hernandez for encouraging me to go to culinary school in the first place. Above all, to my first teacher—Grandma Caceres—who always cooked with love.

I couldn't have made this cookbook without the women who kept my baby safe and happy while I worked, even as he was determined to crawl into the oven. Countless thanks to Jewel, Jennifer, Blanca, and (for this and infinitely more) my mom, Liz, better known these days as Grandma. I also owe much to my life coach Suzanne Morris, who makes people believe they can do anything, then proves them right.

Last, but certainly not least, dearest Abbie. You are a force of nature, and I continue to learn from and be inspired by you. There are so many things you could have spent your time doing (since you can do it all!), I can't tell you how appreciative I am that you chose to spend it writing this book with me. Love you always.

## From Abbie

First, I'd like to thank my family: Shelley, Barry, Jade, Hayden, Zac, and Isabelle. Love you guys dearly. Thank you, also, to my adorable extended (animal) family: India, Soleil, Ysi, Phoenix, Capella, and Buddha. To my awesome mates who were super supportive over the last couple of years during the making of this book: Diego Hernández, Jessie Hill, Michael Lazo, José Padilha, Jennifer Rovero, Michele Knight, Jamie Chung, Bryan Greenberg, Eddie Alcazar, Fabián von Hauske Valtierra, Jeremiah Stone, Rob Salé, Jason Houck, Erin Cunningham, Nichelle Hines, Christopher Scott, Matthew Collins, Gerry Grennell, David Findley, Suli McCullough, Bryan Ling, Joe Komar, and Stacey Komar. Thanks Deb Waknin and Rhea Rachevsky for the beautiful clothes, Gagik at G&G Marble and Granite, and Shroleen at Surfaces USA, for giving me some fine marble offcuts and digging deep into the dungeons to find some unique natural stone. Priceless.

Thanks, Mamma, for helping me pour plaster of Paris onto MDF board like a madwoman late at night in the art studio during our food photography shoot, creating premium, original surfaces that will one day sell for thousands! Just kidding.

Last, but not least, thanks to my dear friend and teacher, Jacqueline, for the light and love you've shared with me in and out of the kitchen. Love you always, too.

# GLOSSARY

**AL DENTE**  Literally meaning "to the tooth" in Italian, al dente pasta is still slightly firm to the bite, not mushy.

**BLANCH**  To briefly plunge foods into boiling water to partially cook. This process sets the color of vegetables, lets you easily peel fruits, and slip the skins off nuts. The food does not cook all the way through, so crisp texture is preserved.

**CHIFFONADE**  Meaning "little ribbons" in French, chiffonade is a slicing technique in which leafy greens or flat-leaved herbs like basil are cut into long, thin strips. This is accomplished by stacking leaves, rolling them tightly lengthwise, then slicing the leaves perpendicular to the roll.

**DEGLAZE**  To add liquid, such as stock or wine, to a pan to loosen and dissolve flavorful food particles that have stuck to the bottom during cooking.

**DEVEIN**  To remove the dark digestive tract, also known as the sand vein, that runs along the back of shrimp.

**DIVIDED**  This is used in the ingredient list to indicate the preceding ingredient will be used in more than one step of the recipe.

**GREASE**  To create a thin coating of fat on a cooking surface to help prevent sticking.

**JULIENNE**  A knife-cut or preparation of food cut into thin strips, measuring approximately ⅛ inch × ⅛ inch × 2 to 3 inches (3 mm × 3 mm × 5 to 8 cm). Also known as the "matchstick" cut.

**MINCE**  To cut into very small pieces, smaller than dice or chop, but not mashed or pureed.

**PARBOIL**  To boil briefly, generally as the first step in a cooking process.

**SCORE**  To make shallow cuts in the surface of foods, often in a diamond pattern. This is done to help foods absorb more flavors and cook faster and more evenly.

**SIMMER**  To cook using liquid at a temperature ranging from 180°F to 200°F (82°C to 94°C) so that bubbles form and gently rise to the surface but the liquid is not yet at a full rolling boil.

**SWEAT**  To cook vegetables, especially aromatic vegetables such as onions, over low heat in a small amount of fat until they soften and release moisture but do not brown.

*"Pull up a chair. Take a taste. Come join us. Life is so endlessly delicious."*

—RUTH REICHL

# INDEX

Note: Page numbers in **bold** indicate recipe category lists and related page references. Page numbers in *italics* indicate photos separate from recipe.

Editor: Sarah Massey
Designer: Laura Palese
Production Manager: Michael Kaserkie

Library of Congress Control Number: 2018936268

ISBN: 978-1-4197-3467-0
eISBN: 978-1-68335-507-6
B&N Exclusive Edition ISBN: 978-1-4197-3988-0

Text copyright © 2019 Dusk, Inc. and Feel Good Kitchen, LLC

Food photography by **Ren Fuller**: pages 4–5, 20–24, 28–52,
54–57, 60–61, 65–84, 87–102, 105–110, 114–123, 126–138, 141–147,
150–168, 170–178, 181, 183–193, 195–212, 215–228, 233, 236–239

Lifestyle photography by **Camraface**: pages 8, 13, 15–19, 27, 53,
58, 62–63, 85, 125, 140, 148, 182, 235

Landscape photography by **Pete Halvorsen**: pages 1, 2–3, 7, 25,
59, 85, 103, 112, 169, 179, 213, 240

Additional lifestyle photography by **Andrew Herrold**: pages 194, 231

Additional lifestyle photography by **Pasha Poosh**: Cover and page 6

Photograph by **Barry Cornish**: page 10; Photograph by **Shelley
Cornish**: page 10; Kzww/Shutterstock.com: page 124; Luboslav
Tiles/Shutterstock.com: page 149

Art direction, food, and prop styling: Abbie Cornish and
Jacqueline King Schiller
Food styling assistants: Adele Fenner and TJ Hardenbergh
Makeup and hair for Jacqueline: Danielle Katherine

Cover © 2019 Abrams

Printed and bound in the United States
10 9 8 7 6 5 4 3 2 1

Abrams books are available at special discounts when purchased
in quantity for premiums and promotions as well as fundraising
or educational use. Special editions can also be created to
specification. For details, contact specialsales@abramsbooks.com
or the address below.

Abrams® is a registered trademark of Harry N. Abrams, Inc.

 **ABRAMS** The Art of Books
195 Broadway, New York, NY 10007
abramsbooks.com